MODERN LIBRARY COLLEGE EDITIONS

A Doll's House

Ghosts

An Enemy of the People

The Master Builder

BY

HENRIK IBSEN

Introduction by
ERIC BENTLEY

THE MODERN LIBRARY · NEW YORK

Contents

INTRODUCTION

By Eric Bentley

IBSEN, PRO AND CON

It must have been a pleasure to welcome Ibsen with open arms when all one's primmer relatives were shaking their fists at him, but the great days of Ibsenism are past. Today the mention of the Norwegian's name elicits, in many quarters, a certain feeling of tedium. After all, the Ibsenites won all too complete a victory: their man was accepted into the dull ranks of fame; he became an academic figure.

A supremely great writer like Shakespeare can survive such acceptance—with whatever wear and tear. It is harder for a genius of the second rank; the livelier reader—the only reader that counts—is apt to think Ibsen well deserves his dim respectability. It would be better if he belonged to the third rank and did not raise such high expectations! Ibsen so often leads us to expect the highest things that we are disturbed when he falls short. He is an author one worries about. From time to time one wonders—as one does not wonder about Shakespeare: is he really good or have I been imposed upon?

If we are to return to him, if we are to read and see him freshly, it cannot be by ignoring such worries. Before hearing a spokesman *for* Ibsen, let us hear a fictitious devil's advocate voice our misgivings.

CON

When we open our Ibsen we enter an unconvincing world: a world created by bad prose, clumsy dramatic structures and stale ideas. Since you will tell me that the bad prose is the work of his translators, I will concentrate on the structures and the ideas.

How could H. L. Mencken feel that Ibsen abolished the artificial "well-made play" and just let the facts "tell themselves"? Hadn't he read *Ghosts*? At the end of Act Two Mrs. Alving's story is just "telling itself" when—lest it all come blurting out before our evening at the theater is done —Ibsen has a sanatorium catch fire. This is disastrously clumsy dramatic construction. The craftsman's machinery overwhelms the poet's vision.

Is not the same true of *A Doll's House*? Krogstad, for example, is a mere pawn of the plot. When convenient to Ibsen, he is a blackmailer (29).* When inconvenient, he is converted (69-70). Ibsen the craftsman is busy constructing relationships between two couples—Torvald and Nora, Krogstad and Mrs. Linde. The parallels and contrasts must work out right, even if the characterization is impaired.

Dr. Rank is not the pawn of the plot—he is not even necessary to it—but he is the pawn of an idea. When Ibsen wants to bring the theme of hereditary disease and death before us he has only to write "Enter Dr. Rank." You will tell me that Dr. Rank is a symbolic character, and that symbolism is one of the elements in the total structure of an Ibsen play. The trouble is that Ibsen's symbolism is so portentous—what with the sanatorium burning to show us that the Alvings are burning and Rank dropping his black cross in the letter box to show us that death is in the background!

In *An Enemy of the People*, *A Doll's House* and *Ghosts* the symbolism is obvious to the point of being tiresome; in *The Master Builder* it is obscure to the point of being confused. I don't mean that the reader of *The Master Builder* has nothing to hold on to. Every little Freudian nowadays knows what to say about the towers and Solness' inability

---

*Figures in parentheses refer to pages in the text.

to climb them. Biographers are at hand to explain that Ibsen was tired of writing "social" plays, as Solness was tired of building homes for human beings. What then? The play as a whole is bewildering. Whatever human reality Ibsen may have meant to show us is hidden behind a wilderness of trolls, birds of prey, helpers and servers, devils (good and bad, blond and brunette), fairy kingdoms and castles in the air. The symbolism proliferates. The total result is a mess.

Then there are the ideas, Ibsen's famous ideas: there should be votes for women; women's rights are equal to men's; hereditary syphilis is a bad thing; mercy killing is sometimes justified; keep germs out of the bathwater; don't be jealous of the younger generation, and so forth. If my phrasing is flippant, blame Ibsen, whose presentation of problems is always either ridiculous or vague: the greatest actress who ever played Mrs. Alving—Eleanora Duse—admitted as much. What, for instance, lies behind the nebulous Victorian terms in which Mrs. Alving's life with her husband is dressed? As a critic has already asked: did she never enjoy it when she went to bed with him? Not the least little bit? Again, if the phrasing is flippant, Ibsen asks for it: his kind of drama raises such questions without supplying the answers. Consequently it is impossible to grasp his characters in the way he seems to want you to grasp them.

Oswald in Paris is as cloudy a figure as his mother in his father's bedroom. A matter we should be clear about is whether his disease *must* have come from his father or whether he could not have contracted syphilis from his own sexual activities. At one moment he seems to say "No" to the latter question. "I have never lived recklessly in any sense. . . . I have never done that" (145), but soon after (147) he says, "I ought to have had nothing to do with the joyous happy life I had lived with my comrades. It had been too much for my strength. So it was my own fault. . . .

My whole life incurably ruined—just because of my own imprudence." This last speech is not conclusive, but that is precisely the trouble: conclusiveness is called for. Perhaps one does not care what the doctors say of Oswald's collapse in Act Three. Perhaps one can forgive Ibsen for his unscrupulously melodramatic timing of the collapse. But there are many details which could be clear and aren't. For example: Oswald argues (117) that the Parisian artists prefer living unmarried with their children's mothers because it is cheaper. But is it?

A picture composed of such unclear details can only come together in our minds as a fog. Is any clear attitude defined to the famous "modern ideas" to be found in the play? And how far do they go? One assumes that the books Mrs. Alving reads—and which Ibsen does not name—are typical of nineteenth-century liberalism. Yet in one curious passage she goes far beyond ordinary enlightenment into the assumption that we should accept even incest (133). Ibsen being Ibsen, the suggestion is not clarified.

If *Ghosts* is not exactly a "drama of ideas" it will be better to instance a play that is—*An Enemy of the People.* Dr. Stockman expects his fellow-townsmen to accept the truth, however they may be affected by it. He finds, however, that people refuse to accept a truth if it interferes with their interests, that the liberal opposition goes along with the interested minority, and that the masses soon follow suit. He therefore decides—in Act Four—that he is against majority rule.

This is straightforward, if not profound. It is in the fifth act that Ibsen proves himself a muddlehead. Vehement as Stockman is in rejecting common folk as "curs" he firmly intends to educate them. He will begin by educating his own boys and a handful of street urchins. He will train the curs to the point where they can drive out the wolves. "You shan't learn a blessed thing ... but I will make liberal-minded and high-minded men out of you" (287). That is to say: "The voice of the people is not the voice of God till the people has been educated by me."

Even if we share Stockman's high opinion of himself we must ask how he can secure his position as an educator in a country where the majority are curs? Even in a more fortunate land how can we make the philosopher a king? *An Enemy of the People* is a manifesto for the petty bourgeois, the petty snob, the petty intellectual. The masses are ignorant, you are cultured, therefore you disbelieve in democracy, you believe in culture. What of it? You haven't made it clear how you can attain power. In any case, as a leader you are self-appointed, and that is a game many can play at: *anyone* can declare himself a leader, cultured or otherwise.

Are you going to say that Stockman is not Ibsen? There is precious little evidence within the play that the latter is critical of his creation. The whole play breathes the perennial self-complacency of the arrogant idealist—from the Pharisee of the first century to the Communist intellectual of today. That Ibsen felt compelled to show the other side of the medal in *The Wild Duck* can hardly comfort the critic of *An Enemy of the People*. It takes more than two one-sided plays to make a single two-sided masterpiece. And *An Enemy* is one-sided, a play of moral blacks and whites. To read it as a subtle study in self-righteousness, like *Le Misanthrope*, would be to conceive another play. Stockman is an Alceste taken pretty much at his own valuation.

As a piece of thinking, *An Enemy of the People* is too superficial to be instructive. As a piece of art, it is too feeble to be influential. In 1950 it would be as easy as it is wise to let Ibsen rest in peace.

PRO

I do not find either Ibsen's ideas or his forms as disastrously "dated" as you assume.

Let me begin where you left off—with the ideas. Are even the ones you mentioned really outmoded? I believe they only *sound* so. "Women's rights," for example. The phrase itself is not in use today—but for that matter it isn't used in *A Doll's House.* The problem as to what women's rights *are* is still real enough. The world is still a man's world, and if the status of women has been raised, it is still a secondary and an awkward status. In 1950 there are still many "doll's houses." As for *Ghosts,* hereditary disease is still with us, mercy killing is still a controversial question. And as for *The Master Builder,* the conflict of the generations is as real as ever.

Even the play you take as the very type of outmoded "drama of ideas"—*An Enemy of the People*—is neither as transparent nor as wrong as you make it appear. Certainly Stockman's philosophy is supererogatory in a country like Germany, where too many people already share it. In America it might be a salutary challenge. The American philosophy of the common man needs constant criticism if it is to be preserved from demagogic sentimentality. The idealism of many people today begins in self-contempt and functions as a flight from the self; Stockman, whatever his failings, knew that morality must start from self-respect. You seem to consider the Ibsen who wrote *An Enemy* facile, trivial, journalistic. Just compare the portrait of a Norwegian community given in Steinbeck's *The Moon Is Down.* There can be no doubt who gives the keener, stricter, more deeply pondered view.

But these are side issues. More essential is the fact that in discussing Ibsen's ideas you mentioned only those that jump to the eyes, the famous "social" ideas that scandalized conservative Victorians and delighted the Ibsenite rebels. Led astray, perhaps, by some of the latter, you, too, seem to expect Ibsen to be primarily a brain. Perhaps you demand that his ideas be brilliant and original and that he juggle them with the skill of a logician. I, on the other hand, shall argue that you have failed to notice what are the most active ideas in Ibsen's plays and that you are therefore unable to see what use he put them to.

What ideas are most active in *Ghosts*? Surely not those you have mentioned. Behind the question of mercy killing is the question of "modern ideas" generally—as against the "established ideas" of Pastor Manders. To perpetrate a mercy killing, a person would have to be emancipated entirely from established ideas. Ibsen brings the matter up, one might almost say, to show that Mrs. Alving is *not* so emancipated. Thus he is less interested in "modern ideas" themselves than in certain ideas that go behind them. In Ibsen one must always look for the idea behind the idea.

Ibsen did not by any means stop with the conflict of modern and established ideas. His special achievement is the depth and body he gives to each of these philosophies as it exists in people's lives. He does this not as an agile arguer but as a poet with a country, a people, a tradition behind him. Abstract ideas take concrete form through (for example) his use of folk imagery. Established ideas he sees as "ghosts," as "the spirits of the dead" of popular belief, and if Mrs. Alving strives after modernity she does so, not as the "new woman" of the Paris boulevards, but as a daughter of the Vikings. Below the surface of "modern," "Christian" civilization Ibsen finds "primitive," "pagan" forces. It is to Norse paganism he looks alike for images of evil and for images of human dignity—here, rather than in those modern books which, so you insinuate, he doesn't even know the titles of. His superior people are to be understood as Vikings *manqués.* Mrs. Alving thinks she ought, like some rash pagan, to countenance incest, but she can't bring herself to do so. The great surprise of *A Doll's House* is our discovery of a Viking spirit in Torvald's little squirrel. Halvard Solness is a man who *had been* a Viking—ten years earlier. If you will agree to call *this* Ibsen's "idea" you will not find *The Master Builder* so bewildering.

Compared with Mrs. Alving, Solness is a strong man. But if the weaker Ibsen characters are held back by "the spirits of the dead," the stronger are goaded on by "the trolls of the mountain."* Early in *A Doll's House* Nora is characterized as a "mad creature" and later, when she dances the tarantella, the "troll in her" takes over. In *The Master Builder* the trolls come for Solness in the person of Hilda Wangel—or that part of her which is a bird of prey. They goad him into attempting the impossible. Being a Viking no longer, he cannot climb as high as he builds. He falls to his death.

I am not offering Norse mythology as a magic key to Ibsen. My point is simply that one can always look in Ibsen for something beyond the clichés of the problem drama. Take the most famous problem play of them all. *A Doll's House* seems to you to be about votes for women, a topic that does not come up in the play at all. What does come up is the matter of woman's place in a man's world, a much larger topic that still bristles with interest today. It even seems to me that Ibsen pushes his investigation towards a further and even deeper subject, the tyranny of one human being over another; in this respect, the play would be just as valid were Torvald the wife and Nora the husband.

Reread the opening pages of *A Doll's House*. Since the text is familiar, you are not just picking up the facts of the story, you are noticing the terms in which Ibsen presents his subject. No words are lost. Nora's tipping the porter (4) a shilling instead of sixpence not only gives us her character but establishes money as one of the topics of the play. The borrowing of money—which lies at the heart

---

* "The troll is not a puck or a goblin; he is truly diabolic. Although the old stories spoke of monstrous three-headed trolls, the troll may look much like a human being; only a little stocky, a little malformed. A troll is humanity minus the specifically human qualities; at once a hideous parody of man and yet only the isolation of his worst potentialities. . . . The troll is the animal version of man, the alternative to man: he is also what man fears he may become."—*Ibsen the Norwegian*, by M. C. Bradbrook, p. 56.

of the action—is mentioned soon (5) and is opposed to the possibility of freedom and beauty. The making of lots of money is seen by Torvald (8) and Nora (11) as a basis for security, a life free from care, yet when we meet someone (13) who actually married for money we have a sense of foreboding. . . . I am mentioning only a few of the references to money. They all lead into the play—taken as a play. (They culminate in Nora's "Torvald, this is a settling of accounts" [84].) You must, after all, regard *A Doll's House* as drama even when your topic is the ideas. The ideas thread their way in and out, as it were, as themes. The theme of money, for example. Money is at the root of so much that happens in *A Doll's House*. Ibsen has, if you like, an "idea" about money. He doesn't philosophize about it. He lets it find expression through the action and the characters.

You managed to speak of four Ibsen plays without noticing an "idea" common to them all—an idea about disease. For Ibsen, disease is not only one of the facts of life in general but a symbol of modern life in particular. You doubtless recall Solness' sickly conscience, Oswald's rotting body and mind, and you mentioned Dr. Rank. Don't you find Ibsen adroit when he introduces the disease-theme in Rank's opening discussion of Krogstad, at once transfers it from the physical to the moral sphere (21), then applies it to society at large (22)?

Admittedly a formula such as "Modern life—a disease" is little or nothing in itself. Ibsen makes dramatic use of it. He sets it in motion. He makes it grow. In *An Enemy of the People,* Act Two, Hovstad explains that the morass which the town is built on is not physical but moral (201). In Act Three, Stockman realizes that "it is the whole of our social life that we have got to purify and disinfect" (225). The idea gathers momentum and has, as it were, a climax, along with the rest of the play's action, in Act Four. "It is not they who are most instrumental in poisoning the sources of our moral life and infecting the ground on which we stand (255)...it is the masses, the majority" (257).

When I turn your attention from the ideas themselves to Ibsen's use of them I don't mean Ibsen didn't take ideas seriously, but that his seriousness about them and the force of the ideas themselves come out more in the way he has them operate than in anything he explicitly says. His criticism of life is made less in general formulations than in ironical juxtaposition of the facts. It has often been shown that Ibsen interweaves, intertwines, interlocks his materials. His dialogue is all implication, all cross-reference. This is his famous method.* It is important to see in it, not a system of meaningless theatrical trickery, but an exquisitely apt expression of Ibsen's awareness.

I grant you that when he became a virtuoso Ibsen succumbed to some of the virtuoso's temptations. His technique is sometimes obtrusive, and often the lines creak and groan beneath the load of double, treble and quadruple significance. I only ask you not, in protesting against the defect, to forget the quality. As to the overall structure of an Ibsen play,** for example, it is misleading to observe that Ibsen used a highly artificial, not to say sensational, pattern borrowed from the Parisian hacks and handed back to them afterwards, if we do not add that this pattern exactly suited Ibsen's deeper purpose. For the hacks, it was a toy— and thus an end in itself, though, by definition, a childish one. For Ibsen, it was the instrument of a vision.

Historians of the drama explain that Ibsen took over from the Parisian hacks the story of the long-buried secret which eventually leaks out with sensational results. They sometimes forget to add that Ibsen saw life itself as a placid surface through which, from time to time, what seemed dead and buried will break—a present into which

---

*How the method works out in *Ghosts* is demonstrated in *The Play: A Critical Anthology*, by Eric Bentley.
**The best descriptions are still to be found in *Playmaking*, by William Archer.

the "vanished" past returns. Perhaps they are indifferent to the meaning of all this—that there is moral continuity between past and present, that concealment (repression, hypocrisy) is the enemy, openness (candor, light, truth) the one thing necessary. If so they miss the point of Ibsen's famous expositions: as pure technique they would be barren exercises; what justifies them is the way they render the interaction of past and present. The curtain goes up ten years after Nora and Mrs. Linde last met, ten years after the death of Alving, ten years after the meeting of Solness and Hilda. Ibsen confronts one decade in his people's lives with another. The plot-pattern gives exact expression alike to his direct vision of life and to his subsequent interpretation of it.

To your contention that Ibsen's plots ride him, rather than he them, I reply that I could give more examples of the contrary. One is to be found at the end of *A Doll's House*. If the plot dominated the play, the culminating point would be Torvald's discovery of Nora's secret. Ibsen's achievement is to have subordinated this external event to Nora's inner realization that Torvald is incapable of nobly taking the blame for what she has done. The dramatically active question of the last act is whether the "wonderful thing" will happen or not. The scene in which Nora realizes that it won't is one of the great scenes in modern drama not only in precipitating some mordant speeches—"It is a thing hundreds of thousands of women have done" (90)— but in occasioning a magnificently dramatic silence—that of Nora gradually realizing that Torvald is a broken reed. A few words escape her but the process of realization is silent (80-83).

I should not leave the subject of Ibsen's dramatic art without a word on his mastery of the theatrical occasion. He isn't writing novels in dialogue form; he is writing for actors before the eyes of an audience. I suspect that, like so many moderns, you are primarily a novel-reader who resents not finding in Ibsen all that he finds in fiction. If you think Ibsen lacks the skills of Henry James you should recognize that he has others which James lacks, the skills of the theater rather than of the book. If of course you simply prefer the novel to the drama, there is no more to be said: you will naturally prefer James's gradual, word-by-word definition of his subject to Ibsen's definition by upheaval. If, on the other hand, you can respect the theatrical medium, you will appreciate the effect on the spectator of, say, Hilda Wangel's first irruption onto the stage with her alpenstock and knapsack, Mrs. Alving's "registering" the offstage laughter of Regina and Oswald, Nora's suddenly appearing in her street clothes. . . . Such things are addressed to the eyes of an audience, not to the imagination of a solitary reader.

"Ibsen and the Actor" is a huge topic, for not only did he write for actors (like every other playwright) ; he gave the actor something essentially new and asked him for something essentially new in return: a new style. He brought to completion a development in the art of acting that had been under way for centuries—the humanizing of the actor, the conversion of a hierophant into a man. In Ibsen that part of man which the ancient mime kept covered—the face—is the very center of the performance. The individual spirit looks out of the eyes and shapes its thoughts with the lips.

But this is no doubt too special a subject for your taste. Let me try to sum up my rejoinder to your protest. I think you have too limited a conception of the way in which an artist teaches. Ibsen, for example, is not—or not in the first instance—providing a list of recommended virtues and deplored vices. In this regard, he is singularly modest. He has written only a preface to morals. He asks for that degree of honor, honesty, integrity, truth, what you will, that is needed before a moral life can exist. We have seen that he tells over and again the story of the disastrous effects of concealment and burial. He is asking us, not necessarily to

be saints and heroes, but at least to stand upright, at least
—like Goethe's Faust—to assume responsibilities and make
ethical distinctions, to be authentic human beings. Ibsen
does not have his people follow the track of any particular
virtue. He shows Nora and Mrs. Alving trying to discover
themselves and reach the threshold of morality, the point
where virtues—and, of course, vices—begin. So much of our
life is too meaningless or too infantile even to be called
vicious.

This criticism of life places Ibsen, not in the piddling
tradition of the problem play, but at the very heart of our
contemporary discussion of ourselves. He is one of the great
modern writers. Like most of the others he has presented
modern life to us in the form of fable, parable, myth and,
once you realize that his medium was theater and not the
book, you will not find his fables inferior to those of other
masters. Ibsen is a poet. Although he gave up verse, he
managed to enrich and intensify his work by so many other
means that the verse plays of the best poets since his time
—T. S. Eliot's, for example—seem dilute and "unpoetic" by
comparison.

Forty years ago a decadent poet—who evidently despised
Ibsen's dialogue in general—could refer to Hilda Wangel's
"harps in the air" as a feeble, if praiseworthy, attempt at
lyricism. Strange that he hadn't more feeling for the *context* of Hilda's phrase, for that dry, prose understatement
against which "harps in the air" comes as a contrast, an
intentionally brief glimpse of another order of experience!
I do not mean to interpret the dry, prose understatement
as a merely negative factor. A generation that has read
Gertrude Stein and Ernest Hemingway knows better than
that. Ibsen is a great realist, not least in his imaginative
use of unimaginative language.

Of recent years those of us who admire Ibsen's "poetry"
have probably understressed his "realism." It is a pity the
two words are used antithetically. Ibsen was a great poet—

that is, he had a great imagination which found its outlet in words—but it would be foolish to try to detach him from the realist movement. He quite consciously channeled his energies into it. It was as a realist that he made his first impact, and, in closing my counter-statement, I shall maintain that it is partly as a realist that he must still make his impact today.

In refusing to squeeze Ibsen into the narrow category of the problem play we need not neglect to view him historically. There is a pedantry of historical scholarship that reduces artists to statistics and vaguely defined abstractions, but there is also history itself—man and all his works in the flux of time. I should prefer to see *any* artist in this context rather than in context of timeless forms and timeless ideas—and Ibsen above all. For, however we stress his artistry and the breadth of his mind, he was a man up to the neck in his time. We find him relevant today partly because we have still not put his time behind us, partly because the artists who become permanent are precisely those who grasp the ephemeral most firmly and not those whose eyes are fixed upon eternity.

A more historical view of Ibsen will keep us from exaggerating the "other-worldliness" of a play like—to come back to your bugbear—*The Master Builder*. For, once we realize that Ibsen was not obsessed with syphilis and votes for women, there is a danger of our locating his interest only in the deepest recesses of the individual consciousness. This would be to consider him just as narrow a specialist—only at the other extreme. The glory of Ibsen is that he refused to make certain fatal separations. He refused (for example) to separate the individual from the collective, the personal from the social.

Halvard Solness is seen in both aspects. There is Solness, the individual artist: *the symbolism of the play drives inwards*, to the rich inner life of the man. There is also Solness, the builder of actual houses: I should not be as much inclined as I once was to regard him as a mere front for the more spiritual figure. As Miss Bradbrook says: "Solness belonged to a class which transformed Norway. The replacing of the old wooden houses ... by modern buildings effected a domestic revolution." *The realism of the play drives outwards,* to the rich outer life of the man. If the symbolism and the realism of *The Master Builder* are imperfectly fused — and that may be the source of your difficulty with the play — one realizes that Ibsen could have "perfected" his work by simplifying his problem, by writing a narrowly "symbolic" or a narrowly "realist" play. Surely one prefers a heroic failure.

Not that the word failure applies to Ibsen's work as a whole. Artistic failures seldom outlive the artist, yet, a hundred years since Ibsen's first play was written, his words sting and burn, if we let them, as fiercely as ever. No playwright has managed to project into his scenes more of the pressure of modern life, its special anxiety, strain and stress. The life of our times courses through his plays in a torrent. And if we are a little more conscious than our grandparents were of the care with which Ibsen controlled the flood — his mastery of form — we must still begin where they began — with shock, with enthrallment, with illumination, as Ibsen's world, which is so large a sector of the modern world, social and personal, outer and inner, unfolds before us.

IBSEN'S LIFE AND WORKS

1881   *Ghosts*

1882   As a result of public outcry against *Ghosts: An Enemy of the People*

1884   Qualifying the extreme position taken in *An Enemy of the People: The Wild Duck*

1885   Pays a visit to Norway but returns to Germany

1886   Following the lead of *The Wild Duck* his plays become less exclusively social, more "mystical": *Rosmersholm*

1888   *The Lady from the Sea*

1890   *Hedda Gabler*

1891   Goes to spend the rest of his days in Norway

1892   Opens his last "series" of plays—more "mystical" still—with *The Master Builder*

1894   *Little Eyolf*

1896   *John Gabriel Borkman*

1899   *When We Dead Awaken*

1900   Has a seizure and never works again

1906   Death

A NOTE ABOUT BOOKS

One should go from the present volume to the Modern Library Giant which contains seven other plays. The only larger collection in English is *The Works of Henrik Ibsen*, edited by William Archer (New York, 1912). Volume XII is *From Ibsen's Workshop*, a valuable collection of notes and first drafts. Among other translations of the various plays at least two are worth special mention: R. Ellis Roberts' version of *Peer Gynt* published separately by the Oxford University Press in the World's Classics Series and Eva LeGallienne's version of *Ghosts* published in *The Play: a Critical Anthology*, edited by Eric Bentley (New York, 1950). For Ibsen's opinions on various subjects, see *The Letters of Henrik Ibsen* (New York, 1905) and *Speeches and New Letters* (Boston, 1910).

The standard biography of Ibsen is Halvdan Koht's *Life of Ibsen* (New York, 1931). The standard exegesis of his plays from *Pillars of Society* on is Hermann J. Weigand's *The Modern Ibsen* (New York, 1924). The most brilliant book Ibsen has ever called forth, and the most influential, is Bernard Shaw's *The Quintessence of Ibsenism* (revised edition: New York, 1912). The best account of Ibsen's craftsmanship is to be found in William Archer's *Playmaking* (Boston, 1923). His intellectual background is best described in Brian W. Downs' *Ibsen: the Intellectual Background* (Cambridge, England, 1946). The importance of Norway in his writings is best brought home by M. C. Bradbrook in her *Ibsen the Norwegian* (London, 1946). A general presentation, good on the biographical side, is A. E. Zucker's *Ibsen the Master Builder* (New York, 1929). The Marxist view of Ibsen is most conveniently found in *Ibsen*, edited by Angel Flores (New York, 1937).

A DOLL'S HOUSE
(1879)

CHARACTERS

Torvald Helmer.
Nora, *his wife*.
Doctor Rank.
Mrs. Linde.
Nils Krogstad.
Helmer's *three young children*.
Anne, *their nurse*.
A Housemaid.
A Porter.

The action takes place in Helmer's *house.*

A DOLL'S HOUSE

ACT I

SCENE.—*A room furnished comfortably and tastefully, but not extravagantly. At the back, a door to the right leads to the entrance hall, another to the left leads to* HELMER'S *study. Between the doors stands a piano. In the middle of the left-hand wall is a door, and beyond it a window. Near the window are a round table, armchairs and a small sofa. In the right-hand wall, at the farther end, another door; and on the same side, nearer the footlights, a stove, two easy chairs and a rocking-chair; between the stove and the door, a small table. Engravings on the walls; a cabinet with china and other small objects; a small book-case with well-bound books. The floors are carpeted, and a fire burns in the stove. It is winter.*

A bell rings in the hall; shortly afterwards the door is heard to open. Enter NORA, *humming a tune and in high spirits. She is in out-door dress and carries a number of parcels; these she lays on the table to the right. She leaves the outer door open after her, and through it is seen a* PORTER *who is carrying a Christmas Tree and a basket, which he gives to the* MAID *who has opened the door.*

Nora. Hide the Christmas Tree carefully, Helen. Be sure the children do not see it till this evening, when it

3

is dressed. *(To the* PORTER, *taking out her purse.)* How much?

Porter. Sixpence.

Nora. There is a shilling. No, keep the change. *(The* PORTER *thanks her, and goes out.* NORA *shuts the door. She is laughing to herself, as she takes off her hat and coat. She takes a packet of macaroons from her pocket and eats one or two; then goes cautiously to her husband's door and listens.)* Yes, he is in.

[*Still humming, she goes to the table on the right.*

Helmer (calls out from his room). Is that my little lark twittering out there?

Nora (busy opening some of the parcels). Yes, it is!

Helmer. Is it my little squirrel bustling about?

Nora. Yes!

Helmer. When did my squirrel come home?

Nora. Just now. *(Puts the bag of macaroons into her pocket and wipes her mouth.)* Come in here, Torvald, and see what I have bought.

Helmer. Don't disturb me. *(A little later, he opens the door and looks into the room, pen in hand.)* Bought, did you say? All these things? Has my little spendthrift been wasting money again?

Nora. Yes, but, Torvald, this year we really can let ourselves go a little. This is the first Christmas that we have not needed to economise.

Helmer. Still, you know, we can't spend money recklessly.

Nora. Yes, Torvald, we may be a wee bit more reckless now, mayn't we? Just a tiny wee bit! You are going to have a big salary and earn lots and lots of money.

Helmer. Yes, after the New Year; but then it will be a whole quarter before the salary is due.

Nora. Pooh! we can borrow till then.

Helmer. Nora! *(Goes up to her and takes her playfully by the ear.)* The same little featherhead! Suppose, now,

that I borrowed fifty pounds to-day, and you spent it all
in the Christmas week, and then on New Year's Eve a
slate fell on my head and killed me, and——

Nora (putting her hands over his mouth). Oh! don't
say such horrid things.

Helmer. Still, suppose that happened,—what then?

Nora. If that were to happen, I don't suppose I should
care whether I owed money or not.

Helmer. Yes, but what about the people who had lent it?

Nora. They? Who would bother about them? I
should not know who they were.

Helmer. That is like a woman! But seriously, Nora,
you know what I think about that. No debt, no borrowing.
There can be no freedom or beauty about a home life that
depends on borrowing and debt. We two have kept bravely
on the straight road so far, and we will go on the same way
for the short time longer that there need be any struggle.

Nora (moving towards the stove). As you please, Torvald.

Helmer (following her). Come, come, my little skylark
must not droop her wings. What is this! Is my little
squirrel out of temper? *(Taking out his purse.)* Nora,
what do you think I have got here?

Nora (turning round quickly). Money!

Helmer. There you are. *(Gives her some money.)* Do
you think I don't know what a lot is wanted for housekeeping at Christmas-time?

Nora (counting). Ten shillings—a pound—two pounds!
Thank you, thank you, Torvald; that will keep me going
for a long time.

Helmer. Indeed it must.

Nora. Yes, yes, it will. But come here and let me show
you what I have bought. And all so cheap! Look, here
is a new suit for Ivar, and a sword; and a horse and a
trumpet for Bob; and a doll and dolly's bedstead for Emmy
—they are very plain, but anyway she will soon break them

in pieces. And here are dress-lengths and handkerchiefs for the maids; old Anne ought really to have something better.

Helmer. And what is in this parcel?

Nora (crying out). No, no! you mustn't see that till this evening.

Helmer. Very well. But now tell me, you extravagant little person, what would you like for yourself?

Nora. For myself? Oh, I am sure I don't want anything.

Helmer. Yes, but you must. Tell me something reasonable that you would particularly like to have.

Nora. No, I really can't think of anything—unless, Torvald——

Helmer. Well?

Nora (playing with his coat buttons, and without raising her eyes to his). If you really want to give me something, you might—you might——

Helmer. Well, out with it!

Nora (speaking quickly). You might give me money, Torvald. Only just as much as you can afford; and then one of these days I will buy something with it.

Helmer. But, Nora——

Nora. Oh, do! dear Torvald; please, please do! Then I will wrap it up in beautiful gilt paper and hang it on the Christmas Tree. Wouldn't that be fun?

Helmer. What are little people called that are always wasting money?

Nora. Spendthrifts—I know. Let us do as you suggest, Torvald, and then I shall have time to think what I am most in want of. That is a very sensible plan, isn't it?

Helmer (smiling). Indeed it is—that is to say, if you were really to save out of the money I give you, and then really buy something for yourself. But if you spend it all on the housekeeping and any number of unnecessary things, then I merely have to pay up again.

Nora. Oh but, Torvald——

Helmer. You can't deny it, my dear little Nora. *(Puts his arm round her waist.)* It's a sweet little spendthrift, but she uses up a deal of money. One would hardly believe how expensive such little persons are!

Nora. It's a shame to say that. I do really save all I can.

Helmer (laughing). That's very true,—all you can. But you can't save anything!

Nora (smiling quietly and happily). You haven't any idea how many expenses we skylarks and squirrels have, Torvald.

Helmer. You are an odd little soul. Very like your father. You always find some new way of wheedling money out of me, and, as soon as you have got it, it seems to melt in your hands. You never know where it has gone. Still, one must take you as you are. It is in the blood; for indeed it is true that you can inherit these things, Nora.

Nora. Ah, I wish I had inherited many of papa's qualities.

Helmer. And I would not wish you to be anything but just what you are, my sweet little skylark. But, do you know, it strikes me that you are looking rather—what shall I say—rather uneasy to-day?

Nora. Do I?

Helmer. You do, really. Look straight at me.

Nora (looks at him). Well?

Helmer (wagging his finger at her). Hasn't Miss Sweet-Tooth been breaking rules in town to-day?

Nora. No; what makes you think that?

Helmer. Hasn't she paid a visit to the confectioner's?

Nora. No, I assure you, Torvald——

Helmer. Not been nibbling sweets?

Nora. No, certainly not.

Helmer. Not even taken a bite at a macaroon or two?

Nora. No, Torvald, I assure you really——

Helmer. There, there, of course I was only joking.

Nora (going to the table on the right). I should not think of going against your wishes.

Helmer. No, I am sure of that! besides, you gave me your word—— *(Going up to her.)* Keep your little Christmas secrets to yourself, my darling. They will all be revealed to-night when the Christmas Tree is lit, no doubt.

Nora. Did you remember to invite Doctor Rank?

Helmer. No. But there is no need; as a matter of course he will come to dinner with us. However, I will ask him when he comes in this morning. I have ordered some good wine. Nora, you can't think how I am looking forward to this evening.

Nora. So am I! And how the children will enjoy themselves, Torvald!

Helmer. It is splendid to feel that one has a perfectly safe appointment, and a big enough income. It's delightful to think of, isn't it?

Nora. It's wonderful?

Helmer. Do you remember last Christmas? For a full three weeks beforehand you shut yourself up every evening till long after midnight, making ornaments for the Christmas Tree and all the other fine things that were to be a surprise to us. It was the dullest three weeks I ever spent!

Nora. I didn't find it dull.

Helmer (smiling). But there was precious little result, Nora.

Nora. Oh, you shouldn't tease me about that again. How could I help the cat's going in and tearing everything to pieces?

Helmer. Of course you couldn't, poor little girl. You had the best of intentions to please us all, and that's the main thing. But it is a good thing that our hard times are over.

Nora. Yes, it is really wonderful.

Helmer. This time I needn't sit here and be dull all

alone, and you needn't ruin your dear eyes and your pretty little hands——

Nora (clapping her hands). No, Torvald, I needn't any longer, need I? It's wonderfully lovely to hear you say so! *(Taking his arm.)* Now I will tell you how I have been thinking we ought to arrange things, Torvald. As soon as Christmas is over—— *(A bell rings in the hall.)* There's the bell. *(She tidies the room a little.)* There's someone at the door. What a nuisance!

Helmer. If it is a caller, remember I am not at home.

Maid (in the doorway). A lady to see you, ma'am,—a stranger.

Nora. Ask her to come in.

Maid (to HELMER*).* The doctor came at the same time, sir.

Helmer. Did he go straight into my room?

Maid. Yes, sir.

> [HELMER *goes into his room. The* MAID *ushers in* MRS. LINDE, *who is in travelling dress, and shuts the door.*

Mrs. Linde (in a dejected and timid voice). How do you do, Nora?

Nora (doubtfully). How do you do——

Mrs. Linde. You don't recognise me, I suppose.

Nora. No, I don't know—yes, to be sure, I seem to—— *(Suddenly.)* Yes! Christine! Is it really you?

Mrs. Linde. Yes, it is I.

Nora. Christine! To think of my not recognising you! And yet how could I—— *(In a gentle voice.)* How you have altered, Christine!

Mrs. Linde. Yes, I have indeed. In nine, ten long years——

Nora. Is it so long since we met? I suppose it is. The last eight years have been a happy time for me, I can tell you. And so now you have come into the town, and have taken this long journey in winter—that was plucky of you.

Mrs. Linde. I arrived by steamer this morning.

Nora. To have some fun at Christmas-time, of course. How delightful! We will have such fun together! But take off your things. You are not cold, I hope. *(Helps her.)* Now we will sit down by the stove, and be cosy. No, take this arm-chair; I will sit here in the rocking-chair. *(Takes her hands.)* Now you look like your old self again; it was only the first moment—— You are a little paler, Christine, and perhaps a little thinner.

Mrs. Linde. And much, much older, Nora.

Nora. Perhaps a little older; very, very little; certainly not much. *(Stops suddenly and speaks seriously.)* What a thoughtless creature I am, chattering away like this. My poor, dear Christine, do forgive me.

Mrs. Linde. What do you mean, Nora?

Nora (gently). Poor Christine, you are a widow.

Mrs. Linde. Yes; it is three years ago now.

Nora. Yes, I knew; I saw it in the papers. I assure you, Christine, I meant ever so often to write to you at the time, but I always put it off and something always prevented me.

Mrs. Linde. I quite understand, dear.

Nora. It was very bad of me, Christine. Poor thing, how you must have suffered. And he left you nothing?

Mrs. Linde. No.

Nora. And no children?

Mrs. Linde. No.

Nora. Nothing at all, then?

Mrs. Linde. Not even any sorrow or grief to live upon.

Nora (looking incredulously at her). But, Christine, is that possible?

Mrs. Linde (smiles sadly and strokes her hair). It sometimes happens, Nora.

Nora. So you are quite alone. How dreadfully sad that must be. I have three lovely children. You can't see them just now, for they are out with their nurse. But now you must tell me all about it.

Mrs. Linde. No, no; I want to hear you.

Nora. No, you must begin. I mustn't be selfish to-day; to-day I must only think of your affairs. But there is one thing I must tell you. Do you know we have just had a great piece of good luck?

Mrs. Linde. No, what is it?

Nora. Just fancy, my husband has been made manager of the Bank!

Mrs. Linde. Your husband? What good luck!

Nora. Yes, tremendous! A barrister's profession is such an uncertain thing, especially if he won't undertake unsavoury cases; and naturally Torvald has never been willing to do that, and I quite agree with him. You may imagine how pleased we are! He is to take up his work in the Bank at the New Year, and then he will have a big salary and lots of commissions. For the future we can live quite differently —we can do just as we like. I feel so relieved and so happy, Christine! It will be splendid to have heaps of money and not need to have any anxiety, won't it?

Mrs. Linde. Yes, anyhow I think it would be delightful to have what one needs.

Nora. No, not only what one needs, but heaps and heaps of money.

Mrs. Linde (smiling). Nora, Nora, haven't you learnt sense yet? In our schooldays you were a great spendthrift.

Nora (laughing). Yes, that is what Torvald says now *(Wags her finger at her.)* But "Nora, Nora" is not so silly as you think. We have not been in a position for me to waste money. We have both had to work.

Mrs. Linde. You too?

Nora. Yes; odds and ends, needlework, crochet-work, embroidery, and that kind of thing. *(Dropping her voice.)* And other things as well. You know Torvald left his office when we were married?   There was no prospect of promotion there, and he had to try and earn more than before. But during the first year he overworked himself dreadfully. You see, he had to make money every way he could, and he worked early and late; but he couldn't stand it, and fell dreadfully ill, and the doctors said it was necessary for him to go south.

Mrs. Linde.   You spent a whole year in Italy, didn't you?

Nora.   Yes.   It was no easy matter to get away, I can tell you.   It was just after Ivar was born; but naturally we had to go.   It was a wonderfully beautiful journey, and it saved Torvald's life.   But it cost a tremendous lot of money, Christine.

Mrs. Linde.   So I should think.

Nora.   It cost about two hundred and fifty pounds. That's a lot, isn't it?

Mrs. Linde.   Yes, and in emergencies like that it is lucky to have the money.

Nora.   I ought to tell you that we had it from papa.

Mrs. Linde.   Oh, I see.   It was just about that time that he died, wasn't it?

Nora.   Yes; and, just think of it, I couldn't go and nurse him.   I was expecting little Ivar's birth every day and I had my poor sick Torvald to look after.   My dear, kind father—I never saw him again, Christine.   That was the saddest time I have known since our marriage.

Mrs. Linde.   I know how fond you were of him.   And then you went off to Italy?

Nora.   Yes; you see we had money then, and the doctors insisted on our going, so we started a month later.

Mrs. Linde.   And your husband came back quite well?

Nora.   As sound as a bell!

Mrs. Linde.   But—the doctor?

Nora.   What doctor?

Mrs. Linde.   I thought your maid said the gentleman who arrived here just as I did, was the doctor?

Nora. Yes, that was Doctor Rank, but he doesn't come here professionally. He is our greatest friend, and comes in at least once every day. No, Torvald has not had an hour's illness since then, and our children are strong and healthy and so am I. *(Jumps up and claps her hands.)* Christine! Christine! it's good to be alive and happy!—— But how horrid of me; I am talking of nothing but my own affairs. *(Sits on a stool near her, and rests her arms on her knees.)* You mustn't be angry with me. Tell me, is it really true that you did not love your husband? Why did you marry him?

Mrs. Linde. My mother was alive then, and was bed-ridden and helpless, and I had to provide for my two younger brothers; so I did not think I was justified in refusing his offer.

Nora. No, perhaps you were quite right. He was rich at that time, then?

Mrs. Linde. I believe he was quite well off. But his business was a precarious one; and, when he died, it all went to pieces and there was nothing left.

Nora. And then?——

Mrs. Linde. Well, I had to turn my hand to anything I could find—first a small shop, then a small school, and so on. The last three years have seemed like one long working-day, with no rest. Now it is at an end, Nora. My poor mother needs me no more, for she is gone; and the boys do not need me either; they have got situations and can shift for themselves.

Nora. What a relief you must feel it——

Mrs. Linde. No, indeed; I only feel my life unspeakably empty. No one to live for any more. *(Gets up restlessly.)* That was why I could not stand the life in my little back-water any longer. I hope it may be easier here to find something which will busy me and occupy my thoughts. If only I could have the good luck to get some regular work—office work of some kind——

Nora. But, Christine, that is so frightfully tiring, and you look tired out now. You had far better go away to some watering-place.

Mrs. Linde (walking to the window). I have no father to give me money for a journey, Nora.

Nora (rising). Oh, don't be angry with me.

Mrs. Linde (going up to her). It is you that must not be angry with me, dear. The worst of a position like mine is that it makes one so bitter. No one to work for, and yet obliged to be always on the look-out for chances. One must live, and so one becomes selfish. When you told me of the happy turn your fortunes have taken—you will hardly believe it—I was delighted not so much on your account as on my own.

Nora. How do you mean?—Oh, I understand. You mean that perhaps Torvald could get you something to do.

Mrs. Linde. Yes, that was what I was thinking of.

Nora. He must, Christine. Just leave it to me; I will broach the subject very cleverly—I will think of something that will please him very much. It will make me so happy to be of some use to you.

Mrs. Linde. How kind you are, Nora, to be so anxious to help me! It is doubly kind in you, for you know so little of the burdens and troubles of life.

Nora. I——? I know so little of them?

Mrs. Linde (smiling). My dear! Small household cares and that sort of thing!—You are a child, Nora.

Nora (tosses her head and crosses the stage). You ought not to be so superior.

Mrs. Linde. No?

Nora. You are just like the others. They all think that I am incapable of anything really serious——

Mrs. Linde. Come, come——

Nora. —that I have gone through nothing in this world of cares.

Mrs. Linde. But, my dear Nora, you have just told me all your troubles.

Nora. Pooh!—those were trifles. *(Lowering her voice.)* I have not told you the important thing.

Mrs. Linde. The important thing? What do you mean?

Nora. You look down upon me altogether, Christine— but you ought not to. You are proud, aren't you, of having worked so hard and so long for your mother?

Mrs. Linde. Indeed, I don't look down on any one. But it is true that I am both proud and glad to think that I was privileged to make the end of my mother's life almost free from care.

Nora. And you are proud to think of what you have done for your brothers.

Mrs. Linde. I think I have the right to be.

Nora. I think so, too. But now, listen to this; I too have something to be proud and glad of.

Mrs. Linde. I have no doubt you have. But what do you refer to?

Nora. Speak low. Suppose Torvald were to hear! He mustn't on any account—no one in the world must know, Christine, except you.

Mrs. Linde. But what is it?

Nora. Come here. *(Pulls her down on the sofa beside her.)* Now I will show you that I too have something to be proud and glad of. It was I who saved Torvald's life.

Mrs. Linde. "Saved"? How?

Nora. I told you about our trip to Italy. Torvald would never have recovered if he had not gone there——

Mrs. Linde. Yes, but your father gave you the necessary funds.

Nora (smiling). Yes, that is what Torvald and all the others think, but——

Mrs. Linde. But——

Nora. Papa didn't give us a shilling. It was I who procured the money.

Mrs. Linde. You? All that large sum?

Nora. Two hundred and fifty pounds. What do you think of that?

Mrs. Linde. But, Nora, how could you possibly do it? Did you win a prize in the Lottery?

Nora (contemptuously). In the Lottery? There would have been no credit in that.

Mrs. Linde. But where did you get it from, then?

Nora (humming and smiling with an air of mystery). Hm, hm! Aha!

Mrs. Linde. Because you couldn't have borrowed it.

Nora. Couldn't I? Why not?

Mrs. Linde. No, a wife cannot borrow without her husband's consent.

Nora (tossing her head). Oh, if it is a wife who has any head for business—a wife who has the wit to be a little bit clever——

Mrs. Linde. I don't understand it at all, Nora.

Nora. There is no need you should. I never said I had borrowed the money. I may have got it some other way. *(Lies back on the sofa.)* Perhaps I got it from some other admirer. When anyone is as attractive as I am——

Mrs. Linde. You are a mad creature.

Nora. Now, you know you're full of curiosity, Christine.

Mrs. Linde. Listen to me, Nora dear. Haven't you been a little bit imprudent?

Nora (sits up straight). Is it imprudent to save your husband's life?

Mrs. Linde. It seems to me imprudent, without his knowledge, to——

Nora. But it was absolutely necessary that he should not know! My goodness, can't you understand that? It was necessary he should have no idea what a dangerous condition he was in. It was to me that the doctors came and said that his life was in danger, and that the only thing to save him was to live in the south. Do you suppose I

didn't try, first of all, to get what I wanted as if it were
for myself? I told him how much I should love to travel
abroad like other young wives; I tried tears and entreaties
with him; I told him that he ought to remember the condition I was in, and that he ought to be kind and indulgent to
me; I even hinted that he might raise a loan. That nearly
made him angry, Christine. He said I was thoughtless,
and that it was his duty as my husband not to indulge me
in my whims and caprices—as I believe he called them.
Very well, I thought, you must be saved—and that was how
I came to devise a way out of the difficulty——

Mrs. Linde. And did your husband never get to know
from your father that the money had not come from him?

Nora. No, never. Papa died just at that time. I had
meant to let him into the secret and beg him never to reveal
it. But he was so ill then—alas, there never was any need
to tell him.

Mrs. Linde. And since then have you never told your
secret to your husband?

Nora. Good Heavens, no! How could you think so?
A man who has such strong opinions about these things!
And besides, how painful and humiliating it would be for
Torvald, with his manly independence, to know that he
owed me anything! It would upset our mutual relations
altogether; our beautiful happy home would no longer be
what it is now.

Mrs. Linde. Do you mean never to tell him about it?

Nora (meditatively, and with a half smile). Yes—some
day, perhaps, after many years, when I am no longer as nice-
looking as I am now. Don't laugh at me! I mean, of
course, when Torvald is no longer as devoted to me as he is
now; when my dancing and dressing-up and reciting have
palled on him; then it may be a good thing to have something in reserve—— *(Breaking off.)* What nonsense!
That time will never come. Now, what do you think of my
great secret, Christine? Do you still think I am of no use?

I can tell you, too, that this affair has caused me a lot of worry. It has been by no means easy for me to meet my engagements punctually. I may tell you that there is something that is called, in business, quarterly interest, and another thing called payment in instalments, and it is always so dreadfully difficult to manage them. I have had to save a little here and there, where I could, you understand. I have not been able to put aside much from my housekeeping money, for Torvald must have a good table. I couldn't let my children be shabbily dressed; I have felt obliged to use up all he gave me for them, the sweet little darlings!

Mrs. Linde. So it has all had to come out of your own necessaries of life, poor Nora?

Nora. Of course. Besides, I was the one responsible for it. Whenever Torvald has given me money for new dresses and such things, I have never spent more than half of it; I have always bought the simplest and cheapest things. Thank Heaven, any clothes look well on me, and so Torvald has never noticed it. But it was often very hard on me, Christine—because it is delightful to be really well dressed, isn't it?

Mrs. Linde. Quite so.

Nora. Well, then I have found other ways of earning money. Last winter I was lucky enough to get a lot of copying to do; so I locked myself up and sat writing every evening until quite late at night. Many a time I was desperately tired; but all the same it was a tremendous pleasure to sit there working and earning money. It was like being a man.

Mrs. Linde. How much have you been able to pay off in that way?

Nora. I can't tell you exactly. You see, it is very difficult to keep an account of a business matter of that kind. I only know that I have paid every penny that I could scrape together. Many a time I was at my wits' end. *(Smiles.)*

Then I used to sit here and imagine that a rich old gentleman had fallen in love with me——

Mrs. Linde. What! Who was it?

Nora. Be quiet!—that he had died; and that when his will was opened it contained, written in big letters, the instruction: "The lovely Mrs. Nora Helmer is to have all I possess paid over to her at once in cash."

Mrs. Linde. But, my dear Nora—who could the man be?

Nora. Good gracious, can't you understand? There was no old gentleman at all; it was only something that I used to sit here and imagine, when I couldn't think of any way of procuring money. But it's all the same now; the tiresome old person can stay where he is, as far as I am concerned; I don't care about him or his will either, for I am free from care now. *(Jumps up.)* My goodness, it's delightful to think of, Christine! Free from care! To be able to be free from care, quite free from care; to be able to play and romp with the children; to be able to keep the house beautifully and have everything just as Torvald likes it! And, think of it, soon the spring will come and the big blue sky! Perhaps we shall be able to take a little trip— perhaps I shall see the sea again! Oh, it's a wonderful thing to be alive and be happy. *(A bell is heard in the hall.)*

Mrs. Linde (rising). There is the bell; perhaps I had better go.

Nora. No, don't go; no one will come in here; it is sure to be for Torvald.

Servant (at the hall door). Excuse me, ma'am—there is a gentleman to see the master, and as the doctor is with him——

Nora. Who is it?

Krogstad (at the door). It is I, Mrs. Helmer. (MRS. LINDE *starts, trembles, and turns to the window.*)

Nora (takes a step towards him, and speaks in a strained,

low voice). You? What is it? What do you want to see my husband about?

Krogstad. Bank business—in a way. I have a small post in the Bank, and I hear your husband is to be our chief now——

Nora. Then it is——

Krogstad. Nothing but dry business matters, Mrs. Helmer; absolutely nothing else.

Nora. Be so good as to go into the study, then. *(She bows indifferently to him and shuts the door into the hall; then comes back and makes up the fire in the stove.)*

Mrs. Linde. Nora—who was that man?

Nora. A lawyer, of the name of Krogstad.

Mrs. Linde. Then it really was he.

Nora. Do you know the man?

Mrs. Linde. I used to—many years ago. At one time he was a solicitor's clerk in our town.

Nora. Yes, he was.

Mrs. Linde. He is greatly altered.

Nora. He made a very unhappy marriage.

Mrs. Linde. He is a widower now, isn't he?

Nora. With several children. There now, it is burning up.

> [*Shuts the door of the stove and moves the rocking-chair aside.*

Mrs. Linde. They say he carries on various kinds of business.

Nora. Really! Perhaps he does; I don't know anything about it. But don't let us think of business; it is so tiresome.

Doctor Rank (comes out of HELMER's *study. Before he shuts the door he calls to him).* No, my dear fellow, I won't disturb you; I would rather go into your wife for a little while. *(Shuts the door and sees* MRS. LINDE.) I beg your pardon; I am afraid I am disturbing you too.

Nora. No, not at all. *(Introducing him.)* Doctor Rank, Mrs. Linde.

Rank. I have often heard Mrs. Linde's name mentioned here. I think I passed you on the stairs when I arrived, Mrs. Linde?

Mrs. Linde. Yes, I go up very slowly; I can't manage stairs well.

Rank. Ah! some slight internal weakness?

Mrs. Linde. No, the fact is I have been overworking myself.

Rank. Nothing more than that? Then I suppose you have come to town to amuse yourself with our entertainments?

Mrs. Linde. I have come to look for work.

Rank. Is that a good cure for overwork?

Mrs. Linde. One must live, Doctor Rank.

Rank. Yes, the general opinion seems to be that it is necessary.

Nora. Look here, Doctor Rank—you know you want to live.

Rank. Certainly. However wretched I may feel, I want to prolong the agony as long as possible. All my patients are like that. And so are those who are morally diseased; one of them, and a bad case too, is at this very moment with Helmer——

Mrs. Linde (sadly). Ah!

Nora. Whom do you mean?

Rank. A lawyer of the name of Krogstad, a fellow you don't know at all. He suffers from a diseased moral character, Mrs. Helmer; but even he began talking of its being highly important that he should live.

Nora. Did he? What did he want to speak to Torvald about?

Rank. I have no idea; I only heard that it was something about the Bank.

Nora. I didn't know this—what's his name—Krogstad
had anything to do with the Bank.

Rank. Yes, he has some sort of appointment there. *(To*
Mrs. Linde.) I don't know whether you find also in your
part of the world that there are certain people who go zeal-
ously snuffing about to smell out moral corruption, and, as
soon as they have found some, put the person concerned into
some lucrative position where they can keep their eye on
him. Healthy natures are left out in the cold.

Mrs. Linde. Still I think the sick are those who most
need taking care of.

Rank (shrugging his shoulders). Yes, there you are.
That is the sentiment that is turning Society into a sick-
house.

> [Nora, *who has been absorbed in her thoughts,*
> *breaks out into smothered laughter and claps her*
> *hands.*

Rank. Why do you laugh at that? Have you any notion what Society really is?

Nora. What do I care about tiresome Society? I am
laughing at something quite different, something extremely
amusing. Tell me, Doctor Rank, are all the people who are
employed in the Bank dependent on Torvald now?

Rank. Is that what you find so extremely amusing?

Nora (smiling and humming). That's my affair!
(Walking about the room.) It's perfectly glorious to think
that we have—that Torvald has so much power over so
many people. *(Takes the packet from her pocket.)* Doctor Rank, what do you say to a macaroon?

Rank. What, macaroons? I thought they were forbidden here.

Nora. Yes, but these are some Christine gave me.

Mrs. Linde. What! I?—

Nora. Oh, well, don't be alarmed! You couldn't know
that Torvald had forbidden them. I must tell you that he
is afraid they will spoil my teeth. But, bah!—once in a

way—— That's so, isn't it, Doctor Rank? By your leave? *(Puts a macaroon into his mouth.)* You must have one too, Christine. And I shall have one, just a little one—. or at most two. *(Walking about.)* I am tremendously happy. There is just one thing in the world now that I should dearly love to do.

Rank. Well, what is that?

Nora. It's something I should dearly love to say, if Torvald could hear me.

Rank. Well, why can't you say it?

Nora. No, I daren't; it's so shocking.

Mrs. Linde. Shocking?

Rank. Well, I should not advise you to say it. Still, with us you might. What is it you would so much like to say if Torvald could hear you?

Nora. I should just love to say—Well, I'm damned!

Rank. Are you mad?

Mrs. Linde. Nora, dear——!

Rank. Say it, here he is!

Nora (hiding the packet). Hush! Hush! Hush!

    [HELMER *comes out of his room, with his coat over his arm and his hat in his hand.*

Nora. Well, Torvald dear, have you got rid of him?

Helmer. Yes, he has just gone.

Nora. Let me introduce you—this is Christine, who has come to town.

Helmer. Christine——? Excuse me, but I don't know

——

Nora. Mrs. Linde, dear; Christine Linde.

Helmer. Of course. A school friend of my wife's, I presume?

Mrs. Linde. Yes, we have known each other since then

Nora. And just think, she has taken a long journey in order to see you.

Helmer. What do you mean?

Mrs. Linde. No, really, I——

Nora. Christine is tremendously clever at book-keeping, and she is frightfully anxious to work under some clever man, so as to perfect herself——

Helmer. Very sensible, Mrs. Linde.

Nora. And when she heard you had been appointed manager of the Bank—the news was telegraphed, you know—she travelled here as quick as she could, Torvald, I am sure you will be able to do something for Christine, for my sake, won't you?

Helmer. Well, it is not altogether impossible. I presume you are a widow, Mrs. Linde?

Mrs. Linde. Yes.

Helmer. And have had some experience of book-keeping?

Mrs. Linde. Yes, a fair amount.

Helmer. Ah! well, it's very likely I may be able to find something for you——

Nora (clapping her hands). What did I tell you? What did I tell you?

Helmer. You have just come at a fortunate moment, Mrs. Linde.

Mrs. Linde. How am I to thank you?

Helmer. There is no need. *(Puts on his coat.)* But to-day you must excuse me——

Rank. Wait a minute; I will come with you.

[*Brings his fur coat from the hall and warms it at the fire.*

Nora. Don't be long away, Torvald dear.

Helmer. About an hour, not more.

Nora. Are you going too, Christine?

Mrs. Linde (putting on her cloak). Yes, I must go and look for a room.

Helmer. Oh, well then, we can walk down the street together.

Nora (helping her). What a pity it is we are so short of space here: I am afraid it is impossible for us——

Mrs. Linde. Please don't think of it! Good-bye, Nora dear, and many thanks.

Nora. Good-bye for the present. Of course you will come back this evening. And you too, Dr. Rank. What do you say? If you are well enough? Oh, you must be! Wrap yourself up well.

> [*They go to the door all talking together. Children's voices are heard on the staircase.*

Nora. There they are. There they are! *(She runs to open the door. The* NURSE *comes in with the children.)* Come in! Come in! *(Stoops and kisses them.)* Oh, you sweet blessings! Look at them, Christine! Aren't they darlings?

Rank. Don't let us stand here in the draught.

Helmer. Come along, Mrs. Linde; the place will only be bearable for a mother now!

> [RANK, HELMER *and* MRS. LINDE *go downstairs. The* NURSE *comes forward with the children;* NORA *shuts the hall door.*

Nora. How fresh and well you look! Such red cheeks! —like apples and roses. *(The children all talk at once while she speaks to them.)* Have you had great fun? That's splendid! What, you pulled both Emmy and Bob along on the sledge?—both at once?—that *was* good. You are a clever boy, Ivar. Let me take her for a little, Anne. My sweet little baby doll! *(Takes the baby from the* MAID *and dances it up and down.)* Yes, yes, mother will dance with Bob too. What! Have you been snowballing? I wish I had been there too! No, no, I will take their things off, Anne; please let me do it, it is such fun. Go in now, you look half frozen. There is some hot coffee for you on the stove.

> [*The* NURSE *goes into the room on the left.* NORA *takes off the children's things and throws them about, while they all talk to her at once.*

Nora. Really! Did a big dog run after you? But it didn't bite you? No, dogs don't bite nice little dolly children. You mustn't look at the parcels, Ivar. What are they? Ah, I daresay you would like to know. No, no— it's something nasty! Come, let us have a game! What shall we play at? Hide and Seek? Yes, we'll play Hide and Seek. Bob shall hide first. Must I hide? Very well, I'll hide first.

> [*She and the children laugh and shout, and romp in and out of the room; at last* NORA *hides under the table, the children rush in and look for her, but do not see her; they hear her smothered laughter, run to the table, lift up the cloth and find her. Shouts of laughter. She crawls forward and pretends to frighten them. Fresh laughter. Meanwhile there has been a knock at the hall door, but none of them has noticed it. The door is half opened, and* KROGSTAD *appears. He waits a little; the game goes on.*

Krogstad. Excuse me, Mr. Helmer.

Nora (with a stifled cry, turns round and gets up on to her knees). Ah! what do you want?

Krogstad. Excuse me, the outer door was ajar; I suppose someone forgot to shut it.

Nora (rising). My husband is out, Mr. Krogstad.

Krogstad. I know that.

Nora. What do you want here, then?

Krogstad. A word with you.

Nora. With me?— *(to the children, gently.)* Go in to nurse. What? No, the strange man won't do mother any harm. When he has gone we will have another game. *(She takes the children into the room on the left, and shuts the door after them.)* You want to speak to me?

Krogstad. Yes, I do.

Nora. To-day? It is not the first of the month yet.

Krogstad. No, it is Christmas Eve, and it will depend on yourself what sort of a Christmas you will spend.

Nora. What do you want? To-day it is absolutely impossible for me——

Krogstad. We won't talk about that till later on. This is something different. I presume you can give me a moment?

Nora. Yes—yes, I can—although——

Krogstad. Good. I was in Olsen's Restaurant and saw your husband going down the street——

Nora. Yes?

Krogstad. With a lady.

Nora. What then?

Krogstad. May I make so bold as to ask if it was a Mrs. Linde?

Nora. It was.

Krogstad. Just arrived in town?

Nora. Yes, to-day.

Krogstad. She is a great friend of yours, isn't she?

Nora. She is. But I don't see——

Krogstad. I knew her too, once upon a time.

Nora. I am aware of that.

Krogstad. Are you? So you know all about it; I thought as much. Then I can ask you, without beating about the bush—is Mrs. Linde to have an appointment in the Bank?

Nora. What right have you to question me, Mr. Krogstad?—You, one of my husband's subordinates! But since you ask, you shall know. Yes, Mrs. Linde *is* to have an appointment. And it was I who pleaded her cause, Mr. Krogstad, let me tell you that.

Krogstad. I was right in what I thought, then.

Nora (walking up and down the stage). Sometimes one has a tiny little bit of influence, I should hope. Because one is a woman, it does not necessarily follow that——. When anyone is in a subordinate position, Mr. Krogstad, they should really be careful to avoid offending anyone who—who——

Krogstad. Who has influence?

Nora. Exactly.

Krogstad (changing his tone). Mrs. Helmer, you will be so good as to use your influence on my behalf.

Nora. What? What do you mean?

Krogstad. You will be so kind as to see that I am allowed to keep my subordinate position in the Bank.

Nora. What do you mean by that? Who proposes to take your post away from you?

Krogstad. Oh, there is no necessity to keep up the pretence of ignorance. I can quite understand that your friend is not very anxious to expose herself to the chance of rubbing shoulders with me; and I quite understand, too, whom I have to thank for being turned off.

Nora. But I assure you——

Krogstad. Very likely; but, to come to the point, the time has come when I should advise you to use your influence to prevent that.

Nora. But, Mr. Krogstad, I *have* no influence.

Krogstad. Haven't you? I thought you said yourself just now——

Nora. Naturally I did not mean you to put that construction on it. I! What should make you think I have any influence of that kind with my husband?

Krogstad. Oh, I have known your husband from our student days. I don't suppose he is any more unassailable than other husbands.

Nora. If you speak slightingly of my husband, I shall turn you out of the house.

Krogstad. You are bold, Mrs. Helmer.

Nora. I am not afraid of you any longer. As soon as the New Year comes, I shall in a very short time be free of the whole thing.

Krogstad (controlling himself). Listen to me, Mrs. Helmer. If necessary, I am prepared to fight for my small post in the Bank as if I were fighting for my life.

Nora. So it seems.

Krogstad. It is not only for the sake of the money; indeed, that weighs least with me in the matter. There is another reason—well, I may as well tell you. My position is this. I daresay you know, like everybody else, that once, many years ago, I was guilty of an indiscretion.

Nora. I think I have heard something of the kind.

Krogstad. The matter never came into court; but every way seemed to be closed to me after that. So I took to the business that you know of. I had to do something; and, honestly, I don't think I've been one of the worst. But now I must cut myself free from all that. My sons are growing up; for their sake I must try and win back as much respect as I can in the town. This post in the Bank was like the first step up for me—and now your husband is going to kick me downstairs again into the mud.

Nora. But you must believe me, Mr. Krogstad; it is not in my power to help you at all.

Krogstad. Then it is because you haven't the will; but I have means to compel you.

Nora. You don't mean that you will tell my husband that I owe you money?

Krogstad. Hm!—suppose I were to tell him?

Nora. It would be perfectly infamous of you. *(Sobbing.)* To think of his learning my secret, which has been my joy and pride, in such an ugly, clumsy way—that he should learn it from you! And it would put me in a horribly disagreeable position——

Krogstad. Only disagreeable?

Nora (impetuously). Well, do it, then!—and it will be the worse for you. My husband will see for himself what a blackguard you are, and you certainly won't keep your post then.

Krogstad. I asked you if it was only a disagreeable scene at home that you were afraid of?

Nora. If my husband does get to know of it, of course he will at once pay you what is still owing, and we shall have nothing more to do with you.

Krogstad (coming a step nearer). Listen to me, Mrs. Helmer. Either you have a very bad memory or you know very little of business. I shall be obliged to remind you of a few details.

Nora. What do you mean?

Krogstad. When your husband was ill, you came to me to borrow two hundred and fifty pounds.

Nora. I didn't know any one else to go to.

Krogstad. I promised to get you that amount——

Nora. Yes, and you did so.

Krogstad. I promised to get you that amount, on certain conditions. Your mind was so taken up with your husband's illness, and you were so anxious to get the money for your journey, that you seem to have paid no attention to the conditions of our bargain. Therefore it will not be amiss if I remind you of them. Now, I promised to get the money on the security of a bond which I drew up.

Nora. Yes, and which I signed.

Krogstad. Good. But below your signature there were a few lines constituting your father a surety for the money; those lines your father should have signed.

Nora. Should? He did sign them.

Krogstad. I had left the date blank; that is to say your father should himself have inserted the date on which he signed the paper. Do you remember that?

Nora. Yes, I think I remember——

Krogstad. Then I gave you the bond to send by post to your father. Is that not so?

Nora. Yes.

Krogstad. And you naturally did so at once, because five

or six days afterwards you brought me the bond with your father's signature. And then I gave you the money.

Nora. Well, haven't I been paying it off regularly?

Krogstad. Fairly so, yes. But—to come back to the matter in hand—that must have been a very trying time for you, Mrs. Helmer?

Nora. It was, indeed.

Krogstad. Your father was very ill, wasn't he?

Nora. He was very near his end.

Krogstad. And died soon afterwards?

Nora. Yes.

Krogstad. Tell me, Mrs. Helmer, can you by any chance remember what day your father died?—on what day of the month, I mean.

Nora. Papa died on the 29th of September.

Krogstad. That is correct; I have ascertained it for myself. And, as that is so, there is a discrepancy *(taking a paper from his pocket)* which I cannot account for.

Nora. What discrepancy? I don't know——

Krogstad. The discrepancy consists, Mrs. Helmer, in the fact that your father signed this bond three days after his death.

Nora. What do you mean? I don't understand——

Krogstad. Your father died on the 29th of September. But, look here; your father has dated his signature the 2nd of October. It is a discrepancy, isn't it? *(Nora is silent.)* Can you explain it to me? *(Nora is still silent.)* It is a remarkable thing, too, that the words "2nd of October," as well as the year, are not written in your father's handwriting but in one that I think I know. Well, of course it can be explained; your father may have forgotten to date his signature, and someone else may have dated it haphazard before they knew of his death. There is no harm in that. It all depends on the signature of the name; and *that* is genuine, I suppose, Mrs. Helmer? It was your father himself who signed his name here?

Nora (after a short pause, throws her head up and looks defiantly at him). No, it was not. It was I that wrote papa's name.

Krogstad. Are you aware that is a dangerous confession?

Nora. In what way? You shall have your money soon.

Krogstad. Let me ask you a question; why did you not send the paper to your father?

Nora. It was impossible; papa was so ill. If I had asked him for his signature, I should have had to tell him what the money was to be used for; and when he was so ill himself I couldn't tell him that my husband's life was in danger—it was impossible.

Krogstad. It would have been better for you if you had given up your trip abroad.

Nora. No, that was impossible. That trip was to save my husband's life; I couldn't give that up.

Krogstad. But did it never occur to you that you were committing a fraud on me?

Nora. I couldn't take that into account; I didn't trouble myself about you at all. I couldn't bear you, because you put so many heartless difficulties in my way, although you knew what a dangerous condition my husband was in.

Krogstad. Mrs. Helmer, you evidently do not realise clearly what it is that you have been guilty of. But I can assure you that my one false step, which lost me all my reputation, was nothing more or nothing worse than what you have done.

Nora. You? Do you ask me to believe that you were brave enough to run a risk to save your wife's life.

Krogstad. The law cares nothing about motives.

Nora. Then it must be a very foolish law.

Krogstad. Foolish or not, it is the law by which you will be judged, if I produce this paper in court.

Nora. I don't believe it. Is a daughter not to be allowed to spare her dying father anxiety and care? Is a wife not to be allowed to save her husband's life? I don't know much about law; but I am certain that there must be laws permitting such things as that. Have you no knowledge of such laws—you who are a lawyer? You must be a very poor lawyer, Mr. Krogstad.

Krogstad. Maybe. But matters of business—such business as you and I have had together—do you think I don't understand that? Very well. Do as you please. But let me tell you this—if I lose my position a second time, you shall lose yours with me.

[*He bows, and goes out through the hall.*

Nora (appears buried in thought for a short time, then tosses her head). Nonsense! Trying to frighten me like that!—I am not so silly as he thinks. *(Begins to busy herself putting the children's things in order.)* And yet——? No, it's impossible! I did it for love's sake.

The Children (in the doorway on the left). Mother, the stranger man has gone out through the gate.

Nora. Yes, dears, I know. But, don't tell anyone about the stranger man. Do you hear? Not even papa.

Children. No, mother; but will you come and play again?

Nora. No, no,—not now.

Children. But, mother, you promised us.

Nora. Yes, but I can't now. Run away in; I have such a lot to do. Run away in, my sweet little darlings. *(She gets them into the room by degrees and shuts the door on them; then sits down on the sofa, takes up a piece of needle-work and sews a few stitches, but soon stops.)* No! *(Throws down the work, gets up, goes to the hall door and calls out.)* Helen! bring the Tree in. *(Goes to the table on the left, opens a drawer, and stops again.)* No, no! it is quite impossible!

Maid (coming in with the Tree). Where shall I put it, ma'am?

Nora. Here, in the middle of the floor.

Maid. Shall I get you anything else?

Nora. No, thank you. I have all I want. [*Exit* MAID.

Nora (begins dressing the tree). A candle here—and flowers here——. The horrible man! It's all nonsense—there's nothing wrong. The Tree shall be splendid! I will do everything I can think of to please you, Torvald!—I will sing for you, dance for you—(HELMER *comes in with some papers under his arm.*) Oh! are you back already?

Helmer. Yes. Has anyone been here?

Nora. Here? No.

Helmer. That is strange. I saw Krogstad going out of the gate.

Nora. Did you? Oh yes, I forgot, Krogstad was here for a moment.

Helmer. Nora, I can see from your manner that he has been here begging you to say a good word for him.

Nora. Yes.

Helmer. And you were to appear to do it of your own accord; you were to conceal from me the fact of his having been here; didn't he beg that of you too?

Nora. Yes, Torvald, but——

Helmer. Nora, Nora, and you would be a party to that sort of thing? To have any talk with a man like that, and give him any sort of promise? And to tell me a lie into the bargain?

Nora. A lie——?

Helmer. Didn't you tell me no one had been here? *(Shakes his finger at her.)* My little song-bird must never do that again. A song-bird must have a clean beak to chirp with—no false notes! *(Puts his arm round her waist.)* That is so, isn't it? Yes, I am sure it is. *(Lets her go.)* We will say no more about it. *(Sits down by the stove.)* How warm and snug it is here!

[*Turns over his papers.*

Nora (after a short pause, during which she busies herself with the Christmas Tree). Torvald!

Helmer. Yes.

Nora. I am looking forward tremendously to the fancy dress ball at the Stenborgs' the day after to-morrow.

Helmer. And I am tremendously curious to see what you are going to surprise me with.

Nora. It was very silly of me to want to do that.

Helmer. What do you mean?

Nora. I can't hit upon anything that will do; everything I think of seems so silly and insignificant.

Helmer. Does my little Nora acknowledge that at last?

Nora (standing behind his chair with her arms on the back of it). Are you very busy, Torvald?

Helmer. Well——

Nora. What are all those papers?

Helmer. Bank business.

Nora. Already?

Helmer. I have got authority from the retiring manager to undertake the necessary changes in the staff and in the rearrangement of the work; and I must make use of the Christmas week for that, so as to have everything in order for the new year.

Nora. Then that was why this poor Krogstad——

Helmer. Hm!

Nora (leans against the back of his chair and strokes his hair). If you hadn't been so busy I should have asked you a tremendously big favour, Torvald.

Helmer. What is that? Tell me.

Nora. There is no one has such good taste as you. And I do so want to look nice at the fancy-dress ball. Torvald, couldn't you take me in hand and decide what I shall go as, and what sort of a dress I shall wear?

Helmer. Aha! so my obstinate little woman is obliged to get someone to come to her rescue?

Nora. Yes, Torvald, I can't get along a bit without your help.

Helmer. Very well, I will think it over, we shall manage to hit upon something.

Nora. That *is* nice of you. *(Goes to the Christmas Tree. A short pause.)* How pretty the red flowers look ——. But, tell me, was it really something very bad that this Krogstad was guilty of?

Helmer. He forged someone's name. Have you any idea what that means?

Nora. Isn't it possible that he was driven to do it by necessity?

Helmer. Yes; or, as in so many cases, by imprudence. I am not so heartless as to condemn a man altogether because of a single false step of that kind.

Nora. No you wouldn't, would you, Torvald?

Helmer. Many a man has been able to retrieve his character, if he has openly confessed his fault and taken his punishment.

Nora. Punishment——?

Helmer. But Krogstad did nothing of that sort; he got himself out of it by a cunning trick, and that is why he has gone under altogether.

Nora. But do you think it would——?

Helmer. Just think how a guilty man like that has to lie and play the hypocrite with everyone, how he has to wear a mask in the presence of those near and dear to him, even before his own wife and children. And about the children— that is the most terrible part of it all, Nora.

Nora. How?

Helmer. Because such an atmosphere of lies infects and poisons the whole life of a home. Each breath the children take in such a house is full of the germs of evil.

Nora (coming nearer him). Are you sure of that?

Helmer. My dear, I have often seen it in the course of my life as a lawyer. Almost everyone who has gone to the bad early in life has had a deceitful mother.

Nora. Why do you only say—mother?

Helmer. It seems most commonly to be the mother's influence, though naturally a bad father's would have the same result. Every lawyer is familiar with the fact. This Krog-stad, now, has been persistently poisoning his own children with lies and dissimulation; that is why I say he has lost all moral character. (*Holds out his hands to her.*) That is why my sweet little Nora must promise me not to plead his cause. Give me your hand on it. Come, come, what is this? Give me your hand. There now, that's settled. I assure you it would be quite impossible for me to work with him; I literally feel physically ill when I am in the company of such people.

Nora (takes her hand out of his and goes to the opposite side of the Christmas Tree). How hot it is in here; and I have such a lot to do.

Helmer (getting up and putting his papers in order). Yes, and I must try and read through some of these before dinner; and I must think about your costume, too. And it is just possible I may have something ready in gold paper to hang up on the Tree. (*Puts his hand on her head.*) My precious little singing-bird!

[*He goes into his room and shuts the door after him.*

Nora (after a pause, whispers). No, no—it isn't true. It's impossible; it must be impossible.

[*The* NURSE *opens the door on the left.*

Nurse. The little ones are begging so hard to be allowed to come in to mamma.

Nora. No, no, no! Don't let them come in to me! You stay with them, Anne.

Nurse. Very well, ma'am. [*Shuts the door.*

Nora (pale with terror). Deprave my little children? Poison my home? (*A short pause. Then she tosses her head.*) It's not true. It can't possibly be true.

ACT II

THE SAME SCENE.—*The Christmas Tree is in the corner by the piano, stripped of its ornaments and with burnt-down candle-ends on its dishevelled branches.* NORA'S *cloak and hat are lying on the sofa. She is alone in the room, walking about uneasily. She stops by the sofa and takes up her cloak.*

Nora (drops the cloak). Someone is coming now! *(Goes to the door and listens.)* No—it is no one. Of course, no one will come to-day, Christmas Day—nor to-morrow either. But, perhaps—*(opens the door and looks out).* No, nothing in the letter-box; it is quite empty. *(Comes forward.)* What rubbish! of course he can't be in earnest about it. Such a thing couldn't happen; it is impossible—I have three little children.

      [*Enter the* NURSE *from the room on the left, carrying a big cardboard box.*

Nurse. At last I have found the box with the fancy dress.

Nora. Thanks; put it on the table.

Nurse (doing so). But it is very much in want of mending.

Nora. I should like to tear it into a hundred thousand pieces.

Nurse. What an idea! It can easily be put in order—just a little patience.

Nora. Yes, I will go and get Mrs. Linde to come and help me with it.

Nurse. What, out again? In this horrible weather? You will catch cold, ma'am, and make yourself ill.

Nora. Well, worse than that might happen. How are the children?

Nurse. The poor little souls are playing with their Christmas presents, but——

Nora. Do they ask much for me?

Nurse. You see, they are so accustomed to have their mamma with them.

Nora. Yes, but, nurse, I shall not be able to be so much with them now as I was before.

Nurse. Oh well, young children easily get accustomed to anything.

Nora. Do you think so? Do you think they would forget their mother if she went away altogether?

Nurse. Good heavens!—went away altogether?

Nora. Nurse, I want you to tell me something I have often wondered about—how could you have the heart to put your own child out among strangers?

Nurse. I was obliged to, if I wanted to be little Nora's nurse.

Nora. Yes, but how could you be willing to do it?

Nurse. What, when I was going to get such a good place by it? A poor girl who has got into trouble should be glad to. Besides, that wicked man didn't do a single thing for me.

Nora. But I suppose your daughter has quite forgotten you.

Nurse. No, indeed she hasn't. She wrote to me when she was confirmed, and when she was married.

Nora (putting her arms round her neck). Dear old Anne, you were a good mother to me when I was little.

Nurse. Little Nora, poor dear, had no other mother but me.

Nora. And if my little ones had no other mother, I am sure you would—— What nonsense I am talking! *(Opens the box.)* Go in to them. Now I must——. You will see to-morrow how charming I shall look.

Nurse. I am sure there will be no one at the ball so charming as you, ma'am.

[*Goes into the room on the left.*

Nora (begins to unpack the box, but soon pushes it away from her). If only I dared go out. If only no one would come. If only I could be sure nothing would happen here in the meantime. Stuff and nonsense! No one will come. Only I mustn't think about it. I will brush my muff. What lovely, lovely gloves! Out of my thoughts, out of my thoughts! One, two, three, four, five, six—— *(Screams.)* Ah! there is someone coming——.

[*Makes a movement towards the door, but stands irresolute.*

[*Enter* MRS. LINDE *from the hall, where she has taken off her cloak and hat.*

Nora. Oh, it's you, Christine. There is no one else out there, is there? How good of you to come!

Mrs. Linde. I heard you were up asking for me.

Nora. Yes, I was passing by. As a matter of fact, it is something you could help me with. Let us sit down here on the sofa. Look here. To-morrow evening there is to be a fancy-dress ball at the Stenborgs', who live above us; and Torvald wants me to go as a Neapolitan fisher-girl, and dance the Tarantella that I learnt at Capri.

Mrs. Linde. I see; you are going to keep up the character.

Nora. Yes, Torvald wants me to. Look, here is the dress; Torvald had it made for me there, but now it is all so torn, and I haven't any idea——

Mrs. Linde. We will easily put that right. It is only some of the trimming come unsewn here and there. Needle and thread? Now then, that's all we want.

Nora. It *is* nice of you.

Mrs. Linde (sewing). So you are going to be dressed up to-morrow, Nora. I will tell you what—I shall come in for a moment and see you in your fine feathers. But I have completely forgotten to thank you for a delightful evening yesterday.

Nora (gets up, and crosses the stage). Well I don't think yesterday was as pleasant as usual. You ought to have come to town a little earlier, Christine. Certainly Torvald does understand how to make a house dainty and attractive.

Mrs. Linde. And so do you, it seems to me; you are not your father's daughter for nothing. But tell me, is Doctor Rank always as depressed as he was yesterday?

Nora. No; yesterday it was very noticeable. I must tell you that he suffers from a very dangerous disease. He has consumption of the spine, poor creature. His father was a horrible man who committed all sorts of excesses; and that is why his son was sickly from childhood, do you understand?

Mrs. Linde (dropping her sewing). But, my dearest Nora, how do you know anything about such things?

Nora (walking about). Pooh! When you have three children, you get visits now and then from—from married women, who know something of medical matters, and they talk about one thing and another.

Mrs. Linde (goes on sewing. A short silence). Does Doctor Rank come here every day?

Nora. Every day regularly. He is Torvald's most intimate friend, and a great friend of mine too. He is just like one of the family.

Mrs. Linde. But tell me this—is he perfectly sincere? I mean, isn't he the kind of man that is very anxious to make himself agreeable?

Nora. Not in the least. What makes you think that?

Mrs. Linde. When you introduced him to me yesterday, he declared he had often heard my name mentioned in this house; but afterwards I noticed that your husband hadn't the slightest idea who I was. So how could Doctor Rank ——?

Nora. That is quite right, Christine. Torvald is so absurdly fond of me that he wants me absolutely to himself, as he says. At first he used to seem almost jealous if I mentioned any of the dear folk at home, so naturally I gave up doing so. But I often talk about such things with Doctor Rank, because he likes hearing about them.

Mrs. Linde. Listen to me, Nora. You are still very like a child in many things, and I am older than you in many ways and have a little more experience. Let me tell you this—you ought to make an end of it with Doctor Rank.

Nora. What ought I to make an end of?

Mrs. Linde. Of two things, I think. Yesterday you talked some nonsense about a rich admirer who was to leave you money——

Nora. An admirer who doesn't exist, unfortunately! But what then?

Mrs. Linde. Is Doctor Rank a man of means?

Nora. Yes, he is.

Mrs. Linde. And has no one to provide for?

Nora. No, no one; but——

Mrs. Linde. And comes here every day?

Nora. Yes, I told you so.

Mrs. Linde. But how can this well-bred man be so tactless?

Nora. I don't understand you at all.

Mrs. Linde. Don't prevaricate, Nora. Do you suppose I don't guess who lent you the two hundred and fifty pounds?

Nora. Are you out of your senses? How can you think of such a thing! A friend of ours, who comes here every day! Do you realise what a horribly painful position that would be?

Mrs. Linde. Then it really isn't he?

Nora. No, certainly not. It would never have entered into my head for a moment. Besides, he had no money to lend then; he came into his money afterwards.

Mrs. Linde. Well, I think that was lucky for you, my dear Nora.

Nora. No, it would never have come into my head to ask Doctor Rank. Although I am quite sure that if I had asked him——

Mrs. Linde. But of course you won't.

Nora. Of course not. I have no reason to think it could possibly be necessary. But I am quite sure that if I told Doctor Rank——

Mrs. Linde. Behind your husband's back?

Nora. I must make an end of it with the other one, and that will be behind his back too. I *must* make an end of it with him.

Mrs. Linde. Yes, that is what I told you yesterday, but——

Nora (walking up and down). A man can put a thing like that straight much easier than a woman——

Mrs. Linde. One's husband, yes.

Nora. Nonsense! *(Standing still.)* When you pay off a debt you get your bond back, don't you?

Mrs. Linde. Yes, as a matter of course.

Nora. And can tear it into a hundred thousand pieces, and burn it up—the nasty dirty paper!

Mrs. Linde (looks hard at her, lays down her sewing and gets up slowly). Nora, you are concealing something from me.

Nora. Do I look as if I were?

Mrs. Linde. Something has happened to you since yesterday morning. Nora, what is it?

Nora (going nearer to her). Christine! *(Listens.)* Hush! there's Torvald come home. Do you mind going in to the children for the present? Torvald can't bear to see dressmaking going on. Let Anne help you.

Mrs. Linde (gathering some of the things together). Certainly—but I am not going away from here till we have had it out with one another.

[*She goes into the room on the left, as* HELMER *comes in from the hall.*

Nora (going up to HELMER*).* I have wanted you so much, Torvald dear.

Helmer. Was that the dressmaker?

Nora. No, it was Christine; she is helping me to put my dress in order. You will see I shall look quite smart.

Helmer. Wasn't that a happy thought of mine, now?

Nora. Splendid! But don't you think it is nice of me, too, to do as you wish?

Helmer. Nice?—because you do as your husband wishes? Well, well, you little rogue, I am sure you did not mean it in that way. But I am not going to disturb you; you will want to be trying on your dress, I expect.

Nora. I suppose you are going to work.

Helmer. Yes. *(Shows her a bundle of papers.)* Look at that. I have just been into the bank.

[*Turns to go into his room.*

Nora. Torvald.

Helmer. Yes.

Nora. If your little squirrel were to ask you for something very, very prettily——?

Helmer. What then?

Nora. Would you do it?

Helmer. I should like to hear what it is, first.

Nora. Your squirrel would run about and do all her tricks if you would be nice, and do what she wants.

Helmer. Speak plainly.

Nora. Your skylark would chirp about in every room, with her song rising and falling——

Helmer. Well, my skylark does that anyhow.

Nora. I would play the fairy and dance for you in the moonlight, Torvald.

Helmer. Nora—you surely don't mean that request you made of me this morning?

Nora (going near him). Yes, Torvald, I beg you so earnestly——

Helmer. Have you really the courage to open up that question again?

Nora. Yes, dear, you *must* do as I ask; you *must* let Krogstad keep his post in the Bank.

Helmer. My dear Nora, it is his post that I have arranged Mrs. Linde shall have.

Nora. Yes, you have been awfully kind about that; but you could just as well dismiss some other clerk instead of Krogstad.

Helmer. This is simply incredible obstinacy! Because you chose to give him a thoughtless promise that you would speak for him, I am expected to——

Nora. That isn't the reason, Torvald. It is for your own sake. This fellow writes in the most scurrilous newspapers; you have told me so yourself. He can do you an unspeakable amount of harm. I am frightened to death of him——

Helmer. Ah, I understand; it is recollections of the past that scare you.

Nora. What do you mean?

Helmer. Naturally you are thinking of your father.

Nora. Yes—yes, of course. Just recall to your mind what these malicious creatures wrote in the papers about papa, and how horribly they slandered him. I believe they would have procured his dismissal if the Department had not sent you over to inquire into it, and if you had not been so kindly disposed and helpful to him.

Helmer. My little Nora, there is an important difference between your father and me. Your father's reputation as a public official was not above suspicion. Mine is, and I hope it will continue to be so, as long as I hold my office.

Nora. You never can tell what mischief these men may contrive. We ought to be so well off, so snug and happy

here in our peaceful home, and have no cares—you and I
and the children, Torvald! That is why I beg you so earnestly——

Helmer. And it is just by interceding for him that you
make it impossible for me to keep him. It is already known
at the Bank that I mean to dismiss Krogstad. Is it to get
about now that the new manager has changed his mind at
his wife's bidding——

Nora. And what if it did?

Helmer. Of course!—if only this obstinate little person
can get her way! Do you suppose I am going to make
myself ridiculous before my whole staff, to let people think
that I am a man to be swayed by all sorts of outside influence? I should very soon feel the consequences of it, I can
tell you! And besides, there is one thing that makes it
quite impossible for me to have Krogstad in the Bank as long
as I am manager.

Nora. Whatever is that?

Helmer. His moral failings I might perhaps have over-
looked, if necessary——

Nora. Yes, you could—couldn't you?

Helmer. And I hear he is a good worker, too. But I
knew him when we were boys. It was one of those rash
friendships that so often prove an incubus in after life. I
may as well tell you plainly, we were once on very intimate
terms with one another. But this tactless fellow lays no
restraint on himself when other people are present. On the
contrary, he thinks it gives him the right to adopt a familiar
tone with me, and every minute it is "I say, Helmer, old
fellow!" and that sort of thing. I assure you it is extremely
painful for me. He would make my position in the Bank
intolerable.

Nora. Torvald, I don't believe you mean that.

Helmer. Don't you? Why not?

Nora. Because it is such a narrow-minded way of looking at things.

Helmer. What are you saying? Narrow-minded? Do you think I am narrow-minded?

Nora. No, just the opposite, dear—and it is exactly for that reason.

Helmer. It's the same thing. You say my point of view is narrow-minded, so I must be so too. Narrow-minded! Very well—I must put an end to this. *(Goes to the hall-door and calls.)* Helen!

Nora. What are you going to do?

Helmer (looking among his papers). Settle it. *(Enter* MAID.*)* Look here; take this letter and go downstairs with it at once. Find a messenger and tell him to deliver it, and be quick. The address is on it, and here is the money.

Maid. Very well, sir.   [*Exit with the letter*

Helmer (putting his papers together). Now then, little Miss Obstinate.

Nora (breathlessly). Torvald—what was that letter?

Helmer. Krogstad's dismissal.

Nora. Call her back, Torvald! There is still time. Oh Torvald, call her back! Do it for my sake—for your own sake—for the children's sake! Do you hear me, Torvald? Call her back! You don't know what that letter can bring upon us.

Helmer. It's too late.

Nora. Yes, it's too late.

Helmer. My dear Nora, I can forgive the anxiety you are in, although really it is an insult to me. It is, indeed. Isn't it an insult to think that I should be afraid of a starving quill-driver's vengeance? But I forgive you nevertheless, because it is such eloquent witness to your great love for me. *(Takes her in his arms.)* And that is as it should be, my own darling Nora. Come what will, you may be sure I shall have both courage and strength if they be needed. You will see I am man enough to take everything upon myself.

Nora (in a horror-stricken voice). What do you mean by that?

Helmer. Everything, I say——

Nora (recovering herself). You will never have to do that.

Helmer. That's right. Well, we will share it, Nora, as man and wife should. That is how it shall be. *(Caressing her.)* Are you content now? There! there!—not these frightened dove's eyes! The whole thing is only the wildest fancy!—Now, you must go and play through the Tarantella and practise with your tambourine. I shall go into the inner office and shut the door, and I shall hear nothing; you can make as much noise as you please. *(Turns back at the door.)* And when Rank comes, tell him where he will find me.

> [*Nods to her, takes his papers and goes into his room, and shuts the door after him.*

Nora (bewildered with anxiety, stands as if rooted to the spot, and whispers). He was capable of doing it. He will do it. He will do it in spite of everything.—No, not that! Never, never! Anything rather than that! Oh, for some help, some way out of it! *(The door-bell rings.)* Doctor Rank! Anything rather than that—anything, whatever it is!

> [*She puts her hands over her face, pulls herself together, goes to the door and opens it.* RANK *is standing without, hanging up his coat. During the following dialogue it begins to grow dark.*

Nora. Good-day, Doctor Rank. I knew your ring. But you mustn't go into Torvald now; I think he is busy with something.

Rank. And you?

Nora (brings him in and shuts the door after him). Oh, you know very well I always have time for you.

Rank. Thank you. I shall make use of as much of it as I can.

Nora. What do you mean by that? As much of it as you can?

Rank. Well, does that alarm you?

Nora. It was such a strange way of putting it. Is anything likely to happen?

Rank. Nothing but what I have long been prepared for. But I certainly didn't expect it to happen so soon.

Nora (gripping him by the arm). What have you found out? Doctor Rank, you must tell me.

Rank (sitting down by the stove). It is all up with me. And it can't be helped.

Nora (with a sigh of relief). Is it about yourself?

Rank. Who else? It is no use lying to one's self. I am the most wretched of all my patients, Mrs. Helmer. Lately I have been taking stock of my internal economy. Bankrupt! Probably within a month I shall lie rotting in the churchyard.

Nora. What an ugly thing to say!

Rank. The thing itself is cursedly ugly, and the worst of it is that I shall have to face so much more that is ugly before that. I shall only make one more examination of myself; when I have done that, I shall know pretty certainly when it will be that the horrors of dissolution will begin. There is something I want to tell you. Helmer's refined nature gives him an unconquerable disgust at everything that is ugly; I won't have him in my sick-room.

Nora. Oh, but, Doctor Rank——

Rank. I won't have him there. Not on any account. I bar my door to him. As soon as I am quite certain that the worst has come, I shall send you my card with a black cross on it, and then you will know that the loathsome end has begun.

Nora. You are quite absurd to-day. And I wanted you so much to be in a really good humour.

Rank. With death stalking beside me?—To have to pay this penalty for another man's sin! Is there any justice in that? And in every single family, in one way or another, some such inexorable retribution is being exacted——

Nora (putting her hands over her ears). Rubbish! Do talk of something cheerful.

Rank. Oh, it's a mere laughing matter, the whole thing. My poor innocent spine has to suffer for my father's youthful amusements.

Nora (sitting at the table on the left). I suppose you mean that he was too partial to asparagus and pâté de foie gras, don't you.

Rank. Yes, and to truffles.

Nora. Truffles, yes. And oysters too, I suppose?

Rank. Oysters, of course, that goes without saying.

Nora. And heaps of port and champagne. It is sad that all these nice things should take their revenge on our bones.

Rank. Especially that they should revenge themselves on the unlucky bones of those who have not had the satisfaction of enjoying them.

Nora. Yes, that's the saddest part of it all.

Rank (with a searching look at her). Hm!——

Nora (after a short pause). Why did you smile?

Rank. No, it was you that laughed.

Nora. No, it was you that smiled, Doctor Rank!

Rank (rising). You are a greater rascal than I thought.

Nora. I am in a silly mood to-day.

Rank. So it seems.

Nora (putting her hands on his shoulders). Dear, dear Doctor Rank, death mustn't take you away from Torvald and me.

Rank. It is a loss you would easily recover from. Those who are gone are soon forgotten.

Nora (looking at him anxiously). Do you believe that?

Rank. People form new ties, and then——

Nora. Who will form new ties?

Rank. Both you and Helmer, when I am gone. You

yourself are already on the high road to it, I think. What did that Mrs. Linde want here last night?

Nora. Oho!—you don't mean to say you are jealous of poor Christine?

Rank. Yes, I am. She will be my successor in this house. When I am done for, this woman will—

Nora. Hush! don't speak so loud. She is in that room.

Rank. To-day again. There, you see.

Nora. She has only come to sew my dress for me. Bless my soul, how unreasonable you are! (*Sits down on the sofa.*) Be nice now, Doctor Rank, and to-morrow you will see how beautifully I shall dance, and you can imagine I am doing it all for you—and for Torvald too, of course. (*Takes various things out of the box.*) Doctor Rank, come and sit down here, and I will show you something.

Rank (sitting down). What is it?

Nora. Just look at those!

Rank. Silk stockings.

Nora. Flesh-coloured. Aren't they lovely? It is so dark here now, but to-morrow—. No, no, no! you must only look at the feet. Oh well, you may have leave to look at the legs too.

Rank. Hm!—

Nora. Why are you looking so critical? Don't you think they will fit me?

Rank. I have no means of forming an opinion about that.

Nora (looks at him for a moment). For shame! (*Hits him lightly on the ear with the stockings.*) That's to punish you. (*Folds them up again.*)

Rank. And what other nice things am I to be allowed to see?

Nora. Not a single thing more, for being so naughty (*She looks among the things, humming to herself.*)

Rank (after a short silence). When I am sitting here,

talking to you as intimately as this, I cannot imagine for a moment what would have become of me if I had never come into this house.

Nora (smiling). I believe you do feel thoroughly at home with us.

Rank (in a lower voice, looking straight in front of him). And to be obliged to leave it all——

Nora. Nonsense, you are not going to leave it.

Rank (as before). And not be able to leave behind one the slightest token of one's gratitude, scarcely even a fleeting regret—nothing but an empty place which the first comer can fill as well as any other.

Nora. And if I asked you now for a—? No!

Rank. For what?

Nora. For a big proof of your friendship——

Rank. Yes, yes!

Nora. I mean a tremendously big favour——

Rank. Would you really make me so happy for once?

Nora. Ah, but you don't know what it is yet.

Rank. No—but tell me.

Nora. I really can't, Doctor Rank. It is something out of all reason; it means advice, and help, and a favour——

Rank. The bigger a thing it is the better. I can't conceive what it is you mean. Do tell me. Haven't I your confidence?

Nora. More than anyone else. I know you are my truest and best friend, and so I will tell you what it is. Well, Doctor Rank, it is something you must help me to prevent. You know how devotedly, how inexpressibly deeply Torvald loves me; he would never for a moment hesitate to give his life for me.

Rank (leaning towards her). Nora—do you think he is the only one——?

Nora (with a slight start). The only one—?

Rank. The only one who would gladly give his life for your sake.

Nora (sadly). Is that it?

Rank. I was determined you should know it before I went away, and there will never be a better opportunity than this. Now you know it, Nora. And now you know, too, that you can trust me as you would trust no one else.

Nora (rises, deliberately and quietly). Let me pass.

Rank (makes room for her to pass him, but sits still) Nora!

Nora (at the hall door). Helen, bring in the lamp. *(Goes over to the stove.)* Dear Doctor Rank, that was really horrid of you.

Rank. To have loved you as much as anyone else does? Was that horrid?

Nora. No, but to go and tell me so. There was really no need——

Rank. What do you mean? Did you know—? *(MAID enters with lamp, puts it down on the table, and goes out.)* Nora—Mrs. Helmer—tell me, had you any idea of this?

Nora. Oh, how do I know whether I had or whether I hadn't? I really can't tell you— To think you could be so clumsy, Doctor Rank! We were getting on so nicely.

Rank. Well, at all events you know now that you can command me, body and soul. So won't you speak out?

Nora (looking at him). After what happened?

Rank. I beg you to let me know what it is.

Nora. I can't tell you anything now.

Rank. Yes, yes. You mustn't punish me in that way. Let me have permission to do for you whatever a man may do.

Nora. You can do nothing for me now. Besides, I really don't need any help at all. You will find that the whole thing is merely fancy on my part. It really is so— of course it is! *(Sits down in the rocking-chair, and looks at him with a smile.)* You are a nice sort of man, Doctor Rank!—don't you feel ashamed of yourself, now the lamp has come?

Rank. Not a bit. But perhaps I had better go—for ever?

Nora. No, indeed, you shall not. Of course you must come here just as before. You know very well Torvald can't do without you.

Rank. Yes, but you?

Nora. Oh, I am always tremendously pleased when you come.

Rank. It is just that, that put me on the wrong track. You are a riddle to me. I have often thought that you would almost as soon be in my company as in Helmer's.

Nora. Yes—you see there are some people one loves best, and others whom one would almost always rather have as companions.

Rank. Yes, there is something in that.

Nora. When I was at home, of course I loved papa best. But I always thought it tremendous fun if I could steal down into the maid's room, because they never moralised at all, and talked to each other about such entertaining things.

Rank. I see—it is *their* place I have taken.

Nora (jumping up and going to him). Oh, dear, nice Doctor Rank, I never meant that at all. But surely you can understand that being with Torvald is a little like being with papa——

[*Enter* MAID *from the hall.*

Maid. If you please, ma'am. *(Whispers and hands her a card.)*

Nora (glancing at the card). Oh! *(Puts it in her pocket.)*

Rank. Is there anything wrong?

Nora. No, no, not in the least. It is only something— it is my new dress——

Rank. What? Your dress is lying there.

Nora. Oh, yes, that one; but this is another. I ordered it Torvald mustn't know about it——

Rank. Oho! Then that was the great secret.

Nora. Of course. Just go in to him; he is sitting in the inner room. Keep him as long as——

Rank. Make your mind easy; I won't let him escape. *(Goes into* HELMER'S *room.)*

Nora (to the MAID*).* And he is standing waiting in the kitchen?

Maid. Yes; he came up the back stairs.

Nora. But didn't you tell him no one was in?

Maid. Yes, but it was no good.

Nora. He won't go away?

Maid. No; he says he won't until he has seen you, ma'am.

Nora. Well, let him come in—but quietly. Helen, you mustn't say anything about it to anyone. It is a surprise for my husband.

Maid. Yes, ma'am, I quite understand. [*Exit.*

Nora. This dreadful thing is going to happen! It will happen in spite of me! No, no, no, it can't happen—it shan't happen!

> [*She bolts the door of* HELMER'S *room. The* MAID *opens the hall door for* KROGSTAD *and shuts it after him. He is wearing a fur coat, high boots and a fur cap.*

Nora (advancing towards him.) Speak low—my husband is at home.

Krogstad. No matter about that.

Nora. What do you want of me?

Krogstad. An explanation of something.

Nora. Make haste then. What is it?

Krogstad. You know, I suppose, that I have got my dismissal.

Nora. I couldn't prevent it, Mr. Krogstad. I fought as hard as I could on your side, but it was no good.

Krogstad. Does your husband love you so little, then? He knows what I can expose you to, and yet he ventures——

Nora. How can you suppose that he has any knowledge of the sort?

Krogstad. I didn't suppose so at all. It would not be the least like our dear Torvald Helmer to show so much courage—

Nora. Mr. Krogstad, a little respect for my husband, please.

Krogstad. Certainly— all the respect he deserves. But since you have kept the matter so carefully to yourself, I make bold to suppose that you have a little clearer idea, than you had yesterday, of what it actually is that you have done?

Nora. More than you could ever teach me.

Krogstad. Yes, such a bad lawyer as I am.

Nora. What is it you want of me?

Krogstad. Only to see how you were, Mrs. Helmer. I have been thinking about you all day long. A mere cashier, a quill-driver, a—well, a man like me—even he has a little of what is called feeling, you know.

Nora. Show it, then; think of my little children.

Krogstad. Have you and your husband thought of mine? But never mind about that. I only wanted to tell you that you need not take this matter too seriously. In the first place there will be no accusation made on my part.

Nora. No, of course not; I was sure of that.

Krogstad. The whole thing can be arranged amicably; there is no reason why anyone should know anything about it. It will remain a secret between us three.

Nora. My husband must never get to know anything about it.

Krogstad. How will you be able to prevent it? Am I to understand that you can pay the balance that is owing?

Nora. No, not just at present.

Krogstad. Or perhaps that you have some expedient for raising the money soon?

Nora. No expedient that I mean to make use of.

Krogstad. Well, in any case, it would have been of no use to you now. If you stood there with ever so much money in your hand, I would never part with your bond.

Nora. Tell me what purpose you mean to put it to.

Krogstad. I shall only preserve it—keep it in my possession. No one who is not concerned in the matter shall have the slightest hint of it. So that if the thought of it has driven you to any desperate resolution——

Nora. It has.

Krogstad. If you had it in your mind to run away from your home——

Nora. I had.

Krogstad. Or even something worse——

Nora. How could you know that?

Krogstad. Give up the idea.

Nora. How did you know I had thought of *that?*

Krogstad. Most of us think of that at first. I did, too —but I hadn't the courage.

Nora (faintly). No more had I.

Krogstad (in a tone of relief). No, that's it, isn't it— you hadn't the courage either?

Nora. No, I haven't—I haven't.

Krogstad. Besides, it would have been a great piece of folly. Once the first storm at home is over—. I have a letter for your husband in my pocket.

Nora. Telling him everything?

Krogstad. In as lenient a manner as I possibly could.

Nora (quickly). He mustn't get the letter. Tear it up. I will find some means of getting money.

Krogstad. Excuse me, Mrs. Helmer, but I think I told you just now——

Nora. I am not speaking of what I owe you. Tell me what sum you are asking my husband for, and I will get the money.

Krogstad. I am not asking your husband for a penny.

Nora. What do you want, then?

Krogstad. I will tell you. I want to rehabilitate myself, Mrs. Helmer; I want to get on; and in that your husband must help me. For the last year and a half I have not had a hand in anything dishonourable, and all that time I have been struggling in most restricted circumstances. I was content to work my way up step by step. Now I am turned out, and I am not going to be satisfied with merely being taken into favour again. I want to get on, I tell you. I want to get into the Bank again, in a higher position. Your husband must make a place for me——

Nora. That he will never do!

Krogstad. He will; I know him; he dare not protest. And as soon as I am in there again with him, then you will see! Within a year I shall be the manager's right hand. It will be Nils Krogstad and not Torvald Helmer who manages the Bank.

Nora. That's a thing you will never see!

Krogstad. Do you mean that you will——?

Nora. I have courage enough for it now.

Krogstad. Oh, you can't frighten me. A fine, spoilt lady like you——

Nora. You will see, you will see.

Krogstad. Under the ice, perhaps? Down into the cold, coal-black water? And then, in the spring, to float up to the surface, all horrible and unrecognisable, with your hair fallen out——

Nora. You can't frighten me.

Krogstad. Nor you me. People don't do such things, Mrs. Helmer. Besides, what use would it be? I should have him completely in my power all the same.

Nora. Afterwards? When I am no longer——

Krogstad. Have you forgotten that it is I who have the keeping of your reputation? *(Nora stands speechlessly looking at him.)* Well, now, I have warned you. Do not do anything foolish. When Helmer has had my letter, I shall expect a message from him. And be sure you remember that it is your husband himself who has forced me into such ways as this again. I will never forgive him for that. Good-bye, Mrs. Helmer.   [*Exit through the hall.*

Nora (goes to the hall door, opens it slightly and listens). He is going. He is not putting the letter in the box. Oh no, no! that's impossible! *(Opens the door by degrees.)* What is that? He is standing outside. He is not going downstairs. Is he hesitating? Can he——

> [*A letter drops into the box; then* KROGSTAD'S *footsteps are heard, till they die away as he goes downstairs.* NORA *utters a stifled cry and runs across the room to the table by the sofa. A short pause.*

Nora. In the letter-box. *(Steals across to the hall door.)* There it lies—Torvald, Torvald, there is no hope for us now!

> [MRS. LINDE *comes in from the room on the left, carrying the dress.*

Mrs. Linde. There, I can't see anything more to mend now. Would you like to try it on——?

Nora (in a hoarse whisper). Christine, come here.

Mrs. Linde (throwing the dress down on the sofa). What is the matter with you? You look so agitated!

Nora. Come here. Do you see that letter? There, look—you can see it through the glass in the letter-box.

Mrs. Linde. Yes, I see it.

Nora. That letter is from Krogstad.

Mrs. Linde. Nora—it was Krogstad who lent you the money!

Nora. Yes, and now Torvald will know all about it.

Mrs. Linde. Believe me, Nora, that's the best thing for both of you.

Nora. You don't know all. I forged a name.

Mrs. Linde. Good heavens——!

Nora. I only want to say this to you, Christine—you must be my witness.

Mrs. Linde. Your witness? What do you mean? What am I to—?

Nora. If I should go out of my mind—and it might easily happen——

Mrs. Linde. Nora!

Nora. Or if anything else should happen to me—anything, for instance, that might prevent my being here—

Mrs. Linde. Nora! Nora! you are quite out of your mind.

Nora. And if it should happen that there were someone who wanted to take all the responsibility, all the blame, you understand——

Mrs. Linde. Yes, yes—but how can you suppose—?

Nora. Then you must be my witness, that it is not true, Christine. I am not out of my mind at all; I am in my right senses now, and I tell you no one else has known anything about it; I, and I alone, did the whole thing. Remember that.

Mrs. Linde. I will, indeed. But I don't understand all this.

Nora. How should you understand it? A wonderful thing is going to happen.

Mrs. Linde. A wonderful thing?

Nora. Yes, a wonderful thing!—But it is so terrible, Christine; it *mustn't* happen, not for all the world.

Mrs. Linde. I will go at once and see Krogstad.

Nora. Don't go to him; he will do you some harm.

Mrs. Linde. There was a time when he would gladly do anything for my sake.

Nora. He?

Mrs. Linde. Where does he live?

Nora. How should I know—? Yes *(feeling in her pocket.)* here is his card. But the letter, the letter——!

Helmer (calls from his room, knocking at the door). Nora!

Nora (cries out anxiously). Oh, what's that? What do you want?

Helmer. Don't be so frightened. We are not coming in; you have locked the door. Are you trying on your dress?

Nora. Yes, that's it. I look so nice, Torvald.

Mrs. Linde (who has read the card). I see he lives at the corner here.

Nora. Yes, but it's no use. It is hopeless. The letter is lying there in the box.

Mrs. Linde. And your husband keeps the key?

Nora. Yes, always.

Mrs. Linde. Krogstad must ask for his letter back unread, he must find some pretence——

Nora. But it is just at this time that Torvald generally——

Mrs. Linde. You must delay him. Go in to him in the meantime. I will come back as soon as I can.

[*She goes out hurriedly through the hall door.*

Nora (goes to HELMER'S *door, opens it and peeps in).* Torvald!

Helmer (from the inner room). Well? May I venture at last to come into my own room again? Come along, Rank, now you will see— *(Halting in the doorway.)* But what is this?

Nora. What is what, dear?

Helmer. Rank led me to expect a splendid transformation.

Rank (in the doorway). I understood so, but evidently I was mistaken.

Nora. Yes, nobody is to have the chance of admiring me in my dress until to-morrow.

Helmer. But, my dear Nora, you look so worn out. Have you been practising too much?

Nora. No, I have not practised at all.

Helmer. But you will need to—

Nora. Yes, indeed I shall, Torvald. But I can't get on a bit without you to help me; I have absolutely forgotten the whole thing.

Helmer. Oh, we will soon work it up again.

Nora. Yes, help me, Torvald. Promise that you will! I am so nervous about it—all the people—. You must give yourself up to me entirely this evening. Not the tiniest bit of business—you mustn't even take a pen in your hand. Will you promise, Torvald dear?

Helmer. I promise. This evening I will be wholly and absolutely at your service, you helpless little mortal. Ah, by the way, first of all I will just——

                                     [*Goes towards the hall door.*

Nora. What are you going to do there?

Helmer. Only see if any letters have come.

Nora. No, no! don't do that, Torvald!

Helmer. Why not?

Nora. Torvald, please don't. There is nothing there.

Helmer. Well, let me look. *(Turns to go to the letter-box.* NORA, *at the piano, plays the first bars of the Tarantella.* HELMER *stops in the doorway.)* Aha!

Nora. I can't dance to-morrow if I don't practise with you.

Helmer (going up to her). Are you really so afraid of it, dear.

Nora. Yes, so dreadfully afraid of it. Let me practise at once; there is time now, before we go to dinner. Sit down and play for me, Torvald dear; criticise me, and correct me as you play.

Helmer. With great pleasure, if you wish me to.

                                     [*Sits down at the piano.*

Nora (takes out of the box a tambourine and a long variegated shawl. She hastily drapes the shawl round her. Then she springs to the front of the stage and calls out). Now play for me! I am going to dance!

[HELMER *plays and* NORA *dances.* RANK *stands*
    by the piano behind HELMER *and looks on.*

Helmer (as he plays). Slower, slower!

Nora. I can't do it any other way.

Helmer. Not so violently, Nora!

Nora. This is the way.

Helmer (stops playing). No, no—that is not a bit right.

Nora (laughing and swinging the tambourine). Didn't
I tell you so?

Rank. Let me play for her.

Helmer (getting up). Yes, do. I can correct her better
then.

[RANK *sits down at the piano and plays.* NORA
    dances more and more wildly. HELMER *has
    taken up a position beside the stove, and during
    her dance gives her frequent instructions. She
    does not seem to hear him; her hair comes down
    and falls over her shoulders; she pays no atten-
    tion to it, but goes on dancing. Enter* MRS.
    LINDE.

Mrs. Linde (standing as if spell-bound in the doorway).
Oh!——

Nora (as she dances). Such fun, Christine!

Helmer. My dear darling Nora, you are dancing as if
your life depended on it.

Nora. So it does.

Helmer. Stop, Rank; this is sheer madness. Stop, I
tell you! (RANK *stops playing, and* NORA *suddenly stands
still.* HELMER *goes up to her.*) I could never have believed it. You have forgotten everything I taught you.

Nora (throwing away the tambourine). There, you see.

Helmer. You will want a lot of coaching.

Nora. Yes, you see how much I need it. You must
coach me up to the last minute. Promise me that, Torvald!

Helmer. You can depend on me.

Nora. You must not think of anything but me, either

to-day or to-morrow; you mustn't open a single letter—not even open the letter-box——

Helmer. Ah, you are still afraid of that fellow——

Nora. Yes, indeed I am.

Helmer. Nora, I can tell from your looks that there is a letter from him lying there.

Nora. I don't know; I think there is; but you must not read anything of that kind now. Nothing horrid must come between us till this is all over.

Rank (whispers to HELMER). You mustn't contradict her.

Helmer (taking her in his arms). The child shall have her way. But to-morrow night, after you have danced——

Nora. Then you will be free.

        [*The* MAID *appears in the doorway to the right.*

Maid. Dinner is served, ma'am.

Nora. We will have champagne, Helen.

Maid. Very good, ma'am.   [*Exit.*

Helmer. Hullo!—are we going to have a banquet?

Nora. Yes, a champagne banquet till the small hours. *(Calls out.)* And a few macaroons, Helen—lots, just for once!

Helmer. Come, come, don't be so wild and nervous. Be my own little skylark, as you used.

Nora. Yes, dear, I will. But go in now and you too, Doctor Rank. Christine, you must help me to do up my hair.

Rank (whispers to HELMER *as they go out).* I suppose there is nothing—she is not expecting anything?

Helmer. Far from it, my dear fellow; it is simply nothing more than this childish nervousness I was telling you of.

        [*They go into the right-hand room.*

Nora. Well!

Mrs. Linde. Gone out of town.

Nora. I could tell from your face.

Mrs. Linde. He is coming home to-morrow evening. I wrote a note for him

Nora. You should have let it alone; you must prevent nothing. After all, it is splendid to be waiting for a wonderful thing to happen.

Mrs. Linde. What is it that you are waiting for?

Nora. Oh, you wouldn't understand. Go in to them, I will come in a moment. *(MRS. LINDE goes into the dining-room. NORA stands still for a little while, as if to compose herself. Then she looks at her watch.)* Five o'clock. Seven hours till midnight; and then four-and-twenty hours till the next midnight. Then the Tarantella will be over. Twenty-four and seven? Thirty-one hours to live.

Helmer (from the doorway on the right). Where's my little skylark?

Nora (going to him with her arms outstretched). Here she is!

ACT III

THE SAME SCENE. *The table has been placed in the middle of the stage, with chairs round it. A lamp is burning on the table. The door into the hall stands open. Dance music is heard in the room above.* MRS. LINDE *is sitting at the table idly turning over the leaves of a book; she tries to read, but does not seem able to collect her thoughts. Every now and then she listens intently for a sound at the outer door.*

Mrs. Linde (looking at her watch). Not yet—and the time is nearly up. If only he does not—. *(Listens again.)* Ah, there he is. *(Goes into the hall and opens the outer door carefully. Light footsteps are heard on the stairs. She whispers.)* Come in. There is no one here.

Krogstad (in the doorway). I found a note from you at home. What does this mean?

Mrs. Linde. It is absolutely necessary that I should have a talk with you.

Krogstad. Really? And is it absolutely necessary that it should be here?

Mrs. Linde. It is impossible where I live; there is no private entrance to my rooms. Come in; we are quite alone. The maid is asleep, and the Helmers are at the dance upstairs.

Krogstad (coming into the room). Are the Helmers really at a dance to-night?

Mrs. Linde. Yes, why not?

Krogstad. Certainly—why not?

66

Mrs. Linde. Now, Nils, let us have a talk.

Krogstad. Can we two have anything to talk about?

Mrs. Linde. We have a great deal to talk about.

Krogstad. I shouldn't have thought so.

Mrs. Linde. No, you have never properly understood me.

Krogstad. Was there anything else to understand except what was obvious to all the world—a heartless woman jilts a man when a more lucrative chance turns up?

Mrs. Linde. Do you believe I am as absolutely heartless as all that? And do you believe that I did it with a light heart?

Krogstad. Didn't you?

Mrs. Linde. Nils, did you really think that?

Krogstad. If it were as you say, why did you write to me as you did at the time?

Mrs. Linde. I could do nothing else. As I had to break with you, it was my duty also to put an end to all that you felt for me.

Krogstad (wringing his hands). So that was it. And all this—only for the sake of money!

Mrs. Linde. You must not forget that I had a helpless mother and two little brothers. We couldn't wait for you, Nils; your prospects seemed hopeless then.

Krogstad. That may be so, but you had no right to throw me over for any one else's sake.

Mrs. Linde. Indeed I don't know. Many a time did I ask myself if I had the right to do it.

Krogstad (more gently). When I lost you, it was as if all the solid ground went from under my feet. Look at me now—I am a shipwrecked man clinging to a bit of wreckage.

Mrs. Linde. But help may be near.

Krogstad. It *was* near; but then you came and stood in my way.

Mrs. Linde. Unintentionally, Nils. It was only to-day that I learnt it was your place I was going to take in the Bank.

Krogstad. I believe you, if you say so. But now that you know it, are you not going to give it up to me?

Mrs. Linde. No, because that would not benefit you in the least.

Krogstad. Oh, benefit, benefit—I would have done it whether or no.

Mrs. Linde. I have learnt to act prudently. Life, and hard, bitter necessity have taught me that.

Krogstad. And life has taught me not to believe in fine speeches.

Mrs. Linde. Then life has taught you something very reasonable. But deeds you must believe in?

Krogstad. What do you mean by that?

Mrs. Linde. You said you were like a shipwrecked man clinging to some wreckage.

Krogstad. I had good reason to say so.

Mrs. Linde. Well, I am like a shipwrecked woman clinging to some wreckage—no one to mourn for, no one to care for.

Krogstad. It was your own choice.

Mrs. Linde. There was no other choice—then.

Krogstad. Well, what now?

Mrs. Linde. Nils, how would it be if we two shipwrecked people could join forces?

Krogstad. What are you saying?

Mrs. Linde. Two on the same piece of wreckage would stand a better chance than each on their own.

Krogstad. Christine!

Mrs. Linde. What do you suppose brought me to town?

Krogstad. Do you mean that you gave me a thought?

Mrs. Linde. I could not endure life without work. All my life, as long as I can remember, I have worked, and it has been my greatest and only pleasure. But now I am quite alone in the world—my life is so dreadfully empty and I feel so forsaken. There is not the least pleasure in working for one's self. Nils, give me someone and something to work for.

Krogstad. I don't trust that. It is nothing but a woman's overstrained sense of generosity that prompts you to make such an offer of yourself.

Mrs. Linde. Have you ever noticed anything of the sort in me?

Krogstad. Could you really do it? Tell me—do you know all about my past life?

Mrs. Linde. Yes.

Krogstad. And do you know what they think of me here?

Mrs. Linde. You seemed to me to imply that with me you might have been quite another man.

Krogstad. I am certain of it.

Mrs. Linde. Is it too late now?

Krogstad. Christine, are you saying this deliberately? Yes, I am sure you are. I see it in your face. Have you really the courage, then—?

Mrs. Linde. I want to be a mother to someone, and your children need a mother. We two need each other. Nils, I have faith in your real character—I can dare anything together with you.

Krogstad (grasps her hands). Thanks, thanks, Christine! Now I shall find a way to clear myself in the eyes of the world. Ah, but I forgot——

Mrs. Linde (listening). Hush! The Tarantella! Go, go!

Krogstad. Why? What is it?

Mrs. Linde. Do you hear them up there? When that is over, we may expect them back.

Krogstad. Yes, yes—I will go. But it is all no use. Of course you are not aware what steps I have taken in the matter of the Helmers.

Mrs. Linde. Yes, I know all about that.

Krogstad. And in spite of that have you the courage to—?

Mrs. Linde. I understand very well to what lengths a man like you might be driven by despair.

Krogstad. If I could only undo what I have done!

Mrs. Linde. You cannot. Your letter is lying in the letter-box now.

Krogstad. Are you sure of that?

Mrs. Linde. Quite sure, but——

Krogstad (with a searching look at her). Is that what it all means?—that you want to save your friend at any cost? Tell me frankly. Is that it?

Mrs. Linde. Nils, a woman who has once sold herself for another's sake, doesn't do it a second time.

Krogstad. I will ask for my letter back.

Mrs. Linde. No, no.

Krogstad. Yes, of course I will. I will wait here till Helmer comes; I will tell him he must give me my letter back—that it only concerns my dismissal—that he is not to read it——

Mrs. Linde. No, Nils, you must not recall your letter.

Krogstad. But, tell me, wasn't it for that very purpose that you asked me to meet you here?

Mrs. Linde. In my first moment of fright, it was. But twenty-four hours have elapsed since then, and in that time I have witnessed incredible things in this house. Helmer must know all about it. This unhappy secret must be disclosed; they must have a complete understanding between them, which is impossible with all this concealment and falsehood going on.

Krogstad. Very well, if you will take the responsibility. But there is one thing I can do in any case, and I shall do it at once.

Mrs. Linde (listening). You must be quick and go! The dance is over; we are not safe a moment longer.

Krogstad. I will wait for you below.

Mrs. Linde. Yes, do. You must see me back to my door.

Krogstad. I have never had such an amazing piece of good fortune in my life.

> [*Goes out through the outer door. The door be-*
> *tween the room and the hall remains open.*

Mrs. Linde (tidying up the room and laying her hat and cloak ready). What a difference! what a difference! Someone to work for and live for—a home to bring comfort into. That I will do, indeed. I wish they would be quick and come— *(Listens.)* Ah, there they are now. I must put on my things.

> [*Takes up her hat and cloak.* HELMER'S *and*
> NORA'S *voices are heard outside; a key is turned,*
> *and* HELMER *brings* NORA *almost by force into*
> *the hall. She is in an Italian costume with a*
> *large black shawl round her; he is in evening*
> *dress and a black domino which is flying open.*

NORA *(hanging back in the doorway, and struggling with him).* No, no, no!—don't take me in. I want to go upstairs again; I don't want to leave so early.

Helmer. But, my dearest Nora——

Nora. Please, Torvald dear—please, *please*—only an hour more.

Helmer. Not a single minute, my sweet Nora. You know that was our agreement. Come along into the room; you are catching cold standing there.

> [*He brings her gently into the room, in spite of*
> *her resistance.*

Mrs. Linde. Good evening.

Nora. Christine!

Helmer. You here, so late, Mrs. Linde?

Mrs. Linde. Yes, you must excuse me; I was so anxious to see Nora in her dress.

Nora. Have you been sitting here waiting for me?

Mrs. Linde. Yes, unfortunately I came too late, you

had already gone upstairs; and I thought I couldn't go away again without having seen you.

Helmer (taking off NORA'S *shawl).* Yes, take a good look at her. I think she is worth looking at. Isn't she charming, Mrs. Linde?

Mrs. Linde. Yes, indeed she is.

Helmer. Doesn't she look remarkably pretty? Everyone thought so at the dance. But she is terribly self-willed, this sweet little person. What are we to do with her? You will hardly believe that I had almost to bring her away by force.

Nora. Torvald, you will repent not having let me stay, even if it were only for half an hour.

Helmer. Listen to her, Mrs. Linde! She had danced her Tarantella, and it had been a tremendous success, as it deserved—although possibly the performance was a trifle too realistic—a little more so, I mean, than was strictly compatible with the limitations of art. But never mind about that! The chief thing is, she had made a success— she had made a tremendous success. Do you think I was going to let her remain there after that, and spoil the effect? No indeed! I took my charming little Capri maiden—my capricious little Capri maiden, I should say—on my arm; took one quick turn round the room; a curtsey on either side, and, as they say in novels, the beautiful apparition disappeared. An exit ought always to be effective, Mrs. Linde; but that is what I cannot make Nora understand. Pooh! this room is hot. *(Throws his domino on a chair and opens the door of his room.)* Hullo! it's all dark in here. Oh, of course—excuse me——.

[*He goes in and lights some candles.*

Nora (in a hurried and breathless whisper). Well?

Mrs. Linde (in a low voice). I have had a talk with him.

Nora. Yes, and——

Mrs. Linde. Nora, you must tell your husband all about it.

Nora (in an expressionless voice). I knew it.

Mrs. Linde. You have nothing to be afraid of as far as Krogstad is concerned; but you must tell him.

Nora. I won't tell him.

Mrs. Linde. Then the letter will.

Nora. Thank you, Christine. Now I know what I must do. Hush——!

Helmer (coming in again). Well, Mrs. Linde, have you admired her?

Mrs. Linde. Yes, and now I will say good-night.

Helmer. What, already? Is this yours, this knitting?

Mrs. Linde (taking it). Yes, thank you, I had very nearly forgotten it.

Helmer. So you knit?

Mrs. Linde. Of course.

Helmer. Do you know, you ought to embroider.

Mrs. Linde. Really? Why?

Helmer. Yes, it's far more becoming. Let me show you. You hold the embroidery thus in your left hand, and use the needle with the right—like this—with a long, easy sweep. Do you see?

Mrs. Linde. Yes, perhaps——

Helmer. But in the case of knitting—that can never be anything but ungraceful; look here—the arms close together, the knitting-needles going up and down—it has a sort of Chinese effect——. That was really excellent champagne they gave us.

Mrs. Linde. Well,—good-night, Nora, and don't be self-willed any more.

Helmer. That's right, Mrs. Linde.

Mrs. Linde. Good-night, Mr. Helmer.

Helmer (accompanying her to the door). Good-night, good-night. I hope you will get home all right. I should be very happy to—but you haven't any great distance to go. Good-night, good-night. *(She goes out; he shuts the door after her, and comes in again.)*   Ah!—at last we have got rid of her   She is a frightful bore, that woman.

Nora.   Aren't you very tired, Torvald?

Helmer.   No, not in the least.

Nora.   Nor sleepy?

Helmer.   Not a bit.   On the contrary, I feel extraordinarily lively.   And you?—you really look both tired and sleepy.

Nora.   Yes, I am very tired.   I want to go to sleep at once.

Helmer.   There, you see it was quite right of me not to let you stay there any longer.

Nora.   Everything you do is quite right, Torvald.

Helmer (kissing her on the forehead).   Now my little skylark is speaking reasonably.   Did you notice what good spirits Rank was in this evening?

Nora.   Really?   Was he?   I didn't speak to him at all.

Helmer.   And I very little, but I have not for a long time seen him in such good form.   *(Looks for a while at her and then goes nearer to her.)*   It is delightful to be at home by ourselves again, to be all alone with you—you fascinating, charming little darling!

Nora.   Don't look at me like that, Torvald.

Helmer.   Why shouldn't I look at my dearest treasure?— at all the beauty that is mine, all my very own?

Nora (going to the other side of the table).   You mustn't say things like that to me to-night.

Helmer (following her).   You have still got the Taran· tella in your blood, I see.   And it makes you more capti-, vating than ever.   Listen—the guests are beginning to go now.   *(In a lower voice.)*   Nora—soon the whole house will be quiet.

Nora.   Yes, I hope so.

Helmer.   Yes, my own darling Nora.   Do you know, when I am out at a party with you like this, why I speak so

little to you, keep away from you, and only send a stolen
glance in your direction now and then?—do you know why
I do that? It is because I make believe to myself that we
are secretly in love, and you are my secretly promised bride,
and that no one suspects there is anything between us.

Nora. Yes, yes—I know very well your thoughts are
with me all the time.

Helmer. And when we are leaving, and I am putting
the shawl over your beautiful young shoulders—on your
lovely neck—then I imagine that you are my young bride
and that we have just come from the wedding, and I am
bringing you for the first time into our home—to be alone
with you for the first time—quite alone with my shy little
darling! All this evening I have longed for nothing but
you. When I watched the seductive figures of the Tarantella, my blood was on fire; I could endure it no longer, and
that was why I brought you down so early——

Nora. Go away, Torvald! You must let me go. I
won't——

Helmer. What's that? You're joking, my little Nora!
You won't—you won't? Am I not your husband—?

[*A knock is heard at the outer door.*

Nora (starting). Did you hear——?

Helmer (going into the hall). Who is it?

Rank (outside). It is I. May I come in for a moment?

Helmer (in a fretful whisper). Oh, what does he want
now? *(Aloud.)* Wait a minute? *(Unlocks the door.)*
Come, that's kind of you not to pass by our door.

Rank. I thought I heard your voice, and felt as if I
should like to look in. *(With a swift glance round.)* Ah,
yes!—these dear familiar rooms. You are very happy and
cosy in here, you two.

Helmer. It seems to me that you looked after yourself
pretty well upstairs too.

Rank. Excellently. Why shouldn't I? Why shouldn't

one enjoy everything in this world?—at any rate as much as one can, and as long as one can. The wine was capital——

Helmer. Especially the champagne.

Rank. So you noticed that too? It is almost incredible how much I managed to put away!

Nora. Torvald drank a great deal of champagne to-night, too.

Rank. Did he?

Nora. Yes, and he is always in such good spirits afterwards.

Rank. Well, why should one not enjoy a merry evening after a well-spent day?

Helmer. Well spent? I am afraid I can't take credit for that.

Rank (clapping him on the back). But I can, you know!

Nora. Doctor Rank, you must have been occupied with some scientific investigation to-day.

Rank. Exactly.

Helmer. Just listen!—little Nora talking about scientific investigations!

Nora. And may I congratulate you on the result?

Rank. Indeed you may.

Nora. Was it favourable, then?

Rank. The best possible, for both doctor and patient—certainty.

Nora (quickly and searchingly). Certainty?

Rank. Absolute certainty. So wasn't I entitled to make a merry evening of it after that?

Nora. Yes, you certainly were, Doctor Rank.

Helmer. I think so too, so long as you don't have to pay for it in the morning.

Rank. Oh well, one can't have anything in this life without paying for it.

Nora. Doctor Rank—are you fond of fancy-dress balls?

Rank. Yes, if there is a fine lot of pretty costumes.

Nora. Tell me—what shall we two wear at the next?

Helmer. Little featherbrain!—are you thinking of the next already?

Rank. We two? Yes, I can tell you. You shall go as a good fairy——

Helmer. Yes, but what do you suggest as an appropriate costume for that?

Rank. Let your wife go dressed just as she is in everyday life.

Helmer. That was really very prettily turned. But can't you tell us what you will be?

Rank. Yes, my dear friend, I have quite made up my mind about that.

Helmer. Well?

Rank. At the next fancy dress ball I shall be invisible.

Helmer. That's a good joke!

Rank. There is a big black hat—have you never heard of hats that make you invisible? If you put one on, no one can see you.

Helmer (suppressing a smile). Yes, you are quite right.

Rank. But I am clean forgetting what I came for. Helmer, give me a cigar—one of the dark Havanas.

Helmer. With the greatest pleasure.

[*Offers him his case.*

Rank (takes a cigar and cuts off the end). Thanks.

Nora (striking a match). Let me give you a light.

Rank. Thank you. *(She holds the match for him to light his cigar.)* And now good-bye!

Helmer. Good-bye, good-bye, dear old man!

Nora. Sleep well, Doctor Rank.

Rank. Thank you for that wish.

Nora. Wish me the same.

Rank. You? Well, if you want me to sleep well! And thanks for the light.

[*He nods to them both and goes out.*

Helmer (in a subdued voice). He has drunk more than he ought.

Nora (absently). Maybe. (HELMER *takes a bunch of keys out of his pocket and goes into the hall.*) Torvald! what are you going to do there?

Helmer. Empty the letter-box; it is quite full; there will be no room to put the newspaper in to-morrow morning.

Nora. Are you going to work to-night?

Helmer. You know quite well I'm not. What is this? Some one has been at the lock.

Nora. At the lock—?

Helmer. Yes, someone has. What can it mean? I should never have thought the maid—. Here is a broken hairpin. Nora, it is one of yours.

Nora (quickly). Then it must have been the children—

Helmer. Then you must get them out of those ways. There, at last I have got it open. (*Takes out the contents of the letter-box, and calls to the kitchen.*) Helen!—Helen, put out the light over the front door. (*Goes back into the room and shuts the door into the hall. He holds out his hand full of letters.*) Look at that—look what a heap of them there are. (*Turning them over.*) What on earth is that?

Nora (at the window). The letter—No! Torvald, no!

Helmer. Two cards—of Rank's.

Nora. Of Doctor Rank's?

Helmer (looking at them). Doctor Rank. They were on the top. He must have put them in when he went out.

Nora. Is there anything written on them?

Helmer. There is a black cross over the name. Look there—what an uncomfortable idea! It looks as if he were announcing his own death.

Nora. It is just what he is doing.

Helmer. What? Do you know anything about it? Has he said anything to you?

Nora. Yes. He told me that when the cards came it

would be his leave-taking from us. He means to shut himself up and die.

Helmer. My poor old friend. Certainly I knew we should not have him very long with us. But so soon! And so he hides himself away like a wounded animal.

Nora. If it has to happen, it is best it should be without a word—don't you think so, Torvald?

Helmer (walking up and down). He had so grown into our lives. I can't think of him as having gone out of them. He, with his sufferings and his loneliness, was like a cloudy background to our sunlit happiness. Well, perhaps it is best so. For him, anyway. *(Standing still.)* And perhaps for us too, Nora. We two are thrown quite upon each other now. *(Puts his arms round her.)* My darling wife, I don't feel as if I could hold you tight enough. Do you know, Nora, I have often wished that you might be threatened by some great danger, so that I might risk my life's blood, and everything, for your sake.

Nora (disengages herself, and says firmly and decidedly). Now you must read your letters, Torvald.

Helmer. No, no; not to-night. I want to be with you, my darling wife.

Nora. With the thought of your friend's death——

Helmer. You are right, it has affected us both. Some-thing ugly has come between us—the thought of the horrors of death. We must try and rid our minds of that. Until then—we will each go to our own room.

Nora (hanging on his neck). Good-night, Torvald— Good-night!

Helmer (kissing her on the forehead). Good-night, my little singing-bird. Sleep sound, Nora. Now I will read my letters through.

[*He takes his letters and goes into his room, shut-ting the door after him.*

Nora (gropes distractedly about, seizes HELMER'S *domino, throws it round her, while she says in quick, hoarse, spas-*

modic whispers). Never to see him again. Never?
Never! *(Puts her shawl over her head.)* Never to see my
children again either—never again. Never! Never!—
Ah! the icy, black water—the unfathomable depths—If only
it were over! He has got it now—now he is reading it.
Good-bye, Torvald and my children!

> [*She is about to rush out through the hall, when*
> HELMER *opens his door hurriedly and stands
> with an open letter in his hand.*

Helmer. Nora!

Nora. Ah!——

HELMER. What is this? Do you know what is in this
letter?

Nora. Yes, I know. Let me go! Let me get out!

Helmer (holding her back). Where are you going?

Nora (trying to get free). You shan't save me, Torvald!

Helmer (reeling). True? Is this true, that I read here?
Horrible! No, no—it is impossible that it can be true.

Nora. It is true. I have loved you above everything
else in the world.

Helmer. Oh, don't let us have any silly excuses.

Nora (taking a step towards him). Torvald——!

Helmer. Miserable creature—what have you done?

Nora. Let me go. You shall not suffer for my sake.
You shall not take it upon yourself.

Helmer. No tragedy airs, please. *(Locks the hall door.)*
Here you shall stay and give me an explanation. Do you
understand what you have done? Answer me? Do you
understand what you have done?

*Nora (looks steadily at him and says with a growing look
of coldness in her face).* Yes, now I am beginning to understand thoroughly.

Helmer (walking about the room). What a horrible
awakening! All these eight years—she who was my joy
and pride—a hypocrite, a liar—worse, worse—a criminal!

The unutterable ugliness of it all! For shame! For
shame! (NORA *is silent and looks steadily at him. He
stops in front of her.*) I ought to have suspected that
something of the sort would happen. I ought to have fore-
seen it. All your father's want of principle—be silent!—
all your father's want of principle has come out in you. No
religion, no morality, no sense of duty—. How I am punished for having winked at what he did! I did it for your
sake, and this is how you repay me.

Nora. Yes, that's just it.

Helmer. Now you have destroyed all my happiness.
You have ruined all my future. It is horrible to think of!
I am in the power of an unscrupulous man; he can do what
he likes with me, ask anything he likes of me, give me any
orders he pleases—I dare not refuse. And I must sink to
such miserable depths because of a thoughtless woman!

Nora. When I am out of the way, you will be free.

Helmer. No fine speeches, please. Your father had always plenty of those ready, too. What good would it be
to me if you were out of the way, as you say? Not the
slightest. He can make the affair known everywhere; and
if he does, I may be falsely suspected of having been a
party to your criminal action. Very likely people will think
I was behind it all—that it was I who prompted you! And
I have to thank you for all this—you whom I have cherished
during the whole of our married life. Do you understand
now what it is you have done for me?

Nora (coldly and quietly). Yes.

Helmer. It is so incredible that I can't take it in. But
we must come to some understanding. Take off that shawl.
Take it off, I tell you. I must try and appease him some
way or another. The matter must be hushed up at any
cost. And as for you and me, it must appear as if everything between us were just as before—but naturally only
in the eyes of the world. You will still remain in my house,
that is a matter of course. But I shall not allow you to

bring up the children; I dare not trust them to you. To think that I should be obliged to say so to one whom I have loved so dearly, and whom I still——. No, that is all over. From this moment happiness is not the question; all that concerns us is to save the remains, the fragments, the appearance——

[*A ring is heard at the front-door bell.*

Helmer (with a start). What is that? So late! Can the worst——? Can he——? Hide yourself, Nora. Say you are ill.

[NORA *stands motionless.* HELMER *goes and un-locks the hall door.*

Maid (half-dressed, comes to the door). A letter for the mistress.

Helmer. Give it to me. *(Takes the letter, and shuts the door.)* Yes, it is from him. You shall not have it; I will read it myself.

Nora. Yes, read it.

Helmer (standing by the lamp). I scarcely have the courage to do it. It may mean ruin for both of us. No, I must know. *(Tears open the letter, runs his eye over a few lines, looks at a paper enclosed and gives a shout of joy.)* Nora! *(She looks at him questioningly.)* Nora!—No, I must read it once again——. Yes, it is true! I am saved! Nora, I am saved!

Nora. And I?

Helmer. You too, of course; we are both saved, both you and I. Look, he sends you your bond back. He says he regrets and repents—that a happy change in his life—never mind what he says! We are saved, Nora! No one can do anything to you. Oh, Nora, Nora!—no, first I must destroy these hateful things. Let me see——. *(Takes a look at the bond.)* No, no, I won't look at it. The whole thing shall be nothing but a bad dream to me. *(Tears up the bond and both letters, throws them all into the stove, and watches them burn.)* There—now it doesn't exist any longer. He says that since Christmas Eve you——. These must have been three dreadful days for you, Nora.

Nora. I have fought a hard fight these three days.

Helmer. And suffered agonies, and seen no way out but——. No, we won't call any of the horrors to mind. We will only shout with joy, and keep saying, "It's all over! It's all over!" Listen to me, Nora. You don't seem to realise that it is all over. What is this?—such a cold, set face! My poor little Nora, I quite understand; you don't feel as if you could believe that I have forgiven you. But it is true, Nora, I swear it; I have forgiven you everything. I know that what you did, you did out of love for me.

Nora. That is true.

Helmer. You have loved me as a wife ought to love her husband. Only you had not sufficient knowledge to judge of the means you used. But do you suppose you are any the less dear to me, because you don't understand how to act on your own responsibility? No, no; only lean on me; I will advise you and direct you. I should not be a man if this womanly helplessness did not just give you a double attractiveness in my eyes. You must not think any more about the hard things I said in my first moment of consternation, when I thought everything was going to overwhelm me. I have forgiven you, Nora; I swear to you I have forgiven you.

Nora. Thank you for your forgiveness.

[*She goes out through the door to the right.*

Helmer. No, don't go——. *(Looks in.)* What are you doing in there?

Nora (from within). Taking off my fancy dress.

Helmer (standing at the open door). Yes, do. Try and calm yourself, and make your mind easy again, my frightened little singing-bird. Be at rest, and feel secure; I have broad wings to shelter you under. *(Walks up and down by the door.)* How warm and cosy our home is, Nora. Here is shelter for you; here I will protect you like a hunted dove that I have saved from a hawk's claws. I will bring peace to your poor beating heart. It will come, little by little, Nora, believe me. Tomorrow morning you will look upon it all quite differently; soon everything will be just as it was before. Very soon you won't need me to assure you that I have forgiven you; you will yourself feel the certainty that I have done so. Can you suppose I should ever think of such a thing as repudiating you, or even reproaching you? You have no idea what a true man's heart is like, Nora. There is something so indescribably sweet and satisfying, to a man, in the knowledge that he has forgiven his wife—forgiven her freely, and with all his heart. It seems as if that had made her, as it were, doubly his own; he has given her a new life, so to speak; and she has in a way become both wife and child to him. So you shall be for me after this, my little scared, helpless darling. Have no anxiety about anything, Nora; only be frank and open with me, and I will serve as will and conscience both to you——. What is this? Not gone to bed? Have you changed your things?

Nora (in everyday dress). Yes, Torvald, I have changed my things now.

Helmer. But what for?—so late as this.

Nora. I shall not sleep to-night.

Helmer. But, my dear Nora——

Nora (looking at her watch). It is not so very late. Sit down here, Torvald. You and I have much to say to one another.

[*She sits down at one side of the table.*

Helmer. Nora—what is this?—this cold, set face?

Nora. Sit down. It will take some time; I have a lot to talk over with you.

Helmer (sits down at the opposite side of the table). You alarm me, Nora!—and I don't understand you.

Nora. No, that is just it. You don't understand me, and I have never understood you either—before to-night. No, you mustn't interrupt me. You must simply listen to what I say. Torvald, this is a settling of accounts.

Helmer. What do you mean by that?

Nora (after a short silence). Isn't there one thing that strikes you as strange in our sitting here like this?

Helmer. What is that?

Nora. We have been married now eight years. Does it not occur to you that this is the first time we two, you and I, husband and wife, have had a serious conversation?

Helmer. What do you mean by serious?

Nora. In all these eight years—longer than that—from the very beginning of our acquaintance, we have never exchanged a word on any serious subject.

Helmer. Was it likely that I would be continually and for ever telling you about worries that you could not help me to bear?

Nora. I am not speaking about business matters. I say that we have never sat down in earnest together to try and get at the bottom of anything.

Helmer. But, dearest Nora, would it have been any good to you?

Nora. That is just it; you have never understood me. I have been greatly wronged, Torvald—first by papa and then by you.

Helmer. What! By us two—by us two, who have loved you better than anyone else in the world?

Nora (shaking her head). You have never loved me. You have only thought it pleasant to be in love with me.

Helmer. Nora, what do I hear you saying?

Nora. It is perfectly true, Torvald. When I was at home with papa, he told me his opinion about everything, and so I had the same opinions; and if I differed from him I concealed the fact, because he would not have liked it. He called me his doll-child, and he played with me just as I used to play with my dolls. And when I came to live with you——

Helmer. What sort of an expression is that to use about our marriage?

Nora (undisturbed). I mean that I was simply transferred from papa's hands into yours. You arranged everything according to your own taste, and so I got the same tastes as you—or else I pretended to, I am really not quite sure which—I think sometimes the one and sometimes the other. When I look back on it, it seems to me as if I had been living here like a poor woman—just from hand to mouth. I have existed merely to perform tricks for you, Torvald. But you would have it so. You and papa have committed a great sin against me. It is your fault that I have made nothing of my life.

Helmer. How unreasonable and how ungrateful you are, Nora! Have you not been happy here?

Nora. No, I have never been happy. I thought I was, but it has never really been so.

Helmer. Not—not happy!

Nora. No, only merry. And you have always been so kind to me. But our home has been nothing but a playroom. I have been your doll-wife, just as at home I was papa's doll-child; and here the children have been my dolls. I thought it great fun when you played with me, just as they thought it great fun when I played with them. That is what our marriage has been, Torvald.

Helmer. There is some truth in what you say—exaggerated and strained as your view of it is. But for the future it shall be different. Playtime shall be over, and lesson-time shall begin.

Nora. Whose lessons? Mine, or the children's?

Helmer. Both yours and the children's, my darling Nora.

Nora. Alas, Torvald, you are not the man to educate me into being a proper wife for you.

Helmer. And you can say that!

Nora. And I—how am I fitted to bring up the children?

Helmer. Nora!

Nora. Didn't you say so yourself a little while ago—that you dare not trust me to bring them up?

Helmer. In a moment of anger! Why do you pay any heed to that?

Nora. Indeed, you were perfectly right. I am not fit for the task. There is another task I must undertake first. I must try and educate myself—you are not the man to help me in that. I must do that for myself. And that is why I am going to leave you now.

Helmer (springing up). What do you say?

Nora. I must stand quite alone, if I am to understand myself and everything about me. It is for that reason that I cannot remain with you any longer.

Helmer. Nora! Nora!

Nora. I am going away from here now, at once. I am sure Christine will take me in for the night——

Helmer. You are out of your mind! I won't allow it! I forbid you!

Nora. It is no use forbidding me anything any longer. I will take with me what belongs to myself. I will take nothing from you, either now or later.

Helmer. What sort of madness is this!

Nora. To-morrow I shall go home—I mean, to my old home. It will be easiest for me to find something to do there.

Helmer. You blind, foolish woman!

Nora. I must try and get some sense, Torvald.

Helmer. To desert your home, your husband and your children! And you don't consider what people will say!

Nora. I cannot consider that at all. I only know that it is necessary for me.

Helmer. It's shocking. This is how you would neglect your most sacred duties.

Nora. What do you consider my most sacred duties?

Helmer. Do I need to tell you that? Are they not your duties to your husband and your children?

Nora. I have other duties just as sacred.

Helmer. That you have not. What duties could those be?

Nora. Duties to myself.

Helmer. Before all else, you are a wife and a mother.

Nora. I don't believe that any longer. I believe that before all else I am a reasonable human being, just as you are—or, at all events, that I must try and become one. I know quite well, Torvald, that most people would think you right, and that views of that kind are to be found in books; but I can no longer content myself with what most people say, or with what is found in books. I must think over things for myself and get to understand them.

Helmer. Can you not understand your place in your own home? Have you not a reliable guide in such matters as that?—have you no religion?

Nora. I am afraid, Torvald, I do not exactly know what religion is.

Helmer. What are you saying?

Nora. I know nothing but what the clergyman said when I went to be confirmed. He told us that religion was this, and that, and the other. When I am away from all this, and am alone, I will look into that matter too. I will see if what the clergyman said is true, or at all events if it is true for me.

Helmer. This is unheard of in a girl of your age! But if religion cannot lead you aright, let me try and awaken your conscience. I suppose you have some moral sense? Or—answer me—am I to think you have none?

Nora. I assure you, Torvald, that is not an easy question to answer. I really don't know. The thing perplexes me altogether. I only know that you and I look at it in quite a different light. I am learning, too, that the law is quite another thing from what I supposed; but I find it impossible to convince myself that the law is right. According to it a woman has no right to spare her old dying father, or to save her husband's life. I can't believe that.

Helmer. You talk like a child. You don't understand the conditions of the world in which you live.

Nora. No, I don't. But now I am going to try. I am going to see if I can make out who is right, the world or I.

Helmer. You are ill, Nora; you are delirious; I almost think you are out of your mind.

Nora. I have never felt my mind so clear and certain as to-night.

Helmer. And is it with a clear and certain mind that you forsake your husband and your children?

Nora. Yes, it is.

Helmer. Then there is only one possible explanation.

Nora. What is that?

Helmer. You do not love me any more.

Nora. No, that is just it.

Helmer. Nora!—and you can say that?

Nora. It gives me great pain, Torvald, for you have always been so kind to me, but I cannot help it. I do not love you any more.

Helmer (regaining his composure). Is that a clear and certain conviction too?

Nora. Yes, absolutely clear and certain. That is the reason why I will not stay here any longer.

Helmer. And can you tell me what I have done to forfeit your love?

Nora. Yes, indeed I can. It was to-night, when the wonderful thing did not happen; then I saw you were not the man I had thought you.

Helmer. Explain yourself better—I don't understand you.

Nora. I have waited so patiently for eight years; for, goodness knows, I knew very well that wonderful things don't happen every day. Then this horrible misfortune came upon me; and then I felt quite certain that the wonderful thing was going to happen at last. When Krogstad's letter was lying out there, never for a moment did I imagine that you would consent to accept this man's conditions. I was so absolutely certain that you would say to him: Publish the thing to the whole world. And when that was done——

Helmer. Yes, what then?—when I had exposed my wife to shame and disgrace?

Nora. When that was done, I was so absolutely certain, you would come forward and take everything upon yourself, and say: I am the guilty one.

Helmer. Nora——!

Nora. You mean that I would never have accepted such a sacrifice on your part? No, of course not. But what would my assurances have been worth against yours? That was the wonderful thing which I hoped for and feared; and it was to prevent that, that I wanted to kill myself.

Helmer. I would gladly work night and day for you, Nora—bear sorrow and want for your sake. But no man would sacrifice his honour for the one he loves.

Nora. It is a thing hundreds of thousands of women have done.

Helmer. Oh, you think and talk like a heedless child.

Nora. Maybe. But you neither think nor talk like the man I could bind myself to. As soon as your fear was over —and it was not fear for what threatened me, but for what might happen to you—when the whole thing was past, as far as you were concerned it was exactly as if nothing at all had happened. Exactly as before, I was your little skylark, your doll, which you would in future treat with doubly gentle care, because it was so brittle and fragile. *(Getting up.)* Torvald—it was then it dawned upon me that for eight years I had been living here with a strange man, and had borne him three children——. Oh, I can't bear to think of it! I could tear myself into little bits!

Helmer (sadly). I see, I see. An abyss has opened between us—there is no denying it. But, Nora, would it not be possible to fill it up?

Nora. As I am now, I am no wife for you.

Helmer. I have it in me to become a different man.

Nora. Perhaps—if your doll is taken away from you.

Helmer. But to part!—to part from you! No, no, Nora, I can't understand that idea.

Nora (going out to the right). That makes it all the more certain that it must be done.

> [*She comes back with her cloak and hat and a small bag which she puts on a chair by the table.*

Helmer. Nora, Nora, not now! Wait till to-morrow.

Nora (putting on her cloak). I cannot spend the night in a strange man's room.

Helmer. But can't we live here like brother and sister——?

Nora (putting on her hat). You know very well that would not last long. *(Puts the shawl round her.)* Good-bye, Torvald. I won't see the little ones. I know they are in better hands than mine. As I am now, I can be of no use to them.

Helmer. But some day, Nora—some day?

Nora. How can I tell? I have no idea what is going to become of me.

Helmer. But you are my wife, whatever becomes of you.

Nora. Listen, Torvald. I have heard that when a wife deserts her husband's house, as I am doing now, he is legally freed from all obligations towards her. In any case I set you free from all your obligations. You are not to feel yourself bound in the slightest way, any more than I shall. There must be perfect freedom on both sides. See here is your ring back. Give me mine.

Helmer. That too?

Nora. That too.

Helmer. Here it is.

Nora. That's right. Now it is all over. I have put the keys here. The maids know all about everything in the house—better than I do. To-morrow, after I have left her,

Christine will come here and pack up my own things that I brought with me from home. I will have them sent after me.

Helmer. All over! All over!—Nora, shall you never think of me again?

Nora. I know I shall often think of you and the children and this house.

Helmer. May I write to you, Nora?

Nora. No—never. You must not do that.

Helmer. But at least let me send you——

Nora. Nothing—nothing——

Helmer. Let me help you if you are in want.

Nora. No. I can receive nothing from a stranger.

Helmer. Nora—can I never be anything more than a stranger to you?

Nora (taking her bag). Ah, Torvald, the most wonderful thing of all would have to happen.

Helmer. Tell me what that would be!

Nora. Both you and I would have to be so changed that——. Oh, Torvald, I don't believe any longer in wonderful things happening.

Helmer. But I will believe in it. Tell me? So changed that——?

Nora. That our life together would be a real wedlock. Good-bye.

[*She goes out through the hall.*

Helmer (sinks down on a chair at the door and buries his face in his hands). Nora! Nora! *(Looks round, and rises.)* Empty. She is gone. *(A hope flashes across his mind.)* The most wonderful thing of all——?

[*The sound of a door shutting is heard from below.*

GHOSTS
(1881)

CHARACTERS

MRS. ALVING, *a widow.*
OSWALD ALVING, *her son, an artist.*
MANDERS, *the Pastor of the parish.*
ENGSTRAND, *a carpenter.*
REGINA ENGSTRAND, *his daughter, in Mrs. Alving's service.*

   The action takes place at MRS. ALVING'S *house on one of the larger fjords of western Norway.*

GHOSTS

ACT I

SCENE.—*A large room looking upon a garden. A door in the left-hand wall, and two in the right. In the middle of the room, a round table with chairs set about it, and books, magazines and newspapers upon it. In the fore-ground on the left, a window, by which is a small sofa with a work-table in front of it. At the back the room opens into a conservatory rather smaller than the room. From the right-hand side of this a door leads to the garden. Through the large panes of glass that form the outer wall of the conservatory, a gloomy fjord land-scape can be discerned, half obscured by steady rain.*

ENGSTRAND *is standing close up to the garden door. His left leg is slightly deformed, and he wears a boot with a clump of wood under the sole.* REGINA, *with an empty garden-syringe in her hand, is trying to prevent his coming in.*

Regina (below her breath). What is it you want? Stay where you are. The rain is dripping off you.

Engstrand. God's good rain, my girl.

Regina. The Devil's own rain, that's what it is!

Engstrand. Lord, how you talk, Regina. *(Takes a few limping steps forward.)* What I wanted to tell you was this——

Regina. Don't clump about like that, stupid! The young master is lying asleep upstairs.

Engstrand. Asleep still? In the middle of the day?

Regina. Well, it's no business of yours.

Engstrand. I was out on the spree last night——

Regina. I don't doubt it.

Engstrand. Yes, we are poor weak mortals, my girl——

Regina. We are indeed.

Engstrand. ——and the temptations of the world are manifold, you know—but, for all that, here I was at my work at half-past five this morning.

Regina. Yes, yes, but make yourself scarce now. I am not going to stand here as if I had a *rendez-vous* with you.

Engstrand. As if you had a what?

Regina. I am not going to have any one find you here: so now you know, and you can go.

Engstrand (coming a few steps nearer). Not a bit of it! Not before we have had a little chat. This afternoon I shall have finished my job down at the school house, and I shall be off home to town by to-night's boat.

Regina (mutters). Pleasant journey to you!

Engstrand. Thanks, my girl. To-morrow is the opening of the Orphanage, and I expect there will be a fine kick-up here and plenty of good strong drink, don't you know. And no one shall say of Jacob Engstrand that he car'+ hold off when temptation comes in his way.

Regina. Oho!

Engstrand. Yes, because there will be a lot of fine folk here to-morrow. Parson Manders is expected from town, too.

Regina. What is more, he's coming to-day.

Engstrand. There you are! And I'm going to be precious careful he doesn't have anything to say against me, do you see?

Regina. Oh, that's your game, is it?

Engstrand. What do you mean?

Regina (with a significant look at him). What is it you want to humbug Mr. Manders out of, this time?

Engstrand. Sh! Sh! Are you crazy? Do you suppose *I* would want to humbug Mr. Manders? No, no—Mr. Manders has always been too kind a friend for me to do that. But what I wanted to talk to you about, was my going back home to-night.

Regina. The sooner you go, the better I shall be pleased.

Engstrand. Yes, only I want to take you with me, Regina.

Regina (open-mouthed). You want to take me——? What did you say?

Engstrand. I want to take you home with me, I said.

Regina (contemptuously). You will never get me home with you.

Engstrand. Ah, we shall see about that.

Regina. Yes, you can be quite certain we *shall* see about that. I, who have been brought up by a lady like Mrs. Alving?—I, who have been treated almost as if I were her own child?—do you suppose I am going home with *you?*—to such a house as yours? Not likely!

Engstrand. What the devil do you mean? Are you setting yourself up against your father, you hussy?

Regina (mutters, without looking at him). You have often told me I was none of yours.

Engstrand. Bah!—why do you want to pay any attention to that?

Regina. Haven't you many and many a time abused me and called me a——? For shame!

Engstrand. I'll swear I never used such an ugly word.

Regina. Oh, it doesn't matter what word you used.

Engstrand. Besides, that was only when I was a bit fuddled—hm! Temptations are manifold in this world, Regina.

Regina. Ugh!

Engstrand. And it was when your mother was in a nasty temper. I had to find some way of getting my knife into her, my girl. She was always so precious genteel.

(Mimicking her.) "Let go, Jacob! Let me be! Please to remember that I was three years with the Alvings at Rosenvold, and they were people who went to Court!" *(Laughs.)* Bless my soul, she never could forget that Captain Alving got a Court appointment while she was in service here.

Regina. Poor mother—you worried her into her grave pretty soon.

Engstrand (shrugging his shoulders). Of course, of course; I have got to take the blame for everything.

Regina (beneath her breath, as she turns away). Ugh— that leg, too!

Engstrand. What are you saying, my girl?

Regina. Pied de mouton.

Engstrand. Is that English?

Regina. Yes.

Engstrand. You have had a good education out here, and no mistake; and it may stand you in good stead now, Regina.

Regina (after a short silence). And what was it you wanted me to come to town for?

Engstrand. Need you ask why a father wants his only child? Ain't I a poor lonely widower?

Regina. Oh, don't come to me with that tale. Why do you want me to go?

Engstrand. Well, I must tell you I am thinking of taking up a new line now.

Regina (whistles). You have tried that so often—but it has always proved a fool's errand.

Engstrand. Ah, but this time you will just see, Regina! Strike me dead if——

Regina (stamping her feet). Stop swearing!

Engstrand. Sh! Sh!—you're quite right, my girl, quite right! What I wanted to say was only this, that I have put by a tidy penny out of what I have made by working at this new Orphanage up here.

Regina. Have you? All the better for you.

Engstrand. What is there for a man to spend his money on, out here in the country?

Regina. Well, what then?

Engstrand. Well, you see, I thought of putting the money into something that would pay. I thought of some kind of an eating-house for seafaring folk——

Regina. Heavens!

Engstrand. Oh, a high-class eating-house, of course,—not a pigsty for common sailors. Damn it, no; it would be a place ships' captains and first mates would come to; really good sort of people, you know.

Regina. And what should I——?

Engstrand. You would help there. But only to make a show, you know. You wouldn't find it hard work, I can promise you, my girl. You should do exactly as you liked.

Regina. Oh, yes, quite so!

Engstrand. But we must have some women in the house; that is as clear as daylight. Because in the evening we must make the place a little attractive—some singing and dancing, and that sort of thing. Remember they are sea-folk—wayfarers on the waters of life! *(Coming nearer to her.)* Now don't be a fool and stand in your own way, Regina. What good are you going to do here? Will this education, that your mistress has paid for, be of any use? You are to look after the children in the new Home, I hear. Is that the sort of work for you? Are you so frightfully anxious to go and wear out your health and strength for the sake of these dirty brats?

Regina. No, if things were to go as I want them to, then——. Well, it may happen; who knows? It may happen!

Engstrand. What may happen?

Regina. Never you mind. Is it much that you have put by, up here?

Engstrand. Taking it all round, I should say about forty or fifty pounds.

Regina. That's not so bad.

Engstrand. It's enough to make a start with, my girl.

Regina. Don't you mean to give me any of the money?

Engstrand. No, I'm hanged if I do.

Regina. Don't you mean to send me as much as a dress-length of stuff, just for once?

Engstrand. Come and live in the town with me and you shall have plenty of dresses.

Regina. Pooh!—I can get that much for myself, if I have a mind to.

Engstrand. But it's far better to have a father's guiding hand, Regina. Just now I can get a nice house in Little Harbour Street. They don't want much money down for it—and we could make it like a sort of seamen's home, don't you know.

Regina. But I have no intention of living with you! I have nothing whatever to do with you. So now, be off!

Engstrand. You wouldn't be living with me long, my girl. No such luck—not if you knew how to play your cards. Such a fine wench as you have grown this last year or two—

Regina. Well——?

Engstrand. It wouldn't be very long before some first mate came along—or perhaps a captain.

Regina. I don't mean to marry a man of that sort. Sailors have no *savoir-vivre.*

Engstrand. What haven't they got?

Regina. I know what sailors are, I tell you. They aren't the sort of people to marry.

Engstrand. Well, don't bother about marrying them. You can make it pay just as well. *(More confidentially.)* That fellow—the Englishman—the one with the yacht—he gave seventy pounds, he did; and she wasn't a bit prettier than you.

Regina (advancing towards him). Get out!

Engstrand (stepping back). Here! here!—you're not going to hit me, I suppose?

Regina. Yes! If you talk like that of mother, I will hit you. Get out, I tell you! *(Pushes him up to the garden door.)* And don't bang the doors. Young Mr. Alving——

Engstrand. Is asleep—I know. It's funny how anxious you are about young Mr. Alving. *(In a lower tone.)* Oho! is it possible that it is *he* that——?

Regina. Get out, and be quick about it! Your wits are wandering, my good man. No, don't go that way; Mr. Manders is just coming along. Be off down the kitchen stairs.

Engstrand (moving towards the right). Yes, yes—all right. But have a bit of a chat with him that's coming along. He's the chap to tell you what a child owes to its father. For I am your father, anyway, you know. I can prove it by the Register.

> [*He goes out through the farther door which RE-GINA has opened. She shuts it after him, looks hastily at herself in the mirror, fans herself with her handkerchief and sets her collar straight; then busies herself with the flowers. MANDERS enters the conservatory through the garden door. He wears an overcoat, carries an umbrella and has a small travelling-bag slung over his shoulder on a strap.*

Manders. Good morning, Miss Engstrand.

Regina (turning round with a look of pleased surprise). Oh, Mr. Manders, good morning. The boat is in, then?

Manders. Just in. *(Comes into the room.)* It is most tiresome, this rain every day.

Regina (following him in). It's a splendid rain for the farmers, Mr. Manders.

Manders. Yes, you are quite right. We town-folk think so little about that.

[Begins to take off his overcoat.

Regina. Oh, let me help you. That's it. Why, how wet it is! I will hang it up in the hall. Give me your umbrella, too; I will leave it open, so that it will dry.

[She goes out with the things by the farther door on the right. MANDERS *lays his bag and his hat down on a chair.* REGINA *re-enters.*

Manders. Ah, it's very pleasant to get indoors. Well, is everything going on well here?

Regina. Yes, thanks.

Manders. Properly busy, though, I expect, getting ready for to-morrow?

Regina. Oh, yes, there is plenty to do.

Manders. And Mrs. Alving is at home, I hope?

Regina. Yes, she is. She has just gone upstairs to take the young master his chocolate.

Manders. Tell me—I heard down at the pier that Oswald had come back.

Regina. Yes, he came the day before yesterday. We didn't expect him till to-day.

Manders. Strong and well, I hope?

Regina. Yes, thank you, well enough. But dreadfully tired after his journey. He came straight from Paris without a stop—I mean, he came all the way without breaking his journey. I fancy he is having a sleep now, so we must talk a little bit more quietly, if you don't mind.

Manders. All right, we will be very quiet.

Regina (while she moves an armchair up to the table). Please sit down, Mr. Manders, and make yourself at home. *(He sits down; she puts a foolstool under his feet.)* There! Is that comfortable?

Manders. Thank you, thank you. That is most comfortable. *(Looks at her.)* I'll tell you what, Miss Engstrand, I certainly think you have grown since I saw you last

Regina. Do you think so? Mrs. Alving says, too, that I have developed.

Manders. Developed? Well, perhaps a little—just suitably. [*A short pause.*

Regina. Shall I tell Mrs. Alving you are here?

Manders. Thanks, there is no hurry, my dear child.— Now tell me, Regina my dear, how has your father been getting on here?

Regina. Thank you, Mr. Manders, he is getting on pretty well.

Manders. He came to see me, the last time he was in town.

Regina. Did he? He is always so glad when he can have a chat with you.

Manders. And I suppose you have seen him pretty regularly every day?

Regina. I? Oh, yes, I do—whenever I have time, that is to say.

Manders. Your father has not a very strong character, Miss Engstrand. He sadly needs a guiding hand.

Regina. Yes, I can quite believe that.

Manders. He needs someone with him that he can cling to, someone whose judgment he can rely on. He acknowledged that freely himself, the last time he came up to see me.

Regina. Yes, he has said something of the same sort to me. But I don't know whether Mrs. Alving could do without me—most of all just now, when we have the new Orphanage to see about. And I should be dreadfully unwilling to leave Mrs. Alving, too; she has always been so good to me.

Manders. But a daughter's duty, my good child——. Naturally we should have to get your mistress' consent first.

Regina. Still I don't know whether it would be quite the thing, at my age, to keep house for a single man.

Manders. What!! My dear Miss Engstrand, it is your own father we are speaking of!

Regina. Yes, I dare say, but still——. Now, if it were in a good house and with a real gentleman——

Manders. But, my dear Regina——

Regina. ——one whom I could feel an affection for, and really feel in the position of a daughter to——

Manders. Come, come—my dear good child——

Regina. I should like very much to live in town. Out here it is terribly lonely; and you know yourself, Mr. Manders, what it is to be alone in the world. And, though I say it, I really am both capable and willing. Don't you know any place that would be suitable for me, Mr. Manders?

Manders. I? No, indeed I don't.

Regina. But, dear Mr. Manders—at any rate don't forget me, in case——

Manders (getting up). No, I won't forget you, Miss Engstrand.

Regina. Because, if I——

Manders. Perhaps you will be so kind as to let Mrs. Alving know I am here?

Regina. I will fetch her at once, Mr. Manders.

> [*Goes out to the left.* MANDERS *walks up and down the room once or twice, stands for a moment at the farther end of the room with his hands behind his back and looks out into the garden. Then he comes back to the table, takes up a book and looks at the title page, gives a start and looks at some of the others.*

Manders. Hm!—Really!

> [MRS. ALVING *comes in by the door on the left. She is followed by* REGINA, *who goes out again at once through the nearer door on the right.*

Mrs. Alving (holding out her hand). I am very glad to see you, Mr. Manders.

Manders. How do you do, Mrs. Alving. Here I am, as I promised.

Mrs. Alving. Always punctual!

Manders. Indeed, I was hard put to it to get away. What with vestry meetings and committees——

Mrs. Alving. It was all the kinder of you to come in such good time; we can settle our business before dinner. But where is your luggage?

Manders (quickly). My things are down at the village shop. I am going to sleep there to-night.

Mrs. Alving (repressing a smile). Can't I really persuade you to stay the night here this time?

Manders. No, no; many thanks all the same; I will put up there, as usual. It is so handy for getting on board the boat again.

Mrs. Alving. Of course you shall do as you please. But it seems to me quite another thing, now we are two old people——

Manders. Ha! ha! You will have your joke! And it's natural you should be in high spirits to-day—first of all there is the great event to-morrow, and also you have got Oswald home.

Mrs. Alving. Yes, am I not a lucky woman! It is more than two years since he was home last, and he has promised to stay the whole winter with me.

Manders. Has he, really? That is very nice and filial of him; because there must be many more attractions in his life in Rome or in Paris, I should think.

Mrs. Alving. Yes, but he has his mother here, you see. Bless the dear boy, he has got a corner in his heart for his mother still.

Manders. Oh, it would be very sad if absence and preoccupation with such a thing as Art were to dull the natural affections.

Mrs. Alving. It would, indeed. But there is no fear of that with him, I am glad to say. I am quite curious to see if you recognise him again. He will be down directly; he is just lying down for a little on the sofa upstairs. But do sit down, my dear friend.

Manders. Thank you. You are sure I am not disturbing you?

Mrs. Alving. Of course not.

> [*She sits down at the table.*

Manders. Good. Then I will show you——. *(He goes
to the chair where his bag is lying and takes a packet of
papers from it; then sits down at the opposite side of the
table and looks for a clear space to put the papers down.)*
Now first of all, here is—*(breaks off)*. Tell me, Mrs. Alving, what are these books doing here?

Mrs. Alving. These books? I am reading them.

Manders. Do you read this sort of thing?

Mrs. Alving. Certainly I do.

Manders. Do you feel any the better or the happier for
reading books of this kind?

Mrs. Alving. I think it makes me, as it were, more self-
reliant.

Manders. That is remarkable. But why?

Mrs. Alving. Well, they give me an explanation or a
confirmation of lots of different ideas that have come into
my own mind. But what surprises me, Mr. Manders, is
that, properly speaking, there is nothing at all new in these
books. There is nothing more in them than what most people think and believe. The only thing is, that most people
either take no account of it or won't admit it to themselves.

Manders. But, good heavens, do you seriously think that
most people——?

Mrs. Alving. Yes, indeed, I do.

Manders. But not here in the country at any rate? Not
here amongst people like ourselves?

Mrs. Alving. Yes, amongst people like ourselves too.

Manders. Well, really, I must say——!

Mrs. Alving. But what is the particular objection that
you have to these books?

Manders. What objection? You surely don't suppose
that I take any particular interest in such productions?

Mrs. Alving. In fact, you don't know anything about what you are denouncing?

Manders. I have read quite enough about these books to disapprove of them.

Mrs. Alving. Yes, but your own opinion——

Manders. My dear Mrs. Alving, there are many occasions in life when one has to rely on the opinion of others. That is the way in this world, and it is quite right that it should be so. What would become of society, otherwise?

Mrs. Alving. Well, you may be right.

Manders. Apart from that, naturally I don't deny that literature of this kind may have a considerable attraction. And I cannot blame you, either, for wishing to make yourself acquainted with the intellectual tendencies which I am told are at work in the wider world in which you have allowed your son to wander for so long. But——

Mrs. Alving. But——?

Manders (lowering his voice). But one doesn't talk about it, Mrs. Alving. One certainly is not called upon to account to every one for what one reads or thinks in the privacy of one's own room.

Mrs. Alving. Certainly not. I quite agree with you.

Manders. Just think of the consideration you owe to this Orphanage, which you decided to build at a time when your thoughts on such subjects were very different from what they are now—as far as I am able to judge.

Mrs. Alving. Yes, I freely admit that. But it was about the Orphanage——

Manders. It was about the Orphanage we were going to talk; quite so. Well—walk warily, dear Mrs. Alving! And now let us turn to the business in hand. *(Opens an envelope and takes out some papers.)* You see these?

Mrs. Alving. The deeds?

Manders. Yes, the whole lot—and everything in order. I can tell you it has been no easy matter to get them in time. I had positively to put pressure on the authorities; they are

almost painfully conscientious when it is a question of settling property.   But here they are at last.   *(Turns over the
papers.)*   Here is the deed of conveyance of that part of the
Rosenvold estate known as the Solvik property, together
with the buildings newly erected thereon—the school, the
masters' houses and the chapel.   And here is the legal sanc-
tion for the statutes of the institution.   Here, you see—
(reads) "Statutes for the Captain Alving Orphanage."

Mrs. Alving (after a long look at the papers).   That
seems all in order.

Manders.   I thought "Captain" was the better title to
use, rather than your husband's Court title of "Chamber-
lain."   "Captain" seems less ostentatious.

Mrs. Alving.   Yes, yes; just as you think best.

Manders.   And here is the certificate for the investment
of the capital in the bank, the interest being earmarked for
the current expenses of the Orphanage.

Mrs. Alving.   Many thanks; but I think it will be most
convenient if you will kindly take charge of them.

Manders.   With pleasure.   I think it will be best to leave
the money in the bank for the present.   The interest is not
very high, it is true; four per cent at six months' call.   Later
on, if we can find some good mortgage—of course it must be
a first mortgage and on unexceptionable security—we can
consider the matter further.

Mrs. Alving.   Yes, yes, my dear Mr. Manders, you know
best about all that.

Manders.   I will keep my eye on it, anyway.   But there
is one thing in connection with it that I have often meant to
ask you about.

Mrs. Alving.   What is that?

Manders.   Shall we insure the buildings, or not?

Mrs. Alving.   Of course we must insure them.

Manders.   Ah, but wait a moment, dear lady.   Let us
look into the matter a little more closely.

Mrs. Alving. Everything of mine is insured—the house and its contents, my livestock—everything.

Manders. Naturally. They are your own property. I do exactly the same, of course. But this, you see, is quite a different case. The Orphanage is, so to speak, dedicated to higher uses.

Mrs. Alving. Certainly, but——

Manders. As far as I am personally concerned, I can conscientiously say that I don't see the smallest objection to our insuring ourselves against all risks.

Mrs. Alving. That is exactly what I think.

Manders. But what about the opinion of the people hereabouts?

Mrs. Alving. Their opinion——?

Manders. Is there any considerable body of opinion here —opinion of some account, I mean—that might take exception to it?

Mrs. Alving. What, exactly, do you mean by opinion of some account?

Manders. Well, I was thinking particularly of persons of such independent and influential position that one could hardly refuse to attach weight to their opinion.

Mrs. Alving. There are a certain number of such people here, who might perhaps take exception to it if we——

Manders. That's just it, you see. In town there are lots of them. All my fellow-clergymen's congregations, for instance! It would be so extremely easy for them to interpret it as meaning that neither you nor I had a proper reliance on Divine protection.

Mrs. Alving. But as far as you are concerned, my dear friend, you have at all events the consciousness that——

Manders. Yes, I know, I know; my own mind is quite easy about it, it is true. But we should not be able to prevent a wrong and injurious interpretation of our action. And that sort of thing, moreover, might very easily end in exercising a hampering influence on the work of the Orphanage.

Mrs. Alving. Oh, well, if that is likely to be the effect of it——

Manders. Nor can I entirely overlook the difficult—indeed, I may say, painful—position I might possibly be placed in. In the best circles in town the matter of this Orphanage is attracting a great deal of attention. Indeed the Orphanage is to some extent built for the benefit of the town too, and it is to be hoped that it may result in the lowering of our poor-rate by a considerable amount. But as I have been your adviser in the matter and have taken charge of the business side of it, I should be afraid that it would be I that spiteful persons would attack first of all——

Mrs. Alving. Yes, you ought not to expose yourself to that.

Manders. Not to mention the attacks that would undoubtedly be made upon me in certain newspapers and reviews——

Mrs. Alving. Say no more about it, dear Mr. Manders; that quite decides it.

Manders. Then you don't wish it to be insured?

Mrs. Alving. No, we will give up the idea.

Manders (leaning back in his chair). But suppose, now, that some acident happened?—one can never tell—would you be prepared to make good the damage?

Mrs. Alving. No; I tell you quite plainly I would not do so under any circumstances.

Manders. Still, you know, Mrs. Alving—after all, it is a serious responsibility that we are taking upon ourselves.

Mrs. Alving. But do you think we can do otherwise?

Manders. No, that's just it. We really can't do otherwise. We ought not to expose ourselves to a mistaken judgment; and we have no right to do anything that will scandalise the community.

Mrs. Alving. You ought not to, as a clergyman, at any rate.

Manders. And, what is more, I certainly think that we may count upon our enterprise being attended by good fortune—indeed, that it will be under a special protection.

Mrs. Alving. Let us hope so, Mr. Manders.

Manders. Then we will leave it alone?

Mrs. Alving. Certainly.

Manders. Very good. As you wish. *(Makes a note.)* No insurance, then.

Mrs. Alving. It's a funny thing that you should just have happened to speak about that to-day——

Manders. I have often meant to ask you about it——

Mrs. Alving. ——because yesterday we very nearly had a fire up there.

Manders. Do you mean it!

Mrs. Alving. Oh, as a matter of fact it was nothing of any consequence. Some shavings in the carpenter's shop caught fire.

Manders. Where Engstrand works?

Mrs. Alving. Yes. They say he is often so careless with matches.

Manders. He has so many things on his mind, poor fellow—so many anxieties. Heaven be thanked, I am told he is really making an effort to live a blameless life.

Mrs. Alving. Really? Who told you so?

Manders. He assured me himself that it is so. He's a good workman, too.

Mrs. Alving. Oh, yes, when he is sober.

Manders. Ah, that sad weakness of his! But the pain in his poor leg often drives him to it, he tells me. The last time he was in town, I was really quite touched by him. He came to my house and thanked me so gratefully for getting him work here, where he could have the chance of being with Regina.

Mrs. Alving. He doesn't see very much of her.

Manders. But he assured me that he saw her every **day.**

Mrs. Alving. Oh well, perhaps he does.

Manders. He feels so strongly that he needs some **one** who can keep a hold on him when temptations assail him. That is the most winning thing about Jacob Engstrand; he comes to one like a helpless child and accuses himself and confesses his frailty. The last time he came and had a talk with me——. Suppose now, Mrs. Alving, that it were really a necessity of his existence to have Regina at home with him again——

Mrs. Alving (standing up suddenly). Regina!

Manders. ——you ought not to set yourself against him.

Mrs. Alving. Indeed, I set myself very definitely against that. And, besides, you know Regina is to have a post in the Orphanage.

Manders. But consider, after all he is her father——

Mrs. Alving. I know best what sort of a father he has been to her. No, she shall never go to him with my consent.

Manders (getting up). My dear lady, don't judge so hastily. It is very sad how you misjudge poor Engstrand. One would really think you were afraid——

Mrs. Alving (more calmly). That is not the question. I have taken Regina into my charge, and in my charge she remains. *(Listens.)* Hush, dear Mr. Manders, don't say any more about it. *(Her face brightens with pleasure.)* Listen! Oswald is coming downstairs. We will only think about him now.

> [Oswald Alving, *in a light overcoat, hat in hand and smoking a big meerschaum pipe, comes in by the door on the left.*

Oswald (standing in the doorway). Oh, I beg your pardon, I thought you were in the office. *(Comes in.)* Good morning, Mr. Manders.

Manders (staring at him). Well! It's most extraordinary——

Mrs. Alving. Yes, what do you think of him, Mr. Manders?

Manders. I—I—no, can it possibly be——?

Oswald. Yes, it really is the prodigal son, Mr. Manders.

Manders. Oh, my dear young friend——

Oswald. Well, the son come home, then.

Mrs. Alving. Oswald is thinking of the time when you were so opposed to the idea of his being a painter.

Manders. We are only fallible, and many steps seem to us hazardous at first, that afterwards—*(grasps his hand).* Welcome, welcome! Really, my dear Oswald—may I still call you Oswald?

Oswald. What else would you think of calling me?

Manders. Thank you. What I mean, my dear Oswald, is that you must not imagine that I have any unqualified disapproval of the artist's life. I admit that there are many who, even in that career, can keep the inner man free from harm.

Oswald. Let us hope so.

Mrs. Alving (beaming with pleasure). I know one who has kept both the inner and the outer man free from harm. Just take a look at him, Mr. Manders.

Oswald (walks across the room). Yes, yes, mother dear, of course.

Manders. Undoubtedly—no one can deny it. And I hear you have begun to make a name for yourself. I have often seen mention of you in the papers—and extremely favourable mention, too. Although, I must admit, latterly I have not seen your name so often.

Oswald (going towards the conservatory). I haven't done so much painting just lately.

Mrs. Alving. An artist must take a rest sometimes, like other people.

Manders. Of course, of course. At those times the artist is preparing and strengthening himself for a greater effort.

Oswald. Yes. Mother, will dinner soon be ready?

Mrs. Alving. In half an hour. He has a fine appetite, thank goodness.

Manders. And a liking for tobacco too.

Oswald. I found father's pipe in the room upstairs, and ——

Manders. Ah, that is what it was!

Mrs. Alving. What?

Manders. When Oswald came in at that door with the pipe in his mouth, I thought for the moment it was his father in the flesh.

Oswald. Really?

Mrs. Alving. How can you say so! Oswald takes after me.

Manders. Yes, but there is an expression about the corners of his mouth—something about the lips—that reminds me so exactly of Mr. Alving—especially when he smokes.

Mrs. Alving. I don't think so at all. To my mind, Oswald has much more of a clergyman's mouth.

Manders. Well, yes—a good many of my colleagues in the church have a similar expression.

Mrs. Alving. But put your pipe down, my dear boy. I don't allow any smoking in here.

Oswald (puts down his pipe). All right, I only wanted to try it, because I smoked it once when I was a child.

Mrs. Alving. You?

Oswald. Yes; it was when I was quite a little chap. And I can remember going upstairs to father's room one evening when he was in very good spirits.

Mrs. Alving. Oh, you can't remember anything about those days.

Oswald. Yes, I remember plainly that he took me on his knee and let me smoke his pipe. "Smoke, my boy," he said, "have a good smoke, boy!" And I smoked as hard as I could, until I felt I was turning quite pale and the perspiration was standing in great drops on my forehead. Then he laughed—such a hearty laugh——

Manders. It was an extremely odd thing to do.

Mrs. Alving. Dear Mr. Manders, Oswald only dreamt it.

Oswald. No indeed, mother, it was no dream. Because —don't you remember—you came into the room and carried me off to the nursery, where I was sick, and I saw that you were crying. Did father often play such tricks?

Manders. In his young days he was full of fun——

Oswald. And, for all that, he did so much with his life— so much that was good and useful, I mean—short as his life was.

Manders. Yes, my dear Oswald Alving, you have inherited the name of a man who undoubtedly was both energetic and worthy. Let us hope it will be a spur to your energies——

Oswald. It ought to be, certainly.

Manders. In any case it was nice of you to come home for the day that is to honour his memory.

Oswald. I could do no less for my father.

Mrs. Alving. And to let me keep him so long here— that's the nicest part of what he has done.

Manders. Yes, I hear you are going to spend the winter at home.

Oswald. I am here for an indefinite time, Mr. Manders. —Oh, it's good to be at home again!

Mrs. Alving (beaming). Yes, isn't it?

Manders (looking sympathetically at him). You went out into the world very young, my dear Oswald.

Oswald. I did. Sometimes I wonder if I wasn't too young.

Mrs. Alving. Not a bit of it. It is the best thing for an active boy, and especially for an only child. It's a pity when they are kept at home with their parents and get spoilt.

Manders. That is a very debatable question, Mrs. Alving. A child's own home is, and always must be, his proper place.

Oswald. There I agree entirely with Mr. Manders.

Manders. Take the case of your own son. Oh yes, we can talk about it before him. What has the result been in his case? He is six or seven and twenty, and has never yet had the opportunity of learning what a well-regulated home means.

Oswald. Excuse me, Mr. Manders, you are quite wrong there.

Manders. Indeed? I imagined that your life abroad had practically been spent entirely in artistic circles.

Oswald. So it has.

Manders. And chiefly amongst the younger artists.

Oswald. Certainly.

Manders. But I imagined that those gentry, as a rule, had not the means necessary for family life and the support of a home.

Oswald. There are a considerable number of them who have not the means to marry, Mr. Manders.

Manders. That is exactly my point.

Oswald. But they can have a home of their own, all the same; a good many of them have. And they are very well-regulated and very comfortable homes, too.

[Mrs. ALVING, *who has listened to him atten-tively, nods assent, but says nothing.*

Manders. Oh, but I am not talking of bachelor estab-lishments. By a home I mean family life—the life a man lives with his wife and children.

Oswald. Exactly, or with his children and his children's mother.

Manders (starts and clasps his hands). Good heavens!

Oswald. What is the matter?

Manders. Lives with—with—his children's mother!

Oswald. Well, would you rather he should repudiate his children's mother?

Manders. Then what you are speaking of are those un-principled conditions known as irregular unions!

Oswald. I have never noticed anything particularly un-principled about these people's lives.

Manders. But do you mean to say that it is possible for a man of any sort of bringing up, and a young woman, to reconcile themselves to such a way of living—and to make no secret of it, either?

Oswald. What else are they to do? A poor artist, and a poor girl—it costs a good deal to get married. What else are they to do?

Manders. What are they to do? Well, Mr. Alving, I will tell you what they ought to do. They ought to keep away from each other from the very beginning—that is what they ought to do!

Oswald. That advice wouldn't have much effect upon hot-blooded young folk who are in love.

Mrs. Alving. No, indeed it wouldn't.

Manders (persistently). And to think that the authorities tolerate such things! That they are allowed to go on, openly! *(Turns to* Mrs. Alving.*)* Had I so little reason, then, to be sadly concerned about your son? In circles where open immorality is rampant—where, one may say, it is honoured——

Oswald. Let me tell you this, Mr. Manders. I have been a constant Sunday guest at one or two of these "irregular" households——

Manders. On Sunday, too!

Oswald. Yes, that is the day of leisure. But never have I heard one objectionable word there, still less have I ever seen anything that could be called immoral. No; but do you know when and where I *have* met with immorality in artists' circles?

Manders. No, thank heaven, I don't!

Oswald. Well, then, I shall have the pleasure of telling you. I have met with it when some one or other of your model husbands and fathers have come out there to have a bit of a look round on their own account, and have done the artists the honour of looking them up in their humble quarters. Then we had a chance of learning something, I can tell you. These gentlemen were able to instruct us about places and things that we had never so much as dreamt of.

Manders. What? Do you want me to believe that honourable men when they get away from home will——

Oswald. Have you never, when these same honourable men come home again, heard them deliver themselves on the subject of the prevalence of immorality abroad?

Manders. Yes, of course, but——

Mrs. Alving. I have heard them, too.

Oswald. Well, you can take their word for it, unhesitatingly. Some of them are experts in the matter. *(Putting his hands to his head.)* To think that the glorious freedom of the beautiful life over there should be so besmirched!

Mrs. Alving. You mustn't get too heated, Oswald; you gain nothing by that.

Oswald. No, you are quite right, mother. Besides, it isn't good for me. It's because I am so infernally tired, you know. I will go out and take a turn before dinner. I beg your pardon, Mr. Manders. It is impossible for you to realise the feeling; but it takes me that way.

[*Goes out by the farther door on the right.*

Mrs. Alving. My poor boy!

Manders. You may well say so. This is what it has brought him to! *(*Mrs. Alving *looks at him, but does not speak.)* He called himself the prodigal son. It's only too true, alas—only too true! *(*Mrs. Alving *looks steadily at him.)* And what do you say to all this?

Mrs. Alving. I say that Oswald was right in every single word he said.

Manders. Right? Right? To hold such principles as that?

Mrs. Alving. In my loneliness here I have come to just

the same opinions as he, Mr. Manders. But I have never presumed to venture upon such topics in conversation. Now there is no need; my boy shall speak for me.

Manders. You deserve the deepest pity, Mrs. Alving. It is my duty to say an earnest word to you. It is no longer your business man and adviser, no longer your old friend and your dead husband's old friend, that stands before you now. It is your priest that stands before you, just as he did once at the most critical moment of your life.

Mrs. Alving. And what is it that my priest has to say to me?

Manders. First of all I must stir your memory. The moment is well chosen. To-morrow is the tenth anniversary of your husband's death; to-morrow the memorial to the departed will be unveiled; to-morrow I shall speak to the whole assembly that will be met together. But to-day I want to speak to you alone.

Mrs. Alving. Very well, Mr. Manders, speak!

Manders. Have you forgotten that after barely a year of married life you were standing at the very edge of a precipice?—that you forsook your house and home?—that you ran away from your husband—yes, Mrs. Alving, ran away, ran away—and refused to return to him in spite of his requests and entreaties?

Mrs. Alving. Have you forgotten how unspeakably unhappy I was during that first year?

Manders. To crave for happiness in this world is simply to be possessed by a spirit of revolt. What right have we to happiness? No! we must do our duty, Mrs. Alving. And your duty was to cleave to the man you had chosen and to whom you were bound by a sacred bond.

Mrs. Alving. You know quite well what sort of a life my husband was living at that time—what excesses he was guilty of.

Manders. I know only too well what rumour used to say of him; and I should be the last person to approve of his conduct as a young man, supposing that rumour spoke the truth. But it is not a wife's part to be her husband's judge. You should have considered it your bounden duty humbly to have borne the cross that a higher will had laid upon you. But, instead of that, you rebelliously cast off your cross, you deserted the man whose stumbling footsteps you should have supported, you did what was bound to imperil your good name and reputation, and came very near to imperilling the reputation of others into the bargain.

Mrs. Alving. Of others? Of one other, you mean.

Manders. It was the height of imprudence, your seeking refuge with me.

Mrs. Alving. With our priest? With our intimate friend?

Manders. All the more on that acount. You should thank God that I possessed the necessary strength of mind —that I was able to turn you from your outrageous intention, and that it was vouchsafed to me to succeed in leading you back into the path of duty and back to your lawful husband.

Mrs. Alving. Yes, Mr. Manders, that certainly was your doing.

Manders. I was but the humble instrument of a higher power. And is it not true that my having been able to bring you again under the yoke of duty and obedience sowed the seeds of a rich blessing on all the rest of your life? Did things not turn out as I foretold to you? Did not your husband turn from straying in the wrong path as a man should? Did he not, after all, live a life of love and good report with you all his days? Did he not become a benefactor to the neighbourhood? Did he not so raise you up to his level, so that by degrees you became his fellow-worker in all his undertakings—and a noble fellow-worker, too, I know, Mrs. Alving; that praise I will give you.—But now I come to the second serious false step in your life.

Mrs. Alving. What do you mean?

Manders. Just as once you forsook your duty as a wife, so, since then, you have forsaken your duty as a mother.

Mrs. Alving. Oh——!

Manders. You have been overmastered all your life by a disastrous spirit of wilfulness. All your impulses have led you towards what is undisciplined and lawless. You have never been willing to submit to any restraint. Anything in life that has seemed irksome to you, you have thrown aside recklessly and unscrupulously, as if it were a burden that you were free to rid yourself of if you would. It did not please you to be a wife any longer, and so you left your husband. Your duties as a mother were irksome to you, so you sent your child away among strangers.

Mrs. Alving. Yes, that is true; I did that.

Manders. And that is why you have become a stranger to him.

Mrs. Alving. No, no, I am not that!

Manders. You are; you must be. And what sort of a son is it that you have got back? Think over it seriously, Mrs. Alving. You erred grievously in your husband's case —you acknowledge as much, by erecting this memorial to him. Now you are bound to acknowledge how much you have erred in your son's case; possibly there may still be time to reclaim him from the paths of wickedness. Turn over a new leaf, and set yourself to reform what there may still be that is capable of reformation in him. Because *(with uplifted forefinger)* in very truth, Mrs. Alving, you are a guilty mother!—That is what I have thought it my duty to say to you.

[*A short silence.*

Mrs. Alving (speaking slowly and with self-control). You have had your say, Mr. Manders, and to-morrow you will be making a public speech in memory of my husband. I shall not speak to-morrow. But now I wish to speak to you for a little, just as you have been speaking to me.

Manders. By all means; no doubt you wish to bring forward some excuses for your behaviour——

Mrs. Alving. No. I only want to tell you something.

Manders. Well?

Mrs. Alving. In all that you said just now about me and
my husband, and about our life together after you had, as
you put it, led me back into the path of duty—there was
nothing that you knew at first hand. From that moment
you never again set foot in our house—you, who had been
our daily companion before that.

Manders. Remember that you and your husband moved
out of town immediately afterwards.

Mrs. Alving. Yes, and you never once came out here to
see us in my husband's lifetime. It was only the business
in connection with the Orphanage that obliged you to come
and see me.

Manders (in a low and uncertain voice). Helen—if that
is a reproach, I can only beg you to consider——

Mrs. Alving. ——the respect you owed to your calling?
—yes. All the more as I was a wife who had tried to run
away from her husband. One can never be too careful to
have nothing to do with such reckless women.

Manders. My dear—Mrs. Alving, you are exaggerating
dreadfully——

Mrs. Alving. Yes, yes,—very well. What I mean is
this, that when you condemn my conduct as a wife you have
nothing more to go upon than ordinary public opinion.

Manders. I admit it. What then?

Mrs. Alving. Well—now, Mr. Manders, now I am going
to tell you the truth. I had sworn to myself that you should
know it one day—you, and you only!

Manders. And what may the truth be?

Mrs. Alving. The truth is this, that my husband died
just as great a profligate as he had been all his life.

Manders (feeling for a chair). What are you saying?

Mrs. Alving. After nineteen years of married life, just

as profligate—in his desires at all events—as he was before you married us.

Manders. And can you talk of his youthful indiscretions —his irregularities—his excesses, if you like—as a profligate life!

Mrs. Alving. That was what the doctor who attended him called it.

Manders. I don't understand what you mean.

Mrs. Alving. It is not necessary you should.

Manders. It makes my brain reel. To think that your marriage—all the years of wedded life you spent with your husband—were nothing but a hidden abyss of misery.

Mrs. Alving. That and nothing else. Now you know.

Manders. This—this bewilders me. I can't understand it! I can't grasp it! How in the world was it possible ——? How could such a state of things remain concealed?

Mrs. Alving. That was just what I had to fight for incessantly, day after day. When Oswald was born, I thought I saw a slight improvement. But it didn't last long. And after that I had to fight doubly hard—fight a desperate fight so that no one should know what sort of a man my child's father was. You know quite well what an attractive manner he had; it seemed as if people could believe nothing but good of him. He was one of those men whose mode of life seems to have no effect upon their reputations. But at last, Mr. Manders—you must hear this too—at last something happened more abominable than everything else.

Manders. More abominable than what you have told me!

Mrs. Alving. I had borne with it all, though I knew only too well what he indulged in in secret, when he was out of the house. But when it came to the point of the scandal coming within our four walls——

Manders. Can you mean it! Here?

Mrs. Alving. Yes, here, in our own home. It was in there *(pointing to the nearer door on the right)* in the din-

ing-room that I got the first hint of it. I had something to
do in there and the door was standing ajar. I heard our
maid come up from the garden with water for the flowers in
the conservatory.

Manders. Well——?

Mrs. Alving. Shortly afterwards I heard my husband
come in too. I heard him say something to her in a low
voice. And then I heard—*(with a short laugh)*—oh, it
rings in my ears still, with its mixture of what was heartbreaking and what was so ridiculous—I heard my own servant whisper: "Let me go, Mr. Alving! Let me be!"

Manders. What unseemly levity on his part! But
surely nothing more than levity, Mrs. Alving, believe me.

Mrs. Alving. I soon knew what to believe. My husband
had his will of the girl—and that intimacy had consequences,
Mr. Manders.

Manders (as if turned to stone). And all that in this
house! In this house!

Mrs. Alving. I have suffered a good deal in this house.
To keep him at home in the evening—and at night—I have
had to play the part of boon companion in his secret drink-
ing-bouts in his room up there. I have had to sit there alone
with him, have had to hobnob and drink with him, have had
to listen to his ribald senseless talk, have had to fight with
brute force to get him to bed——

Manders (trembling). And you were able to endure all
this!

Mrs. Alving. I had my little boy, and endured it for his
sake. But when the crowning insult came—when my own
servant—then I made up my mind that there should be an
end of it. I took the upper hand in the house, absolutely—
both with him and all the others. I had a weapon to use
against him, you see; he didn't dare to speak. It was then
that Oswald was sent away. He was about seven then, and
was beginning to notice things and ask questions as children
will. I could endure all that, my friend. It seemed to me

that the child would be poisoned if he breathed the air of this polluted house. That was why I sent him away. And now you understand, too, why he never set foot here as long as his father was alive. No one knows what it meant to me.

Manders. You have indeed had a pitiable experience.

Mrs. Alving. I could never have gone through with it, if I had not had my work. Indeed, I can boast that I have worked. All the increase in the value of the property, all the improvements, all the useful arrangements that my husband got the honour and glory of—do you suppose that he troubled himself about any of them? He, who used to lie the whole day on the sofa reading old Official Lists! No, you may as well know that too. It was I that kept him up to the mark when he had his lucid intervals; it was I that had to bear the whole burden of it when he began his excesses again or took to whining about his miserable condition.

Manders. And this is the man you are building a memorial to!

Mrs. Alving. There you see the power of an uneasy conscience.

Manders. An uneasy conscience? What do you mean?

Mrs. Alving. I had always before me the fear that it was impossible that the truth should not come out and be believed. That is why the Orphanage is to exist, to silence all rumours and clear away all doubt.

Manders. You certainly have not fallen short of the mark in that, Mrs. Alving.

Mrs. Alving. I had another very good reason. I did not wish Oswald, my own son, to inherit a penny that belonged to his father.

Manders. Then it is with Mr. Alving's property——

Mrs. Alving. Yes. The sums of money that, year after year, I have given towards this Orphanage, make up the amount of property—I have reckoned it carefully—which in the old days made Lieutenant Alving a catch.

Manders. I understand.

Mrs. Alving. That was my purchase money. I don't wish it to pass into Oswald's hands. My son shall have everything from me, I am determined.

[OSWALD *comes in by the farther door on the right. He has left his hat and coat outside.*

Mrs. Alving. Back again, my own dear boy?

Oswald. Yes, what can one do outside in this everlasting rain? I hear dinner is nearly ready. That's good!

[REGINA *comes in from the dining-room, carrying a parcel.*

Regina. This parcel has come for you, ma'am.

[*Gives it to her.*

Mrs. Alving (glancing at MANDERS*).* The ode to be sung to-morrow, I expect.

Manders. Hm——!

Regina. And dinner is ready.

Mrs. Alving. Good. We will come in a moment. I will just—(*begins to open the parcel*).

Regina (to OSWALD*).* Will you drink white or red wine, sir?

Oswald. Both, Miss Engstrand.

Regina. *Bien*—very good, Mr. Alving.

[*Goes into the dining-room.*

Oswald. I may as well help you to uncork it——.

[*Follows her into the dining-room, leaving the door ajar after him.*

Mrs. Alving. Yes, I thought so. Here is the ode, Mr. Manders.

Manders (clasping his hands). How shall I ever have the courage to-morrow to speak the address that——

Mrs. Alving. Oh, you will get through it.

Manders (in a low voice, fearing to be heard in the dining-room). Yes, we must raise no suspicions.

Mrs. Alving (quietly but firmly). No; and then this long dreadful comedy will be at an end. After to-morrow.

I shall feel as if my dead husband had never lived in this house.   There will be no one else here then but my boy and his mother.

> [*From the dining-room is heard the noise of a chair falling; then* REGINA'S *voice is heard in a loud whisper:* Oswald!   Are you mad?   Let me go!

Mrs. Alving (starting in horror).   Oh——!

> [*She stares wildly at the half-open door.* OSWALD *is heard coughing and humming, then the sound of a bottle being uncorked.*

Manders (in an agitated manner).   What's the matter? What is it, Mrs. Alving?

Mrs. Alving (hoarsely).   Ghosts.   The couple in the conservatory—over again.

Manders.   What are you saying!   Regina——?   Is she ——?

Mrs. Alving.   Yes.   Come.   Not a word——!

> [*Grips* MANDERS *by the arm and walks unsteadily with him into the dining-room.*

ACT II

The same scene.   The landscape is still obscured by mist.
    MANDERS *and* MRS. ALVING *come in from the dining-*
    room.

Mrs. Alving (calls into the dining-room from the door-
way).   Aren't you coming in here, Oswald?

Oswald.   No, thanks; I think I will go out for a bit.

Mrs. Alving.   Yes, do; the weather is clearing a little.
(She shuts the dining-room door, then goes to the hall door
and calls.)   Regina!

Regina (from without).   Yes, ma'am?

Mrs. Alving.   Go down into the laundry and help with
the garlands.

Regina.   Yes, ma'am.

        [MRS. ALVING *satisfies herself that she has gone,*
            then shuts the door.

Manders.   I suppose he can't hear us?

Mrs. Alving.   Not when the door is shut.   Besides, he
is going out.

Manders.   I am still quite bewildered.   I don't know
how I managed to swallow a mouthful of your excellent dinner.

Mrs. Alving (walking up and down, and trying to control
her agitation).   Nor I.   But what are we to do?

Manders.   Yes, what are we to do?   Upon my word I
don't know; I am so completely unaccustomed to things of
this kind.

Mrs. Alving.   I am convinced that nothing serious has
happened yet.

Manders. Heaven forbid! But it is most unseemly behaviour, for all that.

Mrs. Alving. It is nothing more than a foolish jest of Oswald's, you may be sure.

Manders. Well, of course, as I said, I am quite inexperienced in such matters; but it certainly seems to me——

Mrs. Alving. Out of the house she shall go—and at once. That part of it is as clear as daylight——

Manders. Yes, that is quite clear.

Mrs. Alving. But where is she to go? We should not be justified in——

Manders. Where to? Home to her father, of course.

Mrs. Alving. To whom, did you say?

Manders. To her——. No, of course Engstrand isn't ——. But, great heavens, Mrs. Alving, how is such a thing possible? You surely may have been mistaken, in spite of everything.

Mrs. Alving. There was no chance of mistake, more's the pity. Joanna was obliged to confess it to me—and my husband couldn't deny it. So there was nothing else to do but to hush it up.

Manders. No, that was the only thing to do.

Mrs. Alving. The girl was sent away at once, and was given a tolerably liberal sum to hold her tongue. She looked after the rest herself when she got to town. She renewed an old acquaintance with the carpenter Engstrand; gave him a hint, I suppose, of how much money she had got, and told him some fairy tale about a foreigner who had been here in his yacht in the summer. So she and Engstrand were married in a great hurry. Why, you married them yourself!

Manders. I can't understand it——. I remember clearly Engstrand's coming to arrange about the marriage. He was full of contrition, and accused himself bitterly for the light conduct he and his fiancée had been guilty of.

Mrs. Alving. Of course he had to take the blame on himself.

Manders. But the deceitfulness of it! And with me, too! I positively would not have believed it of Jacob Engstrand. I shall most certainly give him a serious talking to.—And the immorality of such a marriage! Simply for the sake of the money——! What sum was it that the girl had?

Mrs. Alving. It was seventy pounds.

Manders. Just think of it—for a paltry seventy pounds to let yourself be bound in marriage to a fallen woman!

Mrs. Alving. What about myself, then?—I let myself be bound in marriage to a fallen man.

Manders. Heaven forgive you! what are you saying? A fallen man?

Mrs. Alving. Do you suppose my husband was any purer, when I went with him to the altar, than Joanna was when Engstrand agreed to marry her?

Manders. The two cases are as different as day from night——

Mrs. Alving. Not so very different, after all. It is true there was a great difference in the price paid, between a paltry seventy pounds and a whole fortune.

Manders. How can you compare such totally different things! I presume you consulted your own heart—and your relations.

Mrs. Alving (looking away from him). I thought you understood where what you call my heart had strayed to at that time.

Manders (in a constrained voice). If I had understood anything of the kind, I would not have been a daily guest in your husband's house.

Mrs. Alving. Well, at any rate this much is certain, that I didn't consult myself in the matter at all.

Manders. Still you consulted those nearest to you, as was only right—your mother, your two aunts.

Mrs. Alving. Yes, that is true. The three of them set·

tled the whole matter for me. It seems incredible to me now, how clearly they made out that it would be sheer folly to reject such an offer. If my mother could only see what all that fine prospect has led to!

Manders. No one can be responsible for the result of it. Anyway, there is this to be said, that the match was made in complete conformity with law and order.

Mrs. Alving (going to the window). Oh, law and order! I often think it is that that is at the bottom of all the misery in the world.

Manders. Mrs. Alving, it is very wicked of you to say that.

Mrs. Alving. That may be so; but I don't attach importance to those obligations and considerations any longer. I cannot! I must struggle for my freedom.

Manders. What do you mean?

Mrs. Alving (tapping on the window panes). I ought never to have concealed what sort of a life my husband led. But I had not the courage to do otherwise then—for my own sake, either. I was too much of a coward.

Manders. A coward?

Mrs. Alving. If others had known anything of what happened, they would have said: "Poor man, it is natural enough that he should go astray, when he has a wife that has run away from him."

Manders. They would have had a certain amount of justification for saying so.

Mrs. Alving (looking fixedly at him). If I had been the woman I ought, I would have taken Oswald into my confidence and said to him· "Listen, my son, your father was a dissolute man"——

Manders. Miserable woman——

Mrs. Alving. ——and I would have told him all I have told you, from beginning to end.

Manders. I am almost shocked at you, Mrs. Alving.

Mrs. Alving. I know. I know quite well! I am shocked at myself when I think of it. *(Comes away from the window.)* I am coward enough for that.

Manders. Can you call it cowardice that you simply did your duty! Have you forgotten that a child should love and honour his father and mother?

Mrs. Alving. Don't let us talk in such general terms. Suppose we say: "Ought Oswald to love and honour Mr. Alving?"

Manders. You are a mother—isn't there a voice in your heart that forbids you to shatter your son's ideals?

Mrs. Alving. And what about the truth?

Manders. What about his ideals?

Mrs. Alving. Oh—ideals, ideals! If only I were not such a coward as I am!

Manders. Do not spurn ideals, Mrs. Alving—they have a way of avenging themselves cruelly. Take Oswald's own case, now. He hasn't many ideals, more's the pity. But this much I have seen, that his father is something of an ideal to him.

Mrs. Alving. You are right there.

Manders. And his conception of his father is what you inspired and encouraged by your letters.

Mrs. Alving. Yes, I was swayed by duty and consideration for others; that was why I lied to my son, year in and year out. Oh, what a coward—what a coward I have been!

Manders. You have built up a happy illusion in your son's mind, Mrs. Alving—and that is a thing you certainly ought not to undervalue.

Mrs. Alving. Ah, who knows if that is such a desirable thing after all!—But anyway I don't intend to put up with any goings on with Regina. I am not going to let him get the poor girl into trouble.

Manders. Good heavens, no—that would be a frightful thing!

Mrs. Alving. If only I knew whether he meant it seriously, and whether it would mean happiness for him——

Manders. In what way? I don't understand.

Mrs. Alving. But that is impossible; Regina is not equal to it, unfortunately.

Manders. I don't understand. What do you mean?

Mrs. Alving. If I were not such a miserable coward, I would say to him: "Marry her, or make any arrangement you like with her—only let there be no deceit in the matter."

Manders. Heaven forgive you! Are you actually suggesting anything so abominable, so unheard of, as a marriage between them!

Mrs. Alving. Unheard of, do you call it? Tell me honestly, Mr. Manders, don't you suppose there are plenty of married couples out here in the country that are just as nearly related as they are?

Manders. I am sure I don't understand you.

Mrs. Alving. Indeed you do.

Manders. I suppose you are thinking of cases where possibly——. It is only too true, unfortunately, that family life is not always as stainless as it should be. But as for the sort of thing you hint at—well, it's impossible to tell, at all events with any certainty. Here, on the other hand—for you, a mother, to be willing to allow your——

Mrs. Alving. But I am not willing to allow it. I would not allow it for anything in the world; that is just what I was saying.

Manders. No, because you are a coward, as you put it. But, supposing you were not a coward——! Great heavens —such a revolting union!

Mrs. Alving. Well, for the matter of that, we are all descended from a union of that description, so we are told. And who was it that was responsible for this state of things, Mr. Manders?

Manders. I can't discuss such questions with you, Mrs. Alving; you are by no means in the right frame of mind for that. But for you to dare to say that it is cowardly of you——!

Mrs. Alving. I will tell you what I mean by that. I am frightened and timid, because I am obsessed by the presence of ghosts that I never can get rid of.

Manders. The presence of what?

Mrs. Alving. Ghosts. When I heard Regina and Oswald in there, it was just like seeing ghosts before my eyes. I am half inclined to think we are all ghosts, Mr. Manders. It is not only what we have inherited from our fathers and mothers that exists again in us, but all sorts of old dead ideas and all kinds of old dead beliefs and things of that kind. They are not actually alive in us; but there they are dormant, all the same, and we can never be rid of them. Whenever I take up a newspaper and read it, I fancy I see ghosts creeping between the lines. There must be ghosts all over the world. They must be as countless as the grains of the sands, it seems to me. And we are so miserably afraid of the light, all of us.

Manders. Ah!—there we have the outcome of your reading. Fine fruit it has borne—this abominable, subversive, free-thinking literature!

Mrs. Alving. You are wrong there, my friend. You are the one who made me begin to think; and I owe you my best thanks for it.

Manders. I!

Mrs. Alving. Yes, by forcing me to submit to what you called my duty and my obligations; by praising as right and just what my whole soul revolted against, as it would against something abominable. That was what led me to examine your teachings critically. I only wanted to unravel one point in them; but as soon as I had got that unravelled, the whole fabric came to pieces. And then I realised that it was only machine-made.

Manders (softly, and with emotion). Is that all I accomplished by the hardest struggle of my life?

Mrs. Alving. Call it rather the most ignominious defeat of your life.

Manders. It was the greatest victory of my life, Helen; victory over myself.

Mrs. Alving. It was a wrong done to both of us.

Manders. A wrong?—wrong for me to entreat you as a wife to go back to your lawful husband, when you came to me half distracted and crying: "Here I am, take me!" Was that a wrong?

Mrs. Alving. I think it was.

Manders. We two do not understand one another.

Mrs. Alving. Not now, at all events.

Manders. Never—even in my most secret thoughts—have I for a moment regarded you as anything but the wife of another.

Mrs. Alving. Do you believe what you say?

Manders. Helen——!

Mrs. Alving. One so easily forgets one's own feelings.

Manders. Not I. I am the same as I always was.

Mrs. Alving. Yes, yes—don't let us talk any more about the old days. You are buried up to your eyes now in committees and all sorts of business; and I am here, fighting with ghosts both without and within me.

Manders. I can at all events help you to get the better of those without you. After all that I have been horrified to hear from you to-day, I cannot conscientiously allow a young defenceless girl to remain in your house.

Mrs. Alving. Don't you think it would be best if we could get her settled?—by some suitable marriage, I mean.

Manders. Undoubtedly. I think, in any case, it would have been desirable for her. Regina is at an age now that—well, I don't know much about these things, but——

Mrs. Alving. Regina developed very early.

Manders. Yes, didn't she. I fancy I remember thinking she was remarkably well developed, bodily, at the time I prepared her for Confirmation. But, for the time being she must in any case go home. Under her father's care—no, but of course Engstrand is not——. To think that he, of all men, could so conceal the truth from me!

[*A knock is heard at the hall door.*

Mrs. Alving. Who can that be? Come in!

[ENGSTRAND, *dressed in his Sunday clothes, appears in the doorway.*

Engstrand. I humbly beg pardon, but——

Manders. Aha! Hm!——

Mrs. Alving. Oh, it's you, Engstrand!

Engstrand. There were none of the maids about, so I took the great liberty of knocking.

Mrs. Alving. That's all right. Come in. Do you want to speak to me?

Engstrand (coming in). No, thank you very much, ma'm. It was Mr. Manders I wanted to speak to for a moment.

Manders (walking up and down). Hm!—do you. You want to speak to me, do you?

Engstrand. Yes, sir, I wanted so very much to——

Manders (stopping in front of him). Well, may I ask what it is you want?

Engstrand. It's this way, Mr. Manders. We are being paid off now. And many thanks to you, Mrs. Alving. And now the work is quite finished, I thought it would be so nice and suitable if all of us, who have worked so honestly together all this time, were to finish up with a few prayers this evening.

Manders. Prayers? Up at the Orphanage?

Engstrand. Yes, sir, but if it isn't agreeable to you, then——

Manders. Oh, certainly——but—hm!——

Engstrand. I have made a practice of saying a few prayers there myself each evening——

Mrs. Alving. Have you?

Engstrand. Yes, ma'am, now and then—just as a little

edification, so to speak. But I am only a poor common man, and haven't rightly the gift, alas—and so I thought that as Mr. Manders happened to be here, perhaps——

Manders. Look here, Engstrand. First of all I must ask you a question. Are you in a proper frame of mind for such a thing? Is your conscience free and untroubled?

Engstrand. Heaven have mercy on me a sinner! My conscience isn't worth our speaking about, Mr. Manders.

Manders. But it is just what we must speak about. What do you say to my question?

Engstrand. My conscience? Well—it's uneasy sometimes, of course.

Manders. Ah, you admit that at all events. Now will you tell me, without any concealment—what is your relationship to Regina?

Mrs. Alving (hastily). Mr. Manders!

Manders (calming her).—Leave it to me!

Engstrand. With Regina? Good Lord, how you frightened me! *(Looks at* Mrs. Alving.*)* There is nothing wrong with Regina, is there?

Manders. Let us hope not. What I want to know is, what is your relationship to her? You pass as her father, don't you?

Engstrand (unsteadily). Well—hm!—you know, sir, what happened between me and my poor Joanna.

Manders. No more distortion of the truth! Your late wife made a full confession to Mrs. Alving, before she left her service.

Engstrand. What!—do you mean to say——? Did she do that after all?

Manders. You see it has all come out, Engstrand.

Engstrand. Do you mean to say that she, who gave me her promise and solemn oath——

Manders. Did she take an oath?

Engstrand. Well, no—she only gave me her word, but as seriously as a woman could.

Manders. And all these years you have been hiding the truth from me—from me, who have had such complete and absolute faith in you.

Engstrand. I am sorry to say I have, sir.

Manders. Did I deserve that from you, Engstrand? Haven't I been always ready to help you in word and deed as far as lay in my power? Answer me! Is it not so?

Engstrand. Indeed there's many a time I should have been very badly off without you, sir.

Manders. And this is the way you repay me—by causing me to make false entries in the church registers, and afterwards keeping back from me for years the information which you owed it both to me and to your sense of the truth to divulge. Your conduct has been absolutely inexcusable, Engstrand, and from to-day everything is at an end between us.

Engstrand (with a sigh). Yes, I can see that's what it means.

Manders. Yes, because how can you possibly justify what you did?

Engstrand. Was the poor girl to go and increase her load of shame by talking about it? Just suppose, sir, for a moment that your reverence was in the same predicament as my poor Joanna——

Manders. I!

Engstrand. Good Lord, sir, I don't mean the same predicament. I mean, suppose there were something your reverence were ashamed of in the eyes of the world, so to speak. We men oughtn't to judge a poor woman too hardly, Mr. Manders.

Manders. But I am not doing so at all. It is you I am blaming.

Engstrand. Will your reverence grant me leave to ask you a small question?

Manders. Ask away.

Engstrand. Shouldn't you say it was right for a man to raise up the fallen?

Manders. Of course it is.

Engstrand. And isn't a man bound to keep his word of honour?

Manders. Certainly he is; but——

Engstrand. At the time when Joanna had her misfortune with this Englishman—or maybe he was an American or a Russian, as they call 'em—well, sir, then she came to town. Poor thing, she had refused me once or twice before; she only had eyes for good-looking men in those days, and I had this crooked leg then. Your reverence will remember how I had ventured up into a dancing-saloon where seafaring men were revelling in drunkenness and intoxication, as they say. And when I tried to exhort them to turn from their evil ways——

Mrs. Alving (coughs from the window). Ahem!

Manders. I know, Engstrand, I know—the rough brutes threw you downstairs. You have told me about that incident before. The affliction to your leg is a credit to you.

Engstrand. I don't want to claim credit for it, your reverence. But what I wanted to tell you was that she came then and confided in me with tears and gnashing of teeth. I can tell you, sir, it went to my heart to hear her.

Manders. Did it, indeed, Engstrand? Well, what then?

Engstrand. Well, then I said to her: "The American is roaming about on the high seas, he is. And you, Joanna," I said, "you have committed a sin and are a fallen woman. But here stands Jacob Engstrand," I said, "on two strong legs"—of course that was only speaking in a kind of metaphor, as it were, your reverence.

Manders. I quite understand. Go on.

Engstrand. Well, sir, that was how I rescued her and made her my lawful wife, so that no one should know how recklessly she had carried on with the stranger.

Manders. That was all very kindly done. The only thing I cannot justify was your bringing yourself to accept the money——

Engstrand. Money? I? Not a farthing.

Manders (to MRS. ALVING, *in a questioning tone).* But——

Engstrand. Ah, yes!—wait a bit; I remember now. Joanna did have a trifle of money, you are quite right. But I didn't want to know anything about that. "Fie," I said, "on the mammon of unrighteousness, it's the price of your sin; as for this tainted gold"—or notes, or whatever it was —"we will throw it back in the American's face," I said. But he had gone away and disappeared on the stormy seas, your reverence.

Manders. Was that how it was, my good fellow?

Engstrand. It was, sir. So then Joanna and I decided that the money should go towards the child's bringing-up, and that's what became of it; and I can give a faithful account of every single penny of it.

Manders. This alters the complexion of the affair very considerably.

Engstrand. That's how it was your reverence. And I make bold to say that I have been a good father to Regina —as far as was in my power—for I am a poor erring mortal, alas!

Manders. There, there, my dear Engstrand——

Engstrand. Yes, I do make bold to say that I brought up the child, and made my poor Joanna a loving and careful husband, as the Bible says we ought. But it never occurred to me to go to your reverence and claim credit for it or boast about it because I had done one good deed in this world. No; when Jacob Engstrand does a thing like that, he holds his tongue about it. Unfortunately it doesn't often happen, I know that only too well. And whenever I do come to see your reverence, I never seem to have anything but trouble and wickedness to talk about. Because, as I said just now—and I say it again—conscience can be very hard on us sometimes.

Manders. Give me your hand, Jacob Engstrand.

Engstrand. Oh, sir, I don't like——

Manders. No nonsense. *(Grasps his hand.)* That's it!

Engstrand. And may I make bold humbly to beg your reverence's pardon——

Manders. You? On the contrary it is for me to beg your pardon——

Engstrand. Oh no, sir.

Manders. Yes, certainly it is, and I do it with my whole heart. Forgive me for having so much misjudged you. And I assure you that if I can do anything for you to prove my sincere regret and my goodwill towards you——

Engstrand. Do you mean it, sir?

Manders. It would give me the greatest pleasure.

Engstrand. As a matter of fact, sir, you could do it now. I am thinking of using the honest money I have put away out of my wages up here, in establishing a sort of Sailors' Home in the town.

Mrs. Alving. You?

Engstrand. Yes, to be a sort of Refuge, as it were. There are such manifold temptations lying in wait for sailor men when they are roaming about on shore. But my idea is that in this house of mine they should have a sort of parental care looking after them.

Manders. What do you say to that, Mrs. Alving!

Engstrand. I haven't much to begin such a work with, I know; but Heaven might prosper it, and if I found any helping hand stretched out to me, then——

Manders. Quite so; we will talk over the matter further. Your project attracts me enormously. But in the meantime go back to the Orphanage and put everything tidy and light the lights, so that the occasion may seem a little solemn.

And then we will spend a little edifying time together, my dear Engstrand, for now I am sure you are in a suitable frame of mind.

Engstrand. I believe I am, sir, truly. Good-bye, then, Mrs. Alving, and thank you for all your kindness; and take good care of Regina for me. *(Wipes a tear from his eye.)* Poor Joanna's child—it is an extraordinary thing, but she seems to have grown into my life and to hold me by the heartstrings. That's how I feel about it, truly.

[*Bows and goes out.*

Manders. Now then, what do you think of him, Mrs. Alving! That was quite another explanation that he gave us.

Mrs. Alving. It was, indeed.

Manders. There, you see how exceedingly careful we ought to be in condemning our fellow-men. But at the same time it gives one genuine pleasure to find that one was mistaken. Don't you think so?

Mrs. Alving. What I think is that you are, and always will remain, a big baby, Mr. Manders.

Manders. I?

Mrs. Alving (laying her hands on his shoulders). And I think that I should like very much to give you a good hug.

Manders (drawing back hastily). No, no, good gracious! What an idea!

Mrs. Alving (with a smile). Oh, you needn't be afraid of me.

Manders (standing by the table). You choose such an extravagant way of expressing yourself sometimes. Now I must get these papers together and put them in my bag. *(Does so.)* That's it. And now good-bye, for the present. Keep your eyes open when Oswald comes back. I will come back and see you again presently.

[*He takes his hat and goes out by the hall door.*
Mrs Alving *sighs, glances out of the window,*

puts one or two things tidy in the room and turns to go into the dining-room. She stops in the doorway with a stifled cry.

Mrs. Alving. Oswald, are you still sitting at table!

Oswald (from the dining-room). I am only finishing my cigar.

Mrs. Alving. I thought you had gone out for a little turn.

Oswald (from within the room). In weather like this? *(A glass is heard clinking.* Mrs. Alving *leaves the door open and sits down with her knitting on the couch by the window.)* Wasn't that Mr. Manders that went out just now?

Mrs. Alving. Yes, he has gone over to the Orphanage.

Oswald. Oh.

[*The clink of a bottle on a glass is heard again.*

Mrs. Alving (with an uneasy expression). Oswald, dear, you should be careful with that liqueur. It is strong.

Oswald. It's a good protective against the damp.

Mrs. Alving. Wouldn't you rather come in here?

Oswald. You know you don't like smoking in there.

Mrs. Alving. You may smoke a cigar in here, certainly.

Oswald. All right; I will come in, then. Just one drop more. There! *(Comes in, smoking a cigar, and shuts the door after him. A short silence.)* Where has the parson gone?

Mrs. Alving. I told you he had gone over to the Orphanage.

Oswald. Oh, so you did.

Mrs. Alving. You shouldn't sit so long at table, Oswald

Oswald (holding his cigar behind his back). But it's so nice and cosy, mother dear. *(Caresses her with one hand.)* Think what it means to me—to have come home; to sit at my mother's own table, in my mother's own room, and to enjoy the charming meals she gives me.

Mrs. Alving. My dear, dear boy!

Oswald (a little impatiently, as he walks up and down smoking.) And what else is there for me to do here? I have no occupation——

Mrs. Alving. No occupation?

Oswald. Not in this ghastly weather, when there isn't a blink of sunshine all day long. *(Walks up and down the floor.)* Not to be able to work, it's——!

Mrs. Alving. I don't believe you were wise to come home.

Oswald. Yes, mother; I had to

Mrs. Alving. Because I would ten times rather give up the happiness of having you with me, sooner than that you should——

Oswald (standing still by the table). Tell me, mother— is it really such a great happiness for you to have me at home?

Mrs. Alving. Can you ask?

Oswald (crumpling up a newspaper). I should have thought it would have been pretty much the same to you whether I were here or away.

Mrs. Alving. Have you the heart to say that to your mother, Oswald?

Oswald. But you have been quite happy living without me so far.

Mrs. Alving. Yes, I have lived without you—that is true.

[*A silence. The dusk falls by degrees.* Oswald *walks restlessly up and down. He has laid aside his cigar.*

Oswald (stopping beside Mrs. Alving*).* Mother, may sit on the couch beside you?

Mrs. Alving. Of course, my dear boy.

Oswald (sitting down). Now I must tell you something, mother.

Mrs. Alving (anxiously). What?

Oswald (staring in front of him). I can't bear it any longer.

Mrs. Alving. Bear what? What do you mean?

Oswald (as before). I couldn't bring myself to write to you about it; and since I have been at home——

Mrs. Alving (catching him by the arm). Oswald, what is it?

Oswald. Both yesterday and to-day I have tried to push my thoughts away from me—to free myself from them. But I can't.

Mrs. Alving (getting up). You must speak plainly, Oswald!

Oswald (drawing her down to her seat again). Sit still, and I will try and tell you. I have made a great deal of the fatigue I felt after my journey——

Mrs. Alving. Well, what of that?

Oswald. But that isn't what is the matter. It is no ordinary fatigue——

Mrs. Alving (trying to get up). You are not ill, Oswald!

Oswald (pulling her down again). Sit still, mother. Do take it quietly. I am not exactly ill—not ill in the usual sense. *(Takes his head in his hands.)* Mother, it's my mind that has broken down—gone to pieces—I shall never be able to work any more!

[*Buries his face in his hands and throws himself at her knees in an outburst of sobs.*

Mrs. Alving (pale and trembling). Oswald! Look at me! No, no, it isn't true!

Oswald (looking up with a distracted expression). Never to be able to work any more! Never—never! A living death! Mother, can you imagine anything so horrible!

Mrs. Alving. My poor unhappy boy? How has this terrible thing happened?

Oswald (sitting up again). That is just what I cannot possibly understand. I have never lived recklessly, in any sense. You must believe that of me, mother! I have never done that.

Mrs. Alving. I haven't a doubt of it, Oswald.

Oswald. And yet this comes upon me all the same!—this terrible disaster!

Mrs. Alving. Oh, but it will all come right again, my dear precious boy. It is nothing but overwork. Believe me, that is so.

Oswald (dully). I thought so too, at first; but it isn't so.

Mrs. Alving. Tell me all about it.

Oswald. Yes, I will.

Mrs. Alving. When did you first feel anything?

Oswald. It was just after I had been home last time and had got back to Paris. I began to feel the most violent pains in my head—mostly at the back, I think. It was as if a tight band of iron was pressing on me from my neck upwards.

Mrs. Alving. And then?

Oswald. At first I thought it was nothing but the headaches I always used to be so much troubled with while I was growing.

Mrs. Alving. Yes, yes——

Oswald. But it wasn't; I soon saw that. I couldn't work any longer. I would try and start some big new picture; but it seemed as if all my faculties had forsaken me, as if all my strength were paralysed. I couldn't manage to collect my thoughts; my head seemed to swim—everything went round and round. It was a horrible feeling! At last I sent for a doctor—and from him I learnt the truth.

Mrs. Alving. In what way, do you mean?

Oswald. He was one of the best doctors there. He made me describe what I felt, and then he began to ask me a whole heap of questions which seemed to me to have nothing to do with the matter. I couldn't see what he was driving at——

Mrs. Alving. Well?

Oswald. At last he said: "You have had the canker of

disease in you practically from your birth"—the actual word
he used was *"vermoulu."*

Mrs. Alving (anxiously). What did he mean by that?

Oswald. I couldn't understand, either—and I asked him
for a clearer explanation. And then the old cynic said—
(clenching his fist.) Oh!——

Mrs. Alving. What did he say?

Oswald. He said: "The sins of the fathers are visited on
the children."

Mrs. Alving (getting up slowly). The sins of the
fathers——!

Oswald. I nearly struck him in the face——

Mrs. Alving (walking across the room). The sins of the
fathers——!

Oswald (smiling sadly). Yes, just imagine! Naturally
I assured him that what he thought was impossible. But
do you think he paid any heed to me? No, he persisted
in his opinion; and it was only when I got out your letters
and translated to him all the passages that referred to my
father——

Mrs. Alving. Well, and then?

Oswald. Well, then of course he had to admit that he
was on the wrong tack; and then I learnt the truth—the
incomprehensible truth! I ought to have had nothing to
do with the joyous happy life I had lived with my comrades.
It had been too much for my strength. So it was my own
fault!

Mrs. Alving. No, no, Oswald! Don't believe that!

Oswald. There was no other explanation of it possible,
he said. That is the most horrible part of it. My whole
life incurably ruined—just because of my own imprudence.
All that I wanted to do in the world—not to dare to think
of it any more—not to be *able* to think of it! Oh! if only
I could live my life over again—if only I could undo what I
have done!

[*Throws himself on his face on the couch.* Mrs.
Alving *wrings her hands and walks up and
down silently fighting with herself.*

*Oswald (looks up after a while, raising himself on his el-
bows).* If only it had been something I had inherited—
something I could not help.   But, instead of that, to have
disgracefully, stupidly, thoughtlessly thrown away one's
happiness, one's health, everything in the world—one's future, one's life——

Mrs. Alving. No, no, my darling boy; that is impossible!
(Bending over him.)   Things are not so desperate as you
think.

Oswald.   Ah, you don't know——.   *(Springs up.)*   And
to think, mother, that I should bring all this sorrow upon
you!   Many a time I have almost wished and hoped that
you really did not care so very much for me.

Mrs. Alving. I, Oswald?   My only son!   All that I
have in the world!   The only thing I care about!

Oswald (taking hold of her hands and kissing them).
Yes, yes, I know that is so.   When I am at home I know
that is true.   And that is one of the hardest parts of it to
me.   But now you know all about it; and now we won't
talk any more about it to-day.   I can't stand thinking about
it long at a time.   *(Walks across the room.)*   Let me have
something to drink, mother!

Mrs. Alving.   To drink?   What do you want?

Oswald.   Oh, anything you like.   I suppose you have got
some punch in the house.

Mrs. Alving.   Yes, but my dear Oswald——!

Oswald.   Don't tell me I mustn't, mother.   Do be nice!
I must have something to drown these gnawing thoughts.
(Goes into the conservatory.)   And how—how gloomy it
is here!   *(*Mrs. Alving *rings the bell.)*   And this incessant
rain.   It may go on week after week—a whole month.
Never a ray of sunshine.   I don't remember ever having
seen the sun shine once when I have been at home.

Mrs. Alving. Oswald—you are thinking of going away from me!

Oswald. Hm!—*(sighs deeply).* I am not thinking about anything. I *can't* think about anything! *(In a low voice.)* I have to let that alone.

Regina (coming from the dining-room). Did you ring, ma'am?

Mrs. Alving. Yes, let us have the lamp in.

Regina. In a moment, ma'am; it is all ready lit.

[*Goes out.*

Mrs. Alving (going up to OSWALD). Oswald, don't keep anything back from me.

Oswald. I don't, mother. *(Goes to the table.)* It seems to me I have told you a good lot.

[REGINA *brings the lamp and puts it upon the table.*

Mrs. Alving. Regina, you might bring us a small bottle of champagne.

Regina. Yes, ma'am.   [*Goes out.*

Oswald (taking hold of his mother's face). That's right. I knew my mother wouldn't let her son go thirsty.

Mrs. Alving. My poor dear boy, how could I refuse you anything now?

Oswald (eagerly). Is that true, mother? Do you mean it?

Mrs. Alving. Mean what?

Oswald. That you couldn't deny me anything?

Mrs. Alving. My dear Oswald——

Oswald. Hush!

[REGINA *brings in a tray with a small bottle of champagne and two glasses, which she puts on the table.*

Regina. Shall I open the bottle?

Oswald. No, thank you, I will do it.

[REGINA *goes out.*

Mrs. Alving (sitting down at the table). What did you mean, when you asked if I could refuse you nothing?

Oswald (busy opening the bottle). Let us have a glass first—or two.

> [*He draws the cork, fills one glass and is going to fill the other.*

Mrs. Alving (holding her hand over the second glass). No, thanks—not for me.

Oswald. Oh, well, for me then!

> [*He empties his glass, fills it again and empties it; then sits down at the table.*

Mrs. Alving (expectantly). Now, tell me.

Oswald (without looking at her). Tell me this; I thought you and Mr. Manders seemed so strange—so quiet—at dinner.

Mrs. Alving. Did you notice that?

Oswald. Yes. Ahem! *(After a short pause.)* Tell me —What do you think of Regina?

Mrs. Alving. What do I think of her?

Oswald. Yes, isn't she splendid!

Mrs. Alving. Dear Oswald, you don't know her as well as I do——

Oswald. What of that?

Mrs. Alving. Regina was too long at home, unfortunately. I ought to have taken her under my charge sooner.

Oswald. Yes, but isn't she splendid to look at, mother?

> [*Fills his glass.*

Mrs. Alving. Regina has many serious faults——

Oswald. Yes, but what of that?   [*Drinks.*

Mrs. Alving. But I am fond of her, all the same; and I have made myself responsible for her. I wouldn't for the world she should come to any harm.

Oswald (jumping up). Mother, Regina is my only hope of salvation!

Mrs. Alving (getting up). What do you mean?

Oswald. I can't go on bearing all this agony of mind alone.

Mrs. Alving. Haven't you your mother to help you to bear it?

Oswald. Yes, I thought so; that was why I came home to you. But it is no use; I see that it isn't. I cannot spend my life here.

Mrs. Alving. Oswald!

Oswald. I must live a different sort of life, mother; so I shall have to go away from you. I don't want you watching it.

Mrs. Alving. My unhappy boy! But, Oswald, as long as you are ill like this——

Oswald. If it was only a matter of feeling ill, I would stay with you, mother. You are the best friend I have in the world.

Mrs. Alving. Yes, I am that, Oswald, am I not?

Oswald (walking restlessly about). But all this torment —the regret, the remorse—and the deadly fear. Oh—this horrible fear!

Mrs. Alving (following him). Fear? Fear of what? What do you mean?

Oswald. Oh, don't ask me any more about it. I don't know what it is. I can't put it into words. *(*Mrs. Alving *crosses the room and rings the bell.)* What do you want?

Mrs. Alving. I want my boy to be happy, that's what I want. He mustn't brood over anything. *(To* Regina, *who has come to the door.)* More champagne—a large bottle.

Oswald. Mother!

Mrs. Alving. Do you think we country people don't know how to live?

Oswald. Isn't she splendid to look at? What a figure! And the picture of health!

Mrs. Alving (sitting down at the table). Sit down, Oswald, and let us have a quiet talk.

Oswald (sitting down). You don't know, mother, that I owe Regina a little reparation.

Mrs. Alving. You!

Oswald. Oh, it was only a little thoughtlessness—call it what you like. Something quite innocent, anyway. The last time I was home——

Mrs. Alving. Yes?

Oswald. ——she used often to ask me questions about Paris, and I told her one thing and another about the life there. And I remember saying one day: "Wouldn't you like to go there yourself?"

Mrs. Alving. Well?

Oswald. I saw her blush, and she said: "Yes, I should like to very much." "All right," I said, "I daresay it might be managed"—or something of that sort.

Mrs. Alving. And then?

Oswald. I naturally had forgotten all about it; but the day before yesterday I happened to ask her if she was glad I was to be so long at home——

Mrs. Alving. Well?

Oswald. ——and she looked so queerly at me, and asked: "But what is to become of my trip to Paris?"

Mrs. Alving. Her trip!

Oswald. And then I got it out of her that she had taken the thing seriously, and had been thinking about me all the time, and had set herself to learn French——

Mrs. Alving. So that was why——

Oswald. Mother—when I saw this fine, splendid, handsome girl standing there in front of me—I had never paid any attention to her before then—but now, when she stood there as if with open arms ready for me to take her to myself——

Mrs. Alving. Oswald!

Oswald. ——then I realised that my salvation lay in her, for I saw the joy of life in her.

Mrs. Alving (starting back). The joy of life——? Is there salvation in that?

Regina (coming in from the dining-room with a bottle of champagne). Excuse me for being so long; but I had to go to the cellar.

[*Puts the bottle down on the table.*

Oswald. Bring another glass, too.

Regina (looking at him in astonishment). The mistress's glass is there, sir.

Oswald. Yes, but fetch one for yourself, Regina. (RE-GINA *starts, and gives a quick shy glance at* MRS. ALVING.) Well?

Regina (in a low and hesitating voice). Do you wish me to, ma'am?

Mrs. Alving. Fetch the glass, Regina.

[REGINA *goes into the dining-room.*

Oswald (looking after her). Have you noticed how well she walks?—so firmly and confidently!

Mrs. Alving. It cannot be, Oswald.

Oswald. It is settled. You must see that. It is no use forbidding it. (REGINA *comes in with a glass, which she holds in her hand.*) Sit down, Regina.

[REGINA *looks questioningly at* MRS. ALVING.

Mrs. Alving. Sit down. (REGINA *sits down on a chair near the dining-room door, still holding the glass in her hand.*) Oswald, what was it you were saying about the joy of life?

Oswald. Ah, mother—the joy of life! You don't know very much about that at home here. I shall never realise it here.

Mrs. Alving. Not even when you are with me?

Oswald. Never at home. But you can't understand that.

Mrs. Alving. Yes, indeed I almost think I do understand you—now.

Oswald. That—and the joy of work. They are really

the same thing at bottom. But you don't know anything about that either.

Mrs. Alving. Perhaps you are right. Tell me some more about it, Oswald.

Oswald. Well, all I mean is that here people are brought up to believe that work is a curse and a punishment for sin, and that life is a state of wretchedness and that the sooner we can get out of it the better.

Mrs. Alving. A vale of tears, yes. And we quite conscientiously make it so.

Oswald. But the people over there will have none of that. There is no one there who really believes doctrines of that kind any longer. Over there the mere fact of being alive is thought to be a matter for exultant happiness. Mother, have you noticed that everything I have painted has turned upon the joy of life?—always upon the joy of life, unfailingly. There is light there, and sunshine, and a holiday feeling—and people's faces beaming with happiness. That is why I am afraid to stay at home here with you.

Mrs. Alving. Afraid? What are you afraid of here, with me?

Oswald. I am afraid that all these feelings that are so strong in me would degenerate into something ugly here.

Mrs. Alving (looking steadily at him). Do you think that is what would happen?

Oswald. I am certain it would. Even if one lived the same life at home here, as over there—it would never really be the same life.

Mrs. Alving (who has listened anxiously to him, gets up with a thoughtful expression and says:) Now I see clearly how it all happened.

Oswald. What do you see?

Mrs. Alving. I see it now for the first time. And now I can speak.

Oswald (getting up). Mother, I don't understand you.

Regina (who has got up also). Perhaps I had better go.

Mrs. Alving. No, stay here. Now I can speak. Now, my son, you shall know the whole truth. Oswald! Regina!

Oswald. Hush!—here is the parson——

[MANDERS *comes in by the hall door.*

Manders. Well, my friends, we have been spending an edifying time over there.

Oswald. So have we.

Manders. Engstrand must have help with his Sailors' Home. Regina must go home with him and give him her assistance.

Regina. No, thank you, Mr. Manders.

Manders (perceiving her for the first time). What——? you in here?—and with a wineglass in your hand!

Regina (putting down the glass hastily). I beg your pardon——!

Oswald. Regina is going away with me, Mr. Manders.

Manders. Going away! With you!

Oswald. Yes, as my wife—if she insists on that.

Manders. But, good heavens——!

Regina. It is not my fault, Mr. Manders.

Oswald. Or else she stays here if I stay.

Regina (involuntarily). Here!

Manders. I am amazed at you, Mrs. Alving.

Mrs. Alving. Neither of those things will happen, for now I can speak openly.

Manders. But you won't do that! No, no, no!

Mrs. Alving. Yes, I can and I will. And without destroying any one's ideals.

Oswald. Mother, what is it that is being concealed from me?

Regina (listening). Mrs. Alving! Listen! They are shouting outside.

[*Goes into the conservatory and looks out.*

Oswald (going to the window on the left). What can be the matter? Where does that glare come from?

Regina (calls out). The Orphanage is on fire!

Mrs. Alving (going to the window). On fire?

Manders. On fire? Impossible. I was there just a moment ago.

Oswald. Where is my hat? Oh, never mind that. Father's Orphanage——!

[*Runs out through the garden door.*

Mrs. Alving. My shawl, Regina! The whole place is in flames.

Manders. How terrible! Mrs. Alving, that fire is a judgment on this house of sin!

Mrs. Alving. Quite so. Come, Regina.

[*She and* REGINA *hurry out.*

Manders (clasping his hands). And no insurance!

[*Follows them out.*

ACT III

The same scene. All the doors are standing open. The lamp is still burning on the table. It is dark outside, except for a faint glimmer of light seen through the windows at the back. MRS. ALVING, with a shawl over her head, is standing in the conservatory, looking out. REGINA, also wrapped in a shawl, is standing a little behind her.

Mrs. Alving. Everything burnt—down to the ground.

Regina. It is burning still in the basement.

Mrs. Alving. I can't think why Oswald doesn't come back. There is no chance of saving anything.

Regina. Shall I go and take his hat to him?

Mrs. Alving. Hasn't he even got his hat?

Regina (pointing to the hall). No, there it is, hanging up.

Mrs. Alving. Never mind. He is sure to come back soon. I will go and see what he is doing.

[*Goes out by the garden door.* MANDERS *comes in from the hall.*

Manders. Isn't Mrs. Alving here?

Regina. She has just this moment gone down into the garden.

Manders. I have never spent such a terrible night in my life.

Regina. Isn't it a shocking misfortune, sir!

Manders. Oh, don't speak about it. I scarcely dare to think about it.

Regina. But how can it have happened?

Manders. Don't ask me, Miss Engstrand! How should I know? Are you going to suggest too——? Isn't it enough that your father——?

Regina. What has he done?

Manders. He has nearly driven me crazy.

Engstrand (coming in from the hall). Mr. Manders——!

Manders (turning round with a start). Have you even followed me here!

Engstrand. Yes, God help us all——! Great heavens! What a dreadful thing, your reverence!

Manders (walking up and down). Oh dear, oh dear!

Regina. What do you mean?

Engstrand. Our little prayer-meeting was the cause of it all, don't you see? *(Aside, to* REGINA.*)* Now we've got the old fool, my girl. *(Aloud.)* And to think it is my fault that Mr. Manders should be the cause of such a thing!

Manders. I assure you, Engstrand——

Engstrand. But there was no one else carrying a light there except you, sir.

Manders (standing still). Yes, so you say. But I have no clear recollection of having had a light in my hand.

Engstrand. But I saw quite distinctly your reverence take a candle and snuff it with your fingers and throw away the burning bit of wick among the shavings.

Manders. Did you see that?

Engstrand. Yes, distinctly.

Manders. I can't understand it at all. It is never my habit to snuff a candle with my fingers.

Engstrand. Yes, it wasn't like you to do that, sir. But who would have thought it could be such a dangerous thing to do?

Manders (walking restlessly backwards and forwards). Oh, don't ask me!

Engstrand (following him about). And you hadn't insured it either, had you, sir?

Manders. No, no, no; you heard me say so.

Engstrand. You hadn't insured it— and then went and set light to the whole place! Good Lord, what bad luck!

Manders (wiping the perspiration from his forehead). You may well say so, Engstrand.

Engstrand. And that it should happen to a charitable institution that would have been of service both to the town and the country, so to speak! The newspapers won't be very kind to your reverence, I expect.

Manders. No, that is just what I am thinking of. It is almost the worst part of the whole thing. The spiteful attacks and accusations—it is horrible to think of!

Mrs. Alving (coming in from the garden). I can't get him away from the fire.

Manders. Oh, there you are, Mrs. Alving.

Mrs. Alving. You will escape having to make your inaugural address now, at all events, Mr. Manders.

Manders. Oh, I would so gladly have——

Mrs. Alving (in a dull voice). It is just as well it has happened. This Orphanage would never have come to any good.

Manders. Don't you think so?

Mrs. Alving. Do you?

Manders. But it is none the less an extraordinary piece of ill luck.

Mrs. Alving. We will discuss it simply as a business matter.—Are you waiting for Mr. Manders, Engstrand?

Engstrand (at the hall door). Yes, I am.

Mrs. Alving. Sit down then, while you are waiting.

Engstrand. Thank you, I would rather stand.

Mrs. Alving (to MANDERS*).* I suppose you are going by the boat?

Manders. Yes. It goes in about an hour.

Mrs. Alving. Please take all the documents back with you. I don't want to hear another word about the matter. I have something else to think about now——

Manders. Mrs. Alving——

Mrs. Alving. Later on I will send you a power of attorney to deal with it exactly as you please.

Manders. I shall be most happy to undertake that. I am afraid the original intention of the bequest will have to be entirely altered now.

Mrs. Alving. Of course.

Manders. Provisionally, I should suggest this way of disposing of it. Make over the Solvik property to the parish. The land is undoubtedly not without a certain value; it will always be useful for some purpose or another. And as for the interest on the remaining capital that is on deposit in the bank, possibly I might make suitable use of that in support of some undertaking that promises to be of use to the town.

Mrs. Alving. Do exactly as you please. The whole thing is a matter of indifference to me now.

Engstrand. You will think of my Sailors' Home, Mr. Manders?

Manders. Yes, certainly, that is a suggestion. But we must consider the matter carefully.

Engstrand (aside). Consider!—devil take it! Oh Lord.

Manders (sighing). And unfortunately I can't tell how much longer I may have anything to do with the matter—whether public opinion may not force me to retire from it altogether. That depends entirely upon the result of the enquiry into the cause of the fire.

Mrs. Alving. What do you say?

Manders. And one cannot in any way reckon upon the result beforehand.

Engstrand (going nearer to him). Yes, indeed one can; because here stand I, Jacob Engstrand.

Manders. Quite so, but——

Engstrand (lowering his voice). And Jacob Engstrand isn't the man to desert a worthy benefactor in the hour of need, as the saying is.

Manders. Yes, but, my dear fellow—how——?

Engstrand. You might say Jacob Engstrand is an angel of salvation, so to speak, your reverence.

Manders. No, no, I couldn't possibly accept that.

Engstrand. That's how it will be, all the same. I know some one who has taken the blame for some one else on his shoulders before now, I do.

Manders. Jacob! *(Grasps his hand.)* You are one in a thousand! You shall have assistance in the matter of your Sailors' Home, you may rely upon that.

[ENGSTRAND *tries to thank him, but is prevented by emotion.*

Manders (hanging his wallet over his shoulder). Now we must be off. We will travel together.

Engstrand (by the dining-room door, says aside to RE-GINA). Come with me, you hussy! You shall be as cosy as the yolk in an egg!

Regina (tossing her head). Merci!

[*She goes out into the hall and brings back* MAN-DER'S *luggage.*

Manders. Good-bye, Mrs. Alving! And may the spirit of order and of what is lawful speedily enter into this house.

Mrs. Alving. Good-bye, Mr. Manders.

[*She goes into the conservatory, as she sees* OSWALD *coming in by the garden door.*

Engstrand (as he and REGINA *are helping* MANDERS *on with his coat).* Good-bye, my child. And if anything should happen to you, you know where Jacob Engstrand is to be found. *(Lowering his voice.)* Little Harbour Street, ahem——! *(To* MRS. ALVING *and* OSWALD.*)* And my house for poor seafaring men shall be called the "Alving Home," it shall. And, if I can carry out my own ideas about it, I shall make bold to hope that it may be worthy of bearing the late Mr. Alving's name.

Manders (at the door). Ahem—ahem! Come along, my dear Engstrand. Good-bye—good-bye!

[*He and* ENGSTRAND *go out by the hall door*

Oswald (going to the table).   What house was he speaking about?

Mrs. Alving.   I believe it is some sort of a Home that he and Mr. Manders want to start.

Oswald.   It will be burnt up just like this one.

Mrs. Alving.   What makes you think that?

Oswald.   Everything will be burnt up; nothing will be left that is in memory of my father.   Here am I being burnt up, too.   [REGINA *looks at him in alarm.*

Mrs. Alving.   Oswald!   You should not have stayed so long over there, my poor boy.

Oswald (sitting down at the table).   I almost believe you are right.

Mrs. Alving.   Let me dry your face, Oswald; you are all wet.   [*Wipes his face with her handkerchief.*

Oswald (looking straight before him, with no expression in his eyes).   Thank you, mother.

Mrs. Alving.   And aren't you tired, Oswald?   Don't you want to go to sleep?

Oswald (uneasily).   No, no—not to sleep!   I never sleep; I only pretend to. *(Gloomily.)*   That will come soon enough.

Mrs. Alving (looking at him anxiously).   Anyhow you are really ill, my darling boy.

Regina (intently).   Is Mr. Alving ill?

Oswald (impatiently).   And do shut all the doors!   This deadly fear——

Mrs. Alving.   Shut the doors, Regina. (REGINA *shuts the doors and remains standing by the hall door.* MRS. ALVING *takes off her shawl;* REGINA *does the same.* MRS. ALVING *draws up a chair near to* OSWALD'S *and sits down beside him.)*   That's it!   Now I will sit beside you——

Oswald.   Yes, do.   And Regina must stay in here too. Regina must always be near me.   You must give me a helping hand, you know, Regina.   Won't you do that?

Regina.   I don't understand——

Mrs. Alving. A helping hand?

Oswald. Yes—when there is need for it.

Mrs. Alving. Oswald, have you not your mother to give you a helping hand?

Oswald. You? *(Smiles.)* No, mother, you will never give me the kind of helping hand I mean. *(Laughs grimly.)* You? Ha, ha! *(Looks gravely at her.)* After all, you have the best right. *(Impetuously.)* Why don't you call me by my Christian name, Regina? Why don't you say Oswald?

Regina (in a low voice). I did not think Mrs. Alving would like it.

Mrs. Alving It will not be long before you have the right to do it. Sit down here now beside us, too. (REGINA *sits down quietly and hesitatingly at the other side of the table.)* And now, my poor tortured boy, I am going to take the burden off your mind——

Oswald. You, mother?

Mrs. Alving. ——all that you call remorse and regret and self-reproach.

Oswald. And you think you can do that?

Mrs. Alving. Yes, now I can, Oswald. A little while ago you were talking about the joy of life, and what you said seemed to shed a new light upon everything in my whole life.

Oswald (shaking his head). I don't in the least understand what you mean.

Mrs. Alving. You should have known your father in his young days in the army. He was full of the joy of life, I can tell you.

Oswald. Yes, I know.

Mrs. Alving. It gave me a holiday feeling only to look at him, full of irrepressible energy and exuberant spirits.

Oswald. What then?

Mrs. Alving. Well, then this boy, full of the joy of life —for he was just like a boy, then—had to make his home in a second-rate town which had none of the joy of life to offer him, but only dissipations. He had to come out here and live an aimless life; he had only an official post. He had no work worth devoting his whole mind to; he had nothing more than official routine to attend to. He had not a single companion capable of appreciating what the joy of life meant; nothing but idlers and tipplers——

Oswald. Mother——!

Mrs. Alving. And so the inevitable happened!

Oswald. What was the inevitable?

Mrs. Alving. You said yourself this evening what would happen in your case if you stayed at home.

Oswald. Do you mean by that, that father——?

Mrs. Alving. Your poor father never found any outlet for the overmastering joy of life that was in him. And I brought no holiday spirit into his home, either.

Oswald. You didn't, either?

Mrs. Alving. I had been taught about duty, and the sort of thing that I believed in so long here. Everything seemed to turn upon duty—my duty, or his duty—and I am afraid I made your poor father's home unbearable to him, Oswald.

Oswald. Why did you never say anything about it to me in your letters?

Mrs. Alving. I never looked at it as a thing I could speak of to you, who were his son.

Oswald. What way did you look at it, then?

Mrs. Alving. I only saw the one fact, that your father was a lost man before ever you were born.

Oswald (in a choking voice). Ah——!

.   [*He gets up and goes to the window.*

Mrs. Alving. And then I had the one thought in my mind, day and night, that Regina in fact had as good a right in this house—as my own boy had.

Oswald (turns round suddenly). Regina——?

Regina (gets up and asks in choking tones). I——?

Mrs. Alving. Yes, now you both know it.

Oswald. Regina!

Regina (to herself). So mother was one of that sort too.

Mrs. Alving. Your mother had many good qualities, Regina.

Regina. Yes, but she was one of that sort too, all the same. I have even thought so myself, sometimes, but——. Then, if you please, Mrs. Alving, may I have permission to leave at once?

Mrs. Alving. Do you really wish to, Regina?

Regina. Yes, indeed, I certainly wish to.

Mrs. Alving. Of course you shall do as you like, but——

Oswald (going to REGINA*).* Leave now? This is your home.

Regina. Merci, Mr. Alving—oh, of course I may say Oswald now, but that is not the way I thought it would become allowable.

Mrs. Alving. Regina, I have not been open with you——

Regina. No, I can't say you have! If I had known Oswald was ill——. And now that there can never be anything serious between us——. No, I really can't stay here in the country and wear myself out looking after invalids.

Oswald. Not even for the sake of one who has so near a claim on you?

Regina. No, indeed I can't. A poor girl must make some use of her youth, otherwise she may easily find herself out in the cold before she knows where she is. And I have got the joy of life in me, too, Mrs. Alving!

Mrs. Alving. Yes, unfortunately; but don't throw yourself away, Regina.

Regina. Oh, what's going to happen will happen. If Oswald takes after his father, it is just as likely I take after my mother, I expect.—— May I ask, Mrs. Alving, whether Mr. Manders knows this about me?

Mrs. Alving. Mr. Manders knows everything.

Regina (putting on her shawl). Oh, well then, the best thing I can do is to get away by the boat as soon as I can. Mr. Manders is such a nice gentleman to deal with; and it certainly seems to me that I have just as much right to some of that money as he—as that horrid carpenter.

Mrs. Alving. You are quite welcome to it, Regina.

Regina (looking at her fixedly). You might as well have brought me up like a gentleman's deaughter; it would have been more suitable. *(Tosses her head.)* Oh, well—never mind! *(With a bitter glance at the unopened bottle.)* I daresay some day I shall be drinking champagne with gentlefolk, after all.

Mrs. Alving. If ever you need a home, Regina, come to me.

Regina. No, thank you, Mrs. Alving. Mr. Manders takes an interest in me, I know. And if things should go very badly with me, I know one house at any rate where I shall feel at home.

Mrs. Alving. Where is that?

Regina. In the "Alving Home."

Mrs. Alving. Regina—I can see quite well—you are going to your ruin!

Regina. Pooh!—good-bye.

[*She bows to them and goes out through the hall.*

Oswald (standing by the window and looking out). Has she gone?

Mrs. Alving. Yes.

Oswald (muttering to himself). I think it's all wrong.

Mrs. Alving (going up to him from behind and putting her hands on his shoulders). Oswald, my dear boy—has it been a great shock to you?

Oswald (turning his face towards her). All this about father, do you mean?

Mrs. Alving. Yes, about your unhappy father. I am so afraid it may have been too much for you.

Oswald. What makes you think that? Naturally it has taken me entirely by surprise; but, after all, I don't know that it matters much to me.

Mrs. Alving (drawing back her hands). Doesn't matter! —that your father's life was such a terrible failure!

Oswald. Of course I can feel sympathy for him, just as I would for anyone else, but——

Mrs. Alving. No more than that! For your own father!

Oswald (impatiently). Father—father! I never knew anything of my father. I don't remember anything else about him except that he once made me sick.

Mrs. Alving. It is dreadful to think of!—But surely a child should feel some affection for his father, whatever happens?

Oswald. When the child has nothing to thank his father for? When he has never known him? Do you really cling to that antiquated superstition—you, who are so broad-minded in other things?

Mrs. Alving. You call it nothing but a superstition!

Oswald. Yes, and you can see that for yourself quite well, mother. It is one of those beliefs that are put into circulation in the world, and——

Mrs. Alving. Ghosts of beliefs!

Oswald (walking across the room). Yes, you might call them ghosts.

Mrs. Alving (with an outburst of feeling). Oswald—then you don't love me either.

Oswald. You I know, at any rate——

Mrs. Alving. You know me, yes; but is that all?

Oswald. And I know how fond you are of me, and I ought to be grateful to you for that. Besides, you can be so tremendously useful to me, now that I am ill.

Mrs. Alving. Yes, can't I, Oswald! I could almost bless your illness, as it has driven you home to me. For I see quite well that you are not my very own yet; you must be won.

Oswald (impatiently). Yes, yes, yes; all that is just a way of talking. You must remember I am a sick man, mother. I can't concern myself much with anyone else; I have enough to do, thinking about myself.

Mrs. Alving (gently). I will be very good and patient.

Oswald. And cheerful too, mother!

Mrs. Alving. Yes, my dear boy, you are quite right. *(Goes up to him.)* Now have I taken away all your remorse and self-reproach?

Oswald. Yes, you have done that. But who will take away the fear?

Mrs. Alving. The fear?

Oswald (crossing the room). Regina would have done it for one kind word.

Mrs. Alving. I don't understand you. What fear do you mean—and what has Regina to do with it?

Oswald. Is it very late, mother?

Mrs. Alving. It is early morning. *(Looks out through the conservatory windows.)* The dawn is breaking already on the heights. And the sky is clear, Oswald. In a little while you will see the sun.

Oswald. I am glad of that. After all, there may be many things yet for me to be glad of and to live for——

Mrs. Alving. I should hope so!

Oswald. Even if I am not able to work——

Mrs. Alving. You will soon find you are able to work again now, my dear boy. You have no longer all those painful depressing thoughts to brood over.

Oswald. No, it is a good thing that you have been able to rid me of those fancies. If only, now, I could overcome this one thing——.*(Sits down on the couch.)* Let us have a little chat, mother.

Mrs. Alving. Yes, let us.

> [*Pushes an armchair near to the couch and sits down beside him.*

Oswald. The sun is rising—and you know all about it; so I don't feel the fear any longer.

Mrs. Alving.   I know all about what?

Oswald (without listening to her).   Mother, isn't it the case that you said this evening there was nothing in the world you would not do for me if I asked you?

Mrs. Alving.   Yes, certainly I said so.

Oswald.   And will you be as good as your word, mother?

Mrs. Alving.   You may rely upon that, my own dear boy. I have nothing else to live for, but you.

Oswald.   Yes, yes; well, listen to me, mother. You are very strong-minded, I know. I want you to sit quite quiet when you hear what I am going to tell you.

Mrs. Alving.   But what is this dreadful thing——?

Oswald.   You mustn't scream. Do you hear? Will you promise me that? We are going to sit and talk it over quite quietly. Will you promise me that, mother?

Mrs. Alving.   Yes, yes, I promise—only tell me what it is.

Oswald.   Well, then, you must know that this fatigue of mine—and my not being able to think about my work—all that is not really the illness itself——

Mrs. Alving.   What is the illness itself?

Oswald.   What I am suffering from is hereditary; it—*(touches his forehead, and speaks very quietly)*—it lies here.

Mrs. Alving (almost speechless).   Oswald! No—no!

Oswald.   Don't scream; I can't stand it. Yes, I tell you, it lies here, waiting. And any time, any moment, it may break out.

Mrs. Alving.   How horrible——!

Oswald.   Do keep quiet. That is the state I am in——.

Mrs. Alving (springing up).   It isn't true, Oswald! It is impossible! It can't be that!

Oswald.   I had one attack while I was abroad. It passed off quickly. But when I learnt the condition I had been in then this dreadful haunting fear took possession of me.

Mrs. Alving.   That was the fear, then——

Oswald.   Yes, it is so indescribably horrible, you know

If only it had been an ordinary mortal disease——. I am not so much afraid of dying; though, of course, I should like to live as long as I can.

Mrs. Alving. Yes, yes, Oswald, you must!

Oswald. But this is so appallingly horrible. To become like a helpless child again—to have to be fed, to have to be——. Oh, it's unspeakable!

Mrs. Alving. My child has his mother to tend him.

Oswald (jumping up). No, never; that is just what I won't endure! I dare not think what it would mean to linger on like that for years—to get old and grey like that. And you might die before I did. *(Sits down in* Mrs. Alving's *chair.)* Because it doesn't necessarily have a fatal end quickly, the doctor said. He called it a kind of softening of the brain—or something of that sort. *(Smiles mournfully.)* I think that expression sounds so nice. It always makes me think of cherry-coloured velvet curtains—something that is soft to stroke.

Mrs. Alving (with a scream). Oswald!

Oswald (jumps up and walks about the room). And now you have taken Regina from me! If I had only had her. She would have given me a helping hand, I know.

Mrs. Alving (going up to him). What do you mean, my darling boy? Is there any help in the world I would not be willing to give you?

Oswald. When I had recovered from the attack I had abroad, the doctor told me that when it recurred—and it will recur—there would be no more hope.

Mrs. Alving. And he was heartless enough to——

Oswald. I insisted on knowing. I told him I had arrangements to make——. *(Smiles cunningly.)* And so I had. *(Takes a small box from his inner breast-pocket.)* Mother, do you see this?

Mrs. Alving. What is it?

Oswald. Morphia powders.

Mrs. Alving (looking at him in terror).   Oswald—my boy!

Oswald.   I have twelve of them saved up——

Mrs. Alving (snatching at it).   Give me the box, Oswald!

Oswald.   Not yet, mother.

> [*Puts it back in his pocket.*

Mrs. Alving.   I shall never get over this!

Oswald.   You must.   If I had had Regina here now, I would have told her quietly how things stand with me—and asked her to give me this last helping hand.   She would have helped me, I am certain.

Mrs. Alving.   Never!

Oswald.   If this horrible thing had come upon me and she had seen me lying helpless, like a baby, past help, past saving, past hope—with no chance of recovering——

Mrs. Alving.   Never in the world would Regina have done it.

Oswald.   Regina would have done it.   Regina was so splendidly light-hearted.   And she would very soon have tired of looking after an invalid like me.

Mrs. Alving.   Then thank heaven Regina is not here!

Oswald.   Well, now you have got to give me that helping hand, mother.

Mrs. Alving (with a loud scream).   I!

Oswald.   Who has a better right than you?

Mrs. Alving.   I?   Your mother!

Oswald.   Just for that reason.

Mrs. Alving.   I, who gave you your life!

Oswald.   I never asked you for life.   And what kind of a life was it that you gave me?   I don't want it!   You shall take it back!

Mrs. Alving.   Help!   Help!

> [*Runs into the hall.*

Oswald (following her).   Don't leave me!   Where are you going?

Mrs. Alving (in the hall). To fetch the doctor to you, Oswald! Let me out!

Oswald (going into the hall). You shan't go out. And no one shall come in.

[*Turns the key in the lock.*

Mrs. Alving (coming in again). Oswald! Oswald!— my child!

Oswald (following her). Have you a mother's heart— and can bear to see me suffering this unspeakable terror?

Mrs. Alving (controlling herself, after a moment's silence). There is my hand on it.

Oswald. Will you——?

Mrs. Alving. If it becomes necessary. But it shan't become necessary. No, no—it is impossible it should!

Oswald. Let us hope so. And let us live together as long as we can. Thank you, mother.

[*He sits down in the armchair, which* Mrs. Alving *had moved beside the couch. Day is breaking; the lamp is still burning on the table.*

Mrs. Alving (coming cautiously nearer). Do you feel calmer now?

Oswald. Yes.

Mrs. Alving (bending over him). It has only been a dreadful fancy of yours, Oswald. Nothing but fancy. All this upset has been bad for you. But now you will get some rest, at home with your own mother, my darling boy. You shall have everything you want, just as you did when you were a little child.—There, now. The attack is over. You see how easily it passed off! I knew it would.—And look, Oswald, what a lovely day we are going to have? Brilliant sunshine. Now you will be able to see your home properly.

[*She goes to the table and puts out the lamp. It is sunrise. The glaciers and peaks in the distance are seen bathed in bright morning light.*

Oswald (who has been sitting motionless in the armchair,

with his back to the scene outside, suddenly says:) Mother, give me the sun.

Mrs. Alving (standing at the table, and looking at him in amazement). What do you say?

Oswald (repeats in a dull, toneless voice). The sun—the sun.

Mrs. Alvin (going up to him). Oswald, what is the matter with you? *(OSWALD seems to shrink up in the chair; all his muscles relax; his face loses its expression, and his eyes stare stupidly.* MRS. ALVING *is trembling with terror.)* What is it! *(Screams.)* Oswald! What is the matter with you! *(Throws herself on her knees beside him and shakes him.)* Oswald! Oswald! Look at me! Don't you know me!

Oswald (in an expressionless voice, as before). The sun —the sun.

Mrs. Alving (jumps up despairingly, beats her head with her hands, and screams). I can't bear it! *(Whispers as though paralysed with fear.)* I can't bear it! Never! *(Suddenly.)* Where has he got it? *(Passes her hand quickly over his coat.)* Here! *(Draws back a little way and cries:)* No, no, no!—Yes!—no, no!

> [*She stands a few steps from him, her hands thrust into her hair, and stares at him in speechless terror.*

Oswald (sitting motionless, as before). The sun—the sun.

AN ENEMY OF THE PEOPLE
(1882)

CHARACTERS

DR. THOMAS STOCKMANN, *Medical Officer of the Municipal Baths.*

MRS. STOCKMANN, *his wife.*

PETRA, *their daughter, a teacher.*

EJLIF
MORTEN } *their sons (aged 13 and 10 respectively).*

PETER STOCKMANN, *the Doctor's elder brother; Mayor of the Town and Chief Constable, Chairman of the Baths' Committee, etc., etc.*

MORTEN KIIL, *a tanner* (MRS. STOCKMANN'S *adoptive father*).

HOVSTAD, *editor of the "People's Messenger."*

BILLING, *sub-editor.*

CAPTAIN HORSTER.

ASLAKSEN, *a printer.*

MEN *of various conditions and occupations, some few women, and a troop of schoolboys—the audience at a public meeting.*

   The action takes place in a coast town in southern Norway.

AN ENEMY OF THE PEOPLE

ACT I

SCENE.—DR. STOCKMANN'S *sitting-room. It is evening. The room is plainly but neatly appointed and furnished. In the right-hand wall are two doors; the farther leads out to the hall, the nearer to the doctor's study. In the left-hand wall, opposite the door leading to the hall, is a door leading to the other rooms occupied by the family. In the middle of the same wall stands the stove, and, further forward, a couch with a looking-glass hanging over it and an oval table in front of it. On the table, a lighted lamp, with a lampshade. At the back of the room, an open door leads to the dining-room.* BILLING *is seen sitting at the dining table, on which a lamp is burning. He has a napkin tucked under his chin, and* MRS. STOCKMANN *is standing by the table handing him a large plate-full of roast beef. The other places at the table are empty, and the table somewhat in disorder, a meal having evidently recently been finished.*

Mrs. Stockmann. You see, if you come an hour late, Mr. Billing, you have to put up with cold meat.

Billing (as he eats). It is uncommonly good, thank you —remarkably good.

Mrs. Stockmann. My husband makes such a point of having his meals punctually, you know——

Billing. That doesn't affect me a bit. Indeed, I almost

think I enjoy a meal all the better when I can sit down and eat all by myself and undisturbed.

Mrs. Stockmann. Oh well, as long as you are enjoying it——. *(Turns to the hall door, listening.)* I expect that is Mr. Hovstad coming too.

Billing. Very likely.

> [PETER STOCKMANN *comes in. He wears an over-coat and his official hat, and carries a stick.*

Peter Stockmann. Good evening, Katherine.

Mrs. Stockmann (coming forward into the sitting-room). Ah, good evening—is it you? How good of you to come up and see us!

Peter Stockmann. I happened to be passing, and so—*(looks into the dining-room).* But you have company with you, I see.

Mrs. Stockmann (a little embarrassed). Oh, no—it was quite by chance he came in. *(Hurriedly.)* Won't you come in and have something, too?

Peter Stockmann. I! No, thank you. Good gracious —hot meat at night! Not with my digestion.

Mrs. Stockmann. Oh, but just once in a way——

Peter Stockmann. No, no, my dear lady; I stick to my tea and bread and butter. It is much more wholesome in the long run—and a little more economical, too.

Mrs. Stockmann (smiling). Now you mustn't think that Thomas and I are spendthrifts.

Peter Stockmann. Not you, my dear; I would never think that of you. *(Points to the Doctor's study.)* Is he not at home?

Mrs. Stockmann. No, he went out for a little turn after supper—he and the boys.

Peter Stockmann. I doubt if that is a wise thing to do. *(Listens.)* I fancy I hear him coming now.

Mrs. Stockmann. No, I don't think it is he. *(A knock is heard at the door.)* Come in! *(HOVSTAD comes in from the hall.)* Oh, it is you, Mr. Hovstad!

Hovstad. Yes, I hope you will forgive me, but I was delayed at the printer's. Good evening, Mr. Mayor.

Peter Stockmann (bowing a little distantly). Good evening. You have come on business, no doubt.

Hovstad. Partly. It's about an article for the paper.

Peter Stockmann. So I imagined. I hear my brother has become a prolific contributor to the "People's Messenger."

Hovstad. Yes, he is good enough to write in the "People's Messenger" when he has any home truths to tell.

Mrs. Stockmann (to HOVSTAD*).* But won't you——?
[*Points to the dining-room.*

Peter Stockmann. Quite so, quite so. I don't blame him in the least, as a writer, for addressing himself to the quarters where he will find the readiest sympathy. And, besides that, I personally have no reason to bear any ill will to your paper, Mr. Hovstad.

Hovstad. I quite agree with you.

Peter Stockmann. Taking one thing with another, there is an excellent spirit of toleration in the town—an admirable municipal spirit. And it all springs from the fact of our having a great common interest to unite us—an interest that is in an equally high degree the concern of every right-minded citizen——

Hovstad. The Baths, yes.

Peter Stockmann. Exactly—our fine, new, handsome Baths. Mark my words, Mr. Hovstad—the Baths will become the focus of our municipal life! Not a doubt of it!

Mrs. Stockmann. That is just what Thomas says.

Peter Stockmann. Think how extraordinarily the place has developed within the last year or two! Money has been flowing in, and there is some life and some business doing in the town. Houses and landed property are rising in value every day.

Hovstad. And unemployment is diminishing.

Peter Stockmann. Yes, that is another thing. The bur

den of the poor rates has been lightened, to the great relief of the propertied classes; and that relief will be even greater if only we get a really good summer this year, and lots of visitors—plenty of invalids, who will make the Baths talked about.

Hovstad.   And there is a good prospect of that, I hear.

Peter Stockmann.   It looks very promising.   Enquiries about apartments and that sort of thing are reaching us every day.

Hovstad.   Well, the doctor's article will come in very suitably.

Peter Stockmann.   Has he been writing something just lately?

Hovstad.   This is something he wrote in the winter; a recommendation of the Baths—an account of the excellent sanitary conditions here.   But I held the article over, temporarily.

Peter Stockmann.   Ah,—some little difficulty about it, I suppose?

Hovstad.   No, not at all; I thought it would be better to wait till the spring, because it is just at this time that people begin to think seriously about their summer quarters.

Peter Stockmann.   Quite right; you were perfectly right, Mr. Hovstad.

Hovstad.   Yes, Thomas is really indefatigable when it is a question of the Baths.

Peter Stockmann.   Well—remember, he is the Medical Officer to the Baths.

Hovstad.   Yes, and what is more, they owe their existence to him.

Peter Stockmann.   To him?   Indeed!   It is true I have heard from time to time that some people are of that opinion.   At the same time I must say I imagined that I took a modest part in the enterprise.

Mrs. Stockman.   Yes, that is what Thomas is always saying.

Hovstad. But who denies it, Mr. Stockmann? You set the thing going and made a practical concern of it; we all know that. I only meant that the idea of it came first from the doctor.

Peter Stockmann. Oh, ideas—yes! My brother has had plenty of them in his time—unfortunately. But when it is a question of putting an idea into practical shape, you have to apply to a man of different mettle, Mr. Hovstad. And I certainly should have thought that in this house at least——

Mrs. Stockmann. My dear Peter——

Hovstad. How can you think that——?

Mrs. Stockmann. Won't you go in and have something, Mr. Hovstad? My husband is sure to be back directly.

Hovstad. Thank you, perhaps just a morsel.

[*Goes into the dining-room.*

Peter Stockmann (lowering his voice a little). It is a curious thing that these farmers' sons never seem to lose their want of tact.

Mrs. Stockmann. Surely it is not worth bothering about! Cannot you and Thomas share the credit as brothers?

Peter Stockmann. I should have thought so; but apparently some people are not satisfied with a share.

Mrs. Stockmann. What nonsense! You and Thomas get on so capitally together. *(Listens.)* There he is at last, I think.

[*Goes out and opens the door leading to the hall.*

Dr. Stockmann (laughing and talking outside). Look here—here is another guest for you, Katherine. Isn't that jolly! Come in, Captain Horster; hang your coat up on this peg. Ah, you don't wear an overcoat. Just think, Katherine; I met him in the street and could hardly persuade him to come up! (CAPTAIN HORSTER *comes into the room and greets* MRS. STOCKMANN. *He is followed by* DR. STOCKMANN.*)* Come along in, boys. They are ravenously hungry again, you know. Come along, Captain Horster; you must have a slice of beef.

> [*Pushes* HORSTER *into the dining-room.* EJLIF *and* MORTEN *go in after them.*

Mrs. Stockmann. But, Thomas, don't you see——?

Dr. Stockmann (turning in the doorway). Oh, is it you, Peter? *(Shakes hands with him.)* Now that is very delightful.

Peter Stockmann. Unfortunately I must go in a moment——

Dr. Stockmann. Rubbish! There is some toddy just coming in. You haven't forgotten the toddy, Katherine?

Mrs. Stockmann. Of course not; the water is boiling now.

> [*Goes into the dining-room.*

Peter Stockmann. Toddy too!

Dr. Stockmann. Yes, sit down and we will have it comfortably.

Peter Stockmann. Thanks, I never care about an evening's drinking.

Dr. Stockmann. But this isn't an evening's drinking.

Peter Stockmann. It seems to me——. *(Looks towards the dining-room.)* It is extraordinary how they can put away all that food.

Dr. Stockmann (rubbing his hands). Yes, isn't it splendid to see young people eat? They have always got an appetite, you know! That's as it should be. Lots of food —to build up their strength! They are the people who are going to stir up the fermenting forces of the future, Peter.

Peter Stockmann. May I ask what they will find here to "stir up," as you put it?

Dr. Stockmann. Ah, you must ask the young people that—when the times comes. We shan't be able to see it, of course. That stands to reason—two old fogies, like us——

Peter Stockmann. Really, really! I must say that is an extremely odd expression to——

Dr. Stockmann. Oh, you mustn't take me too literally, Peter. I am so heartily happy and contented, you know. I think it is such an extraordinary piece of good fortune to be in the middle of all this growing, germinating life. It is a splendid time to live in! It is as if a whole new world were being created around one.

Peter Stockmann. Do you really think so?

Dr. Stockmann. Ah, naturally you can't appreciate it as keenly as I. You have lived all your life in these surroundings, and your impressions have got blunted. But I, who have been buried all these years in my little corner up north, almost without ever seeing a stranger who might bring new ideas with him—well, in my case it has just the same effect as if I had been transported into the middle of a crowded city.

Peter Stockmann. Oh, a city——!

Dr. Stockmann. I know, I know; it is all cramped enough here, compared with many other places. But there is life here—there is promise—there are innumerable things to work for and fight for; and that is the main thing *(Calls.)* Katherine, hasn't the postman been here?

Mrs. Stockmann (from the dining-room). No.

Dr. Stockmann. And then to be comfortably off, Peter! That is something one learns to value, when one has been on the brink of starvation, as we have.

Peter Stockmann. Oh, surely——

Dr. Stockmann. Indeed I can assure you we have often been very hard put to it, up there. And now to be able to live like a lord! To-day, for instance, we had roast beef for dinner—and, what is more, for supper too. Won't you come and have a little bit? Or let me show it you, at any rate? Come here——

Peter Stockmann No, no—not for worlds!

Dr. Stockmann. Well, but just come here then. Do you see, we have got a table-cover?

Peter Stockmann. Yes, I noticed it.

Dr. Stockmann. And we have got a lamp-shade too. Do you see? All out of Katherine's savings! It makes the room so cosy. Don't you think so? Just stand here for a moment—no, no, not there—just here, that's it! Look now, when you get the light on it altogether—I really think it looks very nice, doesn't it?

Peter Stockmann. Oh, if you can afford luxuries of this kind——

Dr. Stockmann. Yes, I can afford it now. Katherine tells me I earn almost as much as we spend.

Peter Stockmann. Almost—yes!

Dr. Stockmann. But a scientific man must live in a little bit of style. I am quite sure an ordinary civil servant spends more in a year than I do.

Peter Stockmann. I daresay. A civil servant—a man in a well-paid position——

Dr. Stockmann. Well, any ordinary merchant, then! A man in that position spends two or three times as much as——

Peter Stockmann. It just depends on circumstances.

Dr. Stockmann. At all events I assure you I don't waste money unprofitably. But I can't find it in my heart to deny myself the pleasure of entertaining my friends. I need that sort of thing, you know. I have lived for so long shut out of it all, that it is a necessity of life to me to mix with young, eager, ambitious men, men of liberal and active minds; and that describes every one of those fellows who are enjoying their supper in there. I wish you knew more of Hovstad——

Peter Stockmann. By the way, Hovstad was telling me he was going to print another article of yours.

Dr. Stockmann. An article of mine?

Peter Stockmann. Yes, about the Baths. An article you wrote in the winter.

Dr. Stockmann. Oh, that one! No, I don't intend that to appear just for the present.

Peter Stockmann. Why not? It seems to me that this would be the most opportune moment.

Dr. Stockmann. Yes, very likely—under normal conditions.   [*Crosses the room.*

Peter Stockmann (following him with his eyes). Is there anything abnormal about the present conditions?

Dr. Stockmann (standing still). To tell you the truth, Peter, I can't say just at this moment—at all events not to-night. There may be much that is very abnormal about the present conditions—and it is possible there may be nothing abnormal about them at all. It is quite possible it may be merely my imagination.

Peter Stockmann. I must say it all sounds most mysterious. Is there something going on that I am to be kept in ignorance of? I should have imagined that I, as Chairman of the governing body of the Baths——

Dr. Stockmann. And I should have imagined that I——. Oh, come, don't let us fly out at one another, Peter.

Peter Stockmann. Heaven forbid! I am not in the habit of flying out at people, as you call it. But I am entitled to request most emphatically that all arrangements shall be made in a business-like manner, through the proper channels, and shall be dealt with by the legally constituted authorities. I can allow no going behind our backs by any roundabout means.

Dr. Stockmann. Have I ever at any time tried to go behind your backs!

Peter Stockmann. You have an ingrained tendency to take your own way, at all events; and that is almost equally inadmissible in a well-ordered community. The individual ought undoubtedly to acquiesce in subordinating himself to the community—or, to speak more accurately, to the authorities who have the care of the community's welfare.

Dr. Stockmann. Very likely. But what the deuce has all this got to do with me?

Peter Stockmann. That is exactly what you·never appear to be willing to learn, my dear Thomas. But, mark my words, some day you will have to suffer for it—sooner or later. Now I have told you. Good-bye.

Dr. Stockmann. Have you taken leave of your senses? You are on the wrong scent altogether.

Peter Stockmann. I am not usually that. You must excuse me now if I—*(calls into the dining-room).* Good night, Katherine. Good night, gentlemen.   [*Goes out.*

Mrs. Stockmann (coming from the dining-room). Has he gone?

Dr. Stockmann. Yes, and in such a bad temper.

Mrs. Stockmann. But, dear Thomas, what have you been doing to him again?

Dr. Stockmann. Nothing at all. And, anyhow, he can't oblige me to make my report before the proper time.

Mrs. Stockmann. What have you got to make a report to him about?

Dr. Stockmann. Hm! Leave that to me, Katherine. ——It is an extraordinary thing that the postman doesn't come.

> [Hovstad, Billings *and* Horster *have got up from the table and come into the sitting-room.* Ejlif *and* Morten *come in after them.*

Billing (stretching himself). Ah!—one feels a new man after a meal like that.

Hovstad. The mayor wasn't in a very sweet temper tonight, then.

Dr. Stockmann. It is his stomach; he has a wretched digestion.

Hovstad. I rather think it was us two of the "People's Messenger" that he couldn't digest.

Mrs. Stockmann. I thought you came out of it pretty well with him.

Hovstad. Oh yes; but it isn't anything more than a sort of truce.

Billing. That is just what it is! That word sums up the situation.

Dr. Stockmann. We must remember that Peter is a lonely man, poor chap. He has no home comforts of any kind; nothing but everlasting business. And all that infernal weak tea wash that he pours into himself! Now then, my boys, bring chairs up to the table. Aren't we going to have that toddy, Katherine?

Mrs. Stockmann (going into the dining-room). I am just getting it.

Dr. Stockmann. Sit down here on the couch beside me, Captain Horster. We so seldom see you——. Please sit down, my friends.

> [*They sit down at the table.* MRS. STOCKMANN
> *brings a tray, with a spirit-lamp, glasses, bottles,*
> *etc., upon it.*

Mrs. Stockmann. There you are! This is arrack, and this is rum, and this one is the brandy. Now every one must help himself.

Dr. Stockmann (taking a glass). We will. *(They all mix themselves some toddy.)* And let us have the cigars. Ejlif, you know where the box is. And you, Morten, can fetch my pipe. *(The two boys go into the room on the right.)* I have a suspicion that Ejlif pockets a cigar now and then!—but I take no notice of it. *(Calls out.)* And my smoking-cap too, Morten. Katherine, you can tell him where I left it. Ah, he has got it. *(The boys bring the various things.)* Now, my friends. I stick to my pipe, you know. This one has seen plenty of bad weather with me up north. *(Touches glasses with them.)* Your good health! Ah! it is good to be sitting snug and warm here.

Mrs. Stockmann (who sits knitting).   Do you sail soon, Captain Horster?

Horster.   I expect to be ready to sail next week.

Mrs. Stockmann.   I suppose you are going to America?

Horster.   Yes, that is the plan.

Mrs. Stockmann.   Then you won't be able to take part in the coming election.

Horster.   Is there going to be an election?

Billing.   Didn't you know?

Horster.   No, I don't mix myself up with those things.

Billing.   But do you not take an interest in public affairs?

Horster.   No, I don't know anything about politics.

Billing.   All the same, one ought to vote, at any rate.

Horster.   Even if one doesn't know anything about what is going on?

Billing.   Doesn't know! What do you mean by that? A community is like a ship; every one ought to be prepared to take the helm.

Horster.   May be that is all very well on shore; but on board ship it wouldn't work.

Hovstad.   It is astonishing how little most sailors care about what goes on on shore.

Billing.   Very extraordinary.

Dr. Stockmann.   Sailors are like birds of passage; they feel equally at home in any latitude. And that is only an additional reason for our being all the more keen, Hovstad. Is there to be anything of public interest in to-morrow's "Messenger"?

Hovstad.   Nothing about municipal affairs. But the day after to-morrow I was thinking of printing your article——

Dr. Stockmann.   Ah, devil take it—my article! Look here, that must wait a bit.

Hovstad.   Really? We had just got convenient space for it, and I thought it was just the opportune moment——

Dr. Stockmann. Yes, yes, very likely you are right; but it must wait all the same. I will explain to you later.

> [PETRA *comes in from the hall, in hat and cloak and with a bundle of exercise books under her arm.*

Petra. Good evening.

Dr. Stockmann. Good evening, Petra; come along.

> [*Mutual greetings;* PETRA *takes off her things and puts them down on a chair by the door.*

Petra. And you have all been sitting here enjoying yourselves, while I have been out slaving!

Dr. Stockmann. Well, come and enjoy yourself too!

Billing. May I mix a glass for you?

Petra (coming to the table). Thanks, I would rather do it; you always mix it too strong. But I forgot, father—I have a letter for you.

> [*Goes to the chair where she has laid her things.*

Dr. Stockmann. A letter? From whom?

Petra (looking in her coat pocket). The postman gave it to me just as I was going out——

Dr. Stockmann (getting up and going to her). And you only give to me now!

Petra. I really had not time to run up again. There it is!

Dr. Stockmann (seizing the letter). Let's see, let's see, child! *(Looks at the address.)* Yes, that's all right!

Mrs. Stockmann. Is it the one you have been expecting so anxiously, Thomas?

Dr. Stockmann. Yes, it is. I must go to my room now and——. Where shall I get a light, Katherine? Is there no lamp in my room again?

Mrs. Stockmann. Yes, your lamp is all ready lit on your desk.

Dr. Stockmann. Good, good. Excuse me for a moment——.
> [*Goes into his study*

Petra. What do you suppose it is, mother?

Mrs. Stockmann. I don't know; for the last day or two he has always been asking if the postman has not been.

Billing. Probably some country patient.

Petra. Poor old dad!—he will overwork himself soon. *(Mixes a glass for herself.)* There, that will taste good!

Hovstad. Have you been teaching in the evening school again to-day?

Petra (sipping from her glass). Two hours.

Billing. And four hours of school in the morning——

Petra. Five hours.

Mrs. Stockmann. And you have still got exercises to correct, I see.

Petra. A whole heap, yes.

Horster. You are pretty full up with work too, it seems to me.

Petra. Yes—but that is good. One is so delightfully tired after it.

Billing. Do you like that?

Petra. Yes, because one sleeps so well then.

Morten. You must be dreadfully wicked, Petra.

Petra. Wicked?

Morten. Yes, because you work so much. Mr. Rörlund says work is a punishment for our sins.

Ejlif. Pooh, what a duffer you are, to believe a thing like that!

Mrs. Stockmann. Come, come, Ejlif!

Billing (laughing). That's capital!

Hovstad. Don't you want to work as hard as that, Morten?

Morten. No, indeed I don't.

Hovstad. What do you want to be, then?

Morten. I should like best to be a Viking.

Ejlif. You would have to be a pagan then.

Morten. Well, I could become a pagan, couldn't I?

Billing. I agree with you, Morten! My sentiments. exactly.

Mrs. Stockmann (signalling to him). I am sure that is not true, Mr. Billing.

Billing. Yes, I swear it is! I am a pagan, and I am proud of it. Believe me, before long we shall all be pagans.

Morten. And then shall be allowed to do anything we like?

Billing. Well, you see, Morten——.

Mrs. Stockmann. You must go to your room now, boys; I am sure you have some lessons to learn for to-morrow.

Ejlif. I should like so much to stay a little longer——

Mrs. Stockmann. No, no; away you go, both of you.

[*The boys say good-night and go into the room on the left.*

Hovstad. Do you really think it can do the boys any harm to hear such things?

Mrs. Stockmann. I don't know; but I don't like it.

Petra. But you know, mother, I think you really are wrong about it.

Mrs. Stockmann. Maybe, but I don't like it—not in our own home.

Petra. There is so much falsehood both at home and at school. At home one must not speak, and at school we have to stand and tell lies to the children.

Horster. Tell lies?

Petra. Yes, don't you suppose we have to teach them all sorts of things that we don't believe?

Billing. That is perfectly true.

Petra. If only I had the means I would start a school of my own, and it would be conducted on very different lines.

Billing. Oh, bother the means——!

Horster. Well if you are thinking of that, Miss Stock-mann, I shall be delighted to provide you with a school-room. The great big old house my father left me is stand-

ing almost empty; there is an immense dining-room downstairs——

Petra (laughing). Thank you very much; but I am
afraid nothing will come of it.

Hovstad. No, Miss Petra is much more likely to take to
journalism, I expect. By the way, have you had time to
do anything with that English story you promised to translate for us?

Petra. No, not yet; but you shall have it in good time.

[DR. STOCKMANN *comes in from his room with an
open letter in his hand.*

Dr. Stockmann (waving the letter). Well, now the town
vill have something new to talk about, I can tell you!

Billing. Something new?

Mrs. Stockmann. What is this?

Dr. Stockmann. A great discovery, Katherine.

Hovestad. Really?

Mrs. Stockmann. A discovery of yours?

Dr. Stockmann. A discovery of mine. *(Walks up and
down.)* Just let them come saying, as usual, that it is all
fancy and a crazy man's imagination! But they will be
careful what they say this time, I can tell you!

Petra. But, father, tell us what it is.

Dr. Stockmann. Yes, yes—only give me time, and you
shall know all about it. If only I had Peter here now!
It just shows how we men can go about forming our judg-
ments, when in reality we are as blind as any moles——

Hovstad. What are you driving at, Doctor?

Dr. Stockmann (standing still by the table). Isn't it the
universal opinion that our town is a healthy spot?

Hovstad. Certainly.

Dr. Stockmann. Quite an unusually healthy spot, in
fact—a place that deserves to be recommended in the
warmest possible manner either for invalids or for people
who are well——

Mrs. Stockmann. Yes, but my dear Thomas——

Dr. Stockmann. And we have been recommending it and praising it—I have written and written, both in the "Messenger" and in pamphlets——

Hovstad. Well, what then?

Dr. Stockmann. And the Baths—we have called them the "main artery of the town's life-blood," the "nerve-centre of our town," and the devil knows what else——

Billing. "The town's pulsating heart" was the expression I once used on an important occasion——

Dr. Stockmann. Quite so. Well, do you know what they really are, these great, splendid, much praised Baths, that have cost so much money—do you know what they are?

Hovstad. No, what are they?

Mrs. Stockmann. Yes, what are they?

Dr. Stockmann. The whole place is a pesthouse!

Petra. The Baths, father?

Mrs. Stockmann (at the same time). Our Baths!

Hovstad. But, Doctor——

Billing. Absolutely incredible!

Dr. Stockmann. The whole Bath establishment is a whited, poisoned sepulchre, I tell you—the gravest possible danger to the public health! All the nastiness up at Mölledal, all that stinking filth, is infecting the water in the conduit-pipes leading to the reservoir; and the same cursed, filthy poison oozes out on the shore too——

Horster. Where the bathing-place is?

Dr. Stockmann. Just there.

Hovstad. How do you come to be so certain of all this, Doctor?

Dr. Stockmann. I have investigated the matter most conscientiously. For a long time past I have suspected something of the kind. Last year we had some very strange cases of illness among the visitors—typhoid cases, and cases of gastric fever——

Mrs. Stockmann. Yes, that is quite true.

Dr. Stockmann. At the time, we supposed the visitors had been infected before they came; but later on, in the winter, I began to have a different opinion; and so I set myself to examine the water, as well as I could.

Mrs. Stockmann. Then that is what you have been so busy with?

Dr. Stockmann. Indeed I have been busy, Katherine. But here I had none of the necessary scientific apparatus; so I sent samples, both of the drinking-water and of the sea-water, up to the University, to have an accurate analysis made by a chemist.

Hovstad. And have you got that?

Dr. Stockmann (showing him the letter). Here it is! It proves the presence of decomposing organic matter in the water—it is full of infusoria. The water is absolutely dangerous to use, either internally or externally.

Mrs. Stockmann. What a mercy you discovered it in time.

Dr. Stockmann. You may well say so.

Hovstad. And what do you propose to do now, Doctor?

Dr. Stockmann. To see the matter put right—naturally.

Hovstad. Can that be done?

Dr. Stockmann. It must be done. Otherwise the Baths will be absolutely useless and wasted. But we need not anticipate that; I have a very clear idea what we shall have to do.

Mrs. Stockmann. But why have you kept this all so secret, dear?

Dr. Stockmann. Do you suppose I was going to run about the town gossiping about it, before I had absolute proof? No, thank you. I am not such a fool.

Petra. Still, you might have told us——

Dr. Stockmann. Not a living soul. But to-morrow you may run round to the old Badger——

Mrs. Stockmann. Oh, Thomas! Thomas!

Dr. Stockmann. Well, to your grandfather, then. The

old boy will have something to be astonished at! I know he thinks I am cracked—and there are lots of other people think so too, I have noticed. But now these good folks shall see—they shall just see——! *(Walks about, rubbing his hands.)* There will be a nice upset in the town, Katherine; you can't imagine what it will be. All the conduit-pipes will have to be relaid.

Hovstad (getting up). All the conduit-pipes——?

Dr. Stockmann. Yes, of course. The intake is too low down; it will have to be lifted to a position much higher up.

Petra. Then you were right after all.

Dr. Stockmann. Ah, you remember, Petra—I wrote opposing the plans before the work was begun. But at that time no one would listen to me. Well, I am going to let them have it, now! Of course I have prepared a report for the Baths Committee; I have had it ready for a week, and was only waiting for this to come. *(Shows the letter.)* Now it shall go off at once. *(Goes into his room and comes back with some papers.)* Look at that! Four closely written sheets!—and the letter shall go with them. Give me a bit of paper, Katherine—something to wrap them up in. That will do! Now give it to—to—*(stamps his foot)*—what the deuce is her name?—give it to the maid, and tell her to take it at once to the Mayor.

[MRS. STOCKMAN *takes the packet and goes out through the dining-room.*

Petra. What do you think uncle Peter will say, father?

Dr. Stockmann. What is there for him to say? I should think he would be very glad that such an important truth has been brought to light.

Hovstad. Will you let me print a short note about your discovery in the "Messenger?"

Dr. Stockmann. I shall be very much obliged if you will.

Hovstad. It is very desirable that the public should be informed of it without delay.

Dr. Stockmann. Certainly.

Mrs. Stockmann (coming back). She has just gone with it.

Billing. Upon my soul, Doctor, you are going to be the foremost man in the town!

Dr. Stockmann (walking about happily). Nonsense! As a matter of fact I have done nothing more than my duty. I have only made a lucky find—that's all. Still, all the same——

Billing. Hovstad, don't you think the town ought to give Dr. Stockmann some sort of testimonial?

Hovstad. I will suggest it, anyway.

Billing. And I will speak to Aslaksen about it.

Dr. Stockmann. No, my good friends, don't let us have any of that nonsense. I won't hear of anything of the kind. And if the Baths Committee should think of voting me an increase of salary, I will not accept it. Do you hear, Katherine?—I won't accept it.

Mrs. Stockmann. You are quite right, Thomas.

Petra (lifting her glass). Your health, father!

Hovstad and Billing. Your health, Doctor! Good health!

Horster (touches glasses with Dr. Stockmann*).* I hope it will bring you nothing but good luck.

Dr. Stockmann. Thank you, thank you, my dear fellows! I feel tremendously happy! It is a splendid thing for a man to be able to feel that he has done a service to his native town and to his fellow-citizens. Hurrah, Katherine!

> [*He puts his arms round her and whirls her round
> and round, while she protests with laughing
> cries. They all laugh, clap their hands and
> cheer the* Doctor. *The boys put their heads in
> at the door to see what is going on.*

ACT II

SCENE.—*The same. The door into the dining-room is shut. It is morning.* MRS. STOCKMANN, *with a sealed letter in her hand, comes in from the dining-room, goes to the door of the* DOCTOR'S *study and peeps in.*

Mrs. Stockmann. Are you in, Thomas?

Dr. Stockmann (from within his room). Yes, I have just come in. *(Comes into the room.)* What is it?

Mrs. Stockmann. A letter from your brother.

Dr. Stockmann. Aha, let us see! *(Opens the letter and reads:)* "I return herewith the manuscript you sent me"— *(reads on in a low murmur)* Hm!——

Mrs. Stockmann. What does he say?

Dr. Stockmann (putting the papers in his pocket). Oh, he only writes that he will come up here himself about midday.

Mrs. Stockmann. Well, try and remember to be at home this time.

Dr. Stockmann. That will be all right; I have got through all my morning visits.

Mrs. Stockmann. I am extremely curious to know how he takes it.

Dr. Stockmann. You will see he won't like it's having been I, and not he, that made the discovery.

Mrs. Stockmann. Aren't you a little nervous about that?

Dr. Stockmann. Oh, he really will be pleased enough, you know. But, at the same time, Peter is so confoundedly afraid of anyone's doing any service to the town except himself.

Mrs. Stockmann. I will tell you what, Thomas—you should be good-natured, and share the credit of this with him. Couldn't you make out that it was he who set you on the scent of this discovery?

Dr. Stockmann. I am quite willing. If only I can get the thing set right. I——

[MORTEN KIIL *puts his head in through the door leading from the hall, looks round in an enquiring manner and chuckles.*

Morten Kiil (slyly). Is it—is it true?

Mrs. Stockmann (going to the door). Father!—is it you?

Dr. Stockmann. Ah, Mr. Kiil—good morning, good morning!

Mrs. Stockmann. But come along in.

Morten Kiil. If it is true, I will; if not, I am off.

Dr. Stockmann. If what is true?

Morten Kiil. This tale about the water-supply. Is it true?

Dr. Stockmann. Certainly it is true. But how did you come to hear it?

Morten Kiil (coming in). Petra ran in on her way to the school——

Dr. Stockmann. Did she?

Morten Kiil. Yes; and she declares that——. I thought she was only making a fool of me, but it isn't like Petra to do that.

Dr. Stockmann. Of course not. How could you imagine such a thing!

Morten Kiil. Oh well, it is better never to trust anybody; you may find you have been made a fool of before you know where you are. But it is really true, all the same?

Dr. Stockmann. You can depend upon it that it is true. Won't you sit down? *(Settles him on the couch.)* Isn't it a real bit of luck for the town——

Morten Kiil (suppressing his laughter). A bit of luck for the town?

Dr. Stockmann. Yes, that I made the discovery in good time.

Morten Kiil (as before). Yes, yes, yes!—But I should never have thought you the sort of man to pull your own brother's leg like this!

Dr. Stockmann. Pull his leg!

Mrs. Stockmann. Really, father dear——

Morten Kiil (resting his hands and his chin on the handle of his stick and winking slyly at the Doctor*).* Let me see, what was the story? Some kind of beast that had got into the water-pipes, wasn't it?

Dr. Stockmann. Infusoria—yes.

Morten Kiil. And a lot of these beasts had got in, according to Petra—a tremendous lot.

Dr. Stockmann. Certainly; hundreds of thousands of them, probably.

Morten Kiil. But no one can see them—isn't that so?

Dr. Stockmann. Yes; you can't see them.

Morten Kiil (with a quiet chuckle.). Damme—it's the finest story I have ever heard!

Dr. Stockmann. What do you mean?

Morten Kiil. But you will never get the Mayor to believe a thing like that.

Dr. Stockmann. We shall see.

Morten Kiil. Do you think he will be fool enough to——?

Dr. Stockmann. I hope the whole town will be fools enough.

Morten Kiil. The whole town! Well, it wouldn't be a bad thing. It would just serve them right, and teach them a lesson. They think themselves so much cleverer than we old fellows. They hounded me out of the council; they did, I tell you—they hounded me out. Now they shall pay for it. You pull their legs too, Thomas!

Dr. Stockmann. Really, I——

Morten Kiil. You pull their legs! *(Gets up.)* If you can work it so that the Mayor and his friends all swallow the same bait, I will give ten pounds to a charity—like a shot!

Dr. Stockmann. That is very kind of you.

Morten Kiil. Yes, I haven't got much money to throw away, I can tell you; but if you can work this, I will give five pounds to a charity at Christmas.

[HOVSTAD *comes in by the hall door.*

Hovstad. Good morning! *(Stops.)* Oh, I beg your pardon——

Dr. Stockmann. Not at all; come in.

Morten Kiil (with another chuckle). Oho!—is he in this too?

Hovstad. What do you mean?

Dr. Stockmann. Certainly he is.

Morten Kiil. I might have known it! It must get into the papers. You know how to do it, Thomas! Set your wits to work. Now I must go.

Dr. Stockmann. Won't you stay a little while?

Morten Kiil. No, I must be off now. You keep up this game for all it is worth; you won't repent it, I'm damned if you will!

[*He goes out;* MRS. STOCKMANN *follows him into the hall.*

Dr. Stockmann (laughing). Just imagine—the old chap doesn't believe a word of all this about the water-supply.

Hovstad. Oh that was it, then?

Dr. Stockmann. Yes, that was what we were talking about. Perhaps it is the same thing that brings you here?

Hovstad. Yes, it is. Can you spare me a few minutes, Doctor?

Dr. Stockmann. As long as you like, my dear fellow.

Hovstad. Have you heard from the Mayor yet?

Dr. Stockmann. Not yet. He is coming here later.

Hovstad. I have given the matter a great deal of thought since last night.

Dr. Stockmann. Well?

Hovstad. From your point of view, as a doctor and a man of science, this affair of the water-supply is an isolated matter. I mean, you do not realise that it involves a great many other things.

Dr. Stockmann. How, do you mean?—Let us sit down, my dear fellow. No, sit here on the couch. (HOVSTAD *sits down on the couch,* DR. STOCKMANN *on a chair on the other side of the table.*) Now then. You mean that——?

Hovstad. You said yesterday that the pollution of the water was due to impurities in the soil.

Dr. Stockmann. Yes, unquestionably it is due to that poisonous morass up at Mölledal.

Hovstad. Begging your pardon, doctor, I fancy it is due to quite another morass altogether.

Dr. Stockmann. What morass?

Hovstad. The morass that the whole life of our town is built on and is rotting in.

Dr. Stockmann. What the deuce are you driving at, Hovstad?

Hovstad. The whole of the town's interests have, little by little, got into the hands of a pack of officials.

Dr. Stockmann. Oh, come!—they are not all officials.

Hovstad. No, but those that are not officials are at any rate the officials' friends and adherents; it is the wealthy folk, the old families in the town, that have got us entirely in their hands.

Dr. Stockmann. Yes, but after all they are men of ability and knowledge.

Hovstad. Did they show any ability or knowledge when they laid the conduit-pipes where they are now?

Dr. Stockmann. No, of course that was a great piece of

stupidity on their part. But that is going to be set right now.

Hovstad. Do you think that will be all such plain sailing?

Dr. Stockmann. Plain sailing or no, it has got to be done, anyway.

Hovstad. Yes, provided the press takes up the question.

Dr. Stockmann. I don't think that will be necessary, my dear fellow, I am certain my brother——

Hovstad. Excuse me, doctor; I feel bound to tell you I am inclined to take the matter up.

Dr. Stockmann. In the paper?

Hovstad. Yes. When I took over the "People's Messenger" my idea was to break up this ring of self-opinionated old fossils who had got hold of all the influence.

Dr. Stockmann. But you know you told me yourself what the result had been; you nearly ruined your paper.

Hovstad. Yes, at the time we were obliged to climb down a peg or two, it is quite true; because there was a danger of the whole project of the Baths coming to nothing if they failed us. But now the scheme has been carried through, and we can dispense with these grand gentlemen.

Dr. Stockmann. Dispense with them, yes; but we owe them a great debt of gratitude.

Hovstad. That shall be recognised ungrudgingly. But a journalist of my democratic tendencies cannot let such an opportunity as this slip. The bubble of official infallibility must be pricked. This superstition must be destroyed, like any other.

Dr. Stockmann. I am whole-heartedly with you in that, Mr. Hovstad; if it is a superstition, away with it!

Hovstad. I should be very reluctant to bring the Mayor into it, because he is your brother. But I am sure you will agree with me that truth should be the first consideration.

Dr. Stockmann. That goes without saying. *(With sudden emphasis.)* Yes, but—but——

Hovstad. You must not misjudge me. I am neither more self-interested nor more ambitious than most men.

Dr. Stockmann. My dear fellow—who suggests anything of the kind?

Hovstad. I am of humble origin, as you know; and that has given me opportunities of knowing what is the most crying need in the humbler ranks of life. It is that they should be allowed some part in the direction of public affairs, Doctor. That is what will develop their faculties and intelligence and self-respect——

Dr. Stockmann. I quite appreciate that.

Hovstad. Yes—and in my opinion a journalist incurs a heavy responsibility if he neglects a favourable opportunity of emancipating the masses—the humble and oppressed. I know well enough that in exalted circles I shall be called an agitator, and all that sort of thing; but they may call what they like. If only my conscience doesn't reproach me, then

———

Dr. Stockmann. Quite right! Quite right, Mr. Hovstad. But all the same—devil take it! *(A knock is heard at the door.)* Come in!

[ASLAKSEN *appears at the door. He is poorly but decently dressed, in black, with a slightly crumpled white neckcloth; he wears gloves and has a felt hat in his hand.*

Aslaksen (bowing). Excuse my taking the liberty, Doctor——

Dr. Stockmann (getting up). Ah, it is you, Aslaksen!

Aslaksen. Yes, Doctor.

Hovstad (standing up). Is it me you want, Aslaksen?

Aslaksen. No; I didn't know I should find you here. No, it was the Doctor I——

Dr. Stockmann. I am quite at your service. What is it?

Aslaksen. Is what I heard from Mr. Billing true, sir—that you mean to improve our water-supply?

Dr. Stockmann. Yes, for the Baths.

Aslaksen. Quite so, I understand. Well, I have come to say that I will back that up by every means in my power.

Hovstad (to the DOCTOR). You see!

Dr. Stockmann. I shall be very grateful to you, but——

Aslaksen. Because it may be no bad thing to have us small tradesmen at your back. We form, as it were, a compact majority in the town—if we choose. And it is always a good thing to have the majority with you, Doctor.

Dr. Stockmann. That is undeniably true; but I confess I don't see why such unusual precautions should be necessary in this case. It seems to me that such a plain, straight-forward thing——

Aslaksen. Oh, it may be very desirable, all the same. I know our local authorities so well; officials are not generally very ready to act on proposals that come from other people. That is why I think it would not be at all amiss if we made a little demonstration.

Hovstad. That's right.

Dr. Stockmann. Demonstration, did you say? What on earth are you going to make a demonstration about?

Aslaksen. We shall proceed with the greatest moderation, Doctor. Moderation is always my aim; it is the greatest virtue in a citizen—at least, I think so.

Dr. Stockmann. It is well known to be a characteristic of yours, Mr. Aslaksen.

Aslaksen. Yes, I think I may pride myself on that. And this matter of the water-supply is of the greatest importance to us small tradesmen. The Baths promise to be a regular gold-mine for the town. We shall all make our living out of them, especially those of us who are householders. That is why we will back up the project as strongly as possible. And as I am at present Chairman of the Householders' Association——

Dr. Stockmann. Yes——?

Aslaksen. And, what is more, local secretary of the Temperance Society—you know, sir, I suppose, that I am a worker in the temperance cause?

Dr. Stockmann. Of course, of course.

Aslaksen. Well, you can understand that I come into contact with a great many people. And as I have the reputation of a temperate and law-abiding citizen—like yourself, Doctor—I have a certain influence in the town, a little bit of power, if I may be allowed to say so.

Dr. Stockmann. I know that quite well, Mr. Aslaksen.

Aslaksen. So you see it would be an easy matter for me to set on foot some testimonial, if necessary.

Dr. Stockmann. A testimonial?

Aslaksen. Yes, some kind of an address of thanks from the townsmen for your share in a matter of such importance to the community. I need scarcely say that it would have to be drawn up with the greatest regard to moderation, so as not to offend the authorities—who, after all, have the reins in their hands. If we pay strict attention to that, no one can take it amiss, I should think!

Hovstad. Well, and even supposing they didn't like it——

Aslaksen. No, no, no; there must be no discourtesy to the authorities, Mr. Hovstad. It is no use falling foul of those upon whom our welfare so closely depends. I have done that in my time, and no good ever comes of it. But no one can take exception to a reasonable and frank expression of a citizen's views.

Dr. Stockmann (shaking him by the hand). I can't tell you, dear Mr. Aslaksen, how extremely pleased I am to find such hearty support among my fellow-citizens. I am de lighted—delighted! Now, you will take a small glass of sherry, eh?

Aslaksen. No, thank you; I never drink alcohol of that kind.

Dr. Stockmann. Well, what do you say to a glass of beer, then?

Aslaksen. Nor that either, thank you, Doctor. I never drink anything as early as this. I am going into town now to talk this over with one or two householders, and prepare the ground.

Dr. Stockmann. It is tremendously kind of you, Mr. Aslaksen; but I really cannot understand the necessity for all these precautions. It seems to me that the thing should go of itself.

Aslaksen. The authorities are somewhat slow to move, Doctor. Far be it from me to seem to blame them——

Hovstad. We are going to stir them up in the paper to-morrow, Aslaksen.

Aslaksen. But not violently, I trust, Mr. Hovstad. Proceed with moderation, or you will do nothing with them. You may take my advice; I have gathered my experience in the school of life. Well, I must say good-bye, Doctor. You know now that we small tradesmen are at your back at all events, like a solid wall. You have the compact majority on your side, Doctor.

Dr. Stockmann. I am very much obliged, dear Mr. Aslaksen. *(Shakes hands with him.)* Good-bye, good-bye.

Aslaksen Are you going my way, towards the printing-office, Mr. Hovstad?

Hovstad. I will come later; I have something to settle up first.

Aslaksen. Very well.

[*Bows and goes out;* STOCKMANN *follows him into the hall.*

Hovstad (as STOCKMANN *comes in again).* Well, what do you think of that, Doctor? Don't you think it is high time we stirred a little life into all this slackness and vacillation and cowardice?

Dr. Stockmann. Are you referring to Aslaksen?

Hovstad. Yes, I am. He is one of those who are floundering in a bog—decent enough fellow though he may be, otherwise. And most of the people here are in just the same case—see-sawing and edging first to one side and then to the other, so overcome with caution and scruple that they never dare to take any decided step.

Dr. Stockmann. Yes, but Aslaksen seemed to me so thoroughly well-intentioned.

Hovstad. There is one thing I esteem higher than that; and that is for a man to be self-reliant and sure of himself.

Dr. Stockmann. I think you are perfectly right there.

Hovstad. That is why I want to seize this opportunity, and try if I cannot manage to put a little virility into these well-intentioned people for once. The idol of Authority must be shattered in this town. This gross and inexcusable blunder about the water-supply must be brought home to the mind of every municipal voter.

Dr. Stockmann. Very well; if you are of opinion that it is for the good of the community, so be it. But not until I have had a talk with my brother.

Hovstad. Anyway, I will get a leading article ready; and if the Mayor refuses to take the matter up——

Dr. Stockmann. How can you suppose such a thing possible?

Hovstad. It is conceivable. And in that case——

Dr. Stockmann. In that case I promise you——. Look here, in that case you may print my report—every word of it.

Hovstad. May I? Have I your word for it?

Dr. Stockmann (giving him the MS.). Here it is; take it with you. It can do no harm for you to read it through, and you can give it me back later on.

Hovstad. Good, good! That is what I will do. And now good-bye, Doctor.

Dr. Stockmann. Good-bye, good-bye. You will see everything will run quite smoothly, Mr. Hovstad—quite smoothly.

Hovstad. Hm!—we shall see.   [*Bows and goes out.*

Dr. Stockmann (opens the dining-room door and looks in). Katherine!   Oh, you are back, Petra?

Petra (coming in).   Yes, I have just come from the school.

Mrs. Stockmann (coming in).   Has he not been here yet?

Dr. Stockmann.   Peter?   No.   But I have had a long talk with Hovstad.   He is quite excited about my discovery. I find it has a much wider bearing than I at first imagined. And he has put his paper at my disposal if necessity should arise.

Mrs. Stockmann.   Do you think it will?

Dr. Stockmann.   Not for a moment.   But at all events it makes me feel proud to know that I have the liberal-minded independent press on my side.   Yes, and—just imagine—I have had a visit from the Chairman of the Householders' Association!

Mrs. Stockmann.   Oh!   What did he want?

Dr. Stockmann.   To offer me his support too.   They will support me in a body if it should be necessary.   Katherine —do you know what I have got behind me?

Mrs. Stockmann.   Behind you?   No, what have you got behind you?

Dr. Stockmann.   The compact majority.

Mrs. Stockmann.   Really?   Is that a good thing for you, Thomas?

Dr. Stockmann.   I should think it was a good thing. *(Walks up and down rubbing his hands.)*   By Jove, it's a fine thing to feel this bond of brotherhood between oneself and one's fellow-citizens!

Petra.   And to be able to do so much that is good and useful, father!

Dr. Stockmann.   And for one's own native town into the bargain, my child!

Mrs. Stockmann.   That was a ring at the bell.

Dr. Stockmann.   It must be he, then.   *(A knock is heard at the door.)*   Come in!

Peter Stockmann (comes in from the hall).   Good morning.

Dr. Stockmann.   Glad to see you, Peter!

Mrs. Stockmann.   Good morning, Peter. How are you?

Peter Stockmann.   So so, thank you. *(To* Dr. Stockmann.)*   I received from you yesterday, after office-hours, a report dealing with the condition of the water at the Baths.

Dr. Stockmann.   Yes. Have you read it?

Peter Stockmann.   Yes, I have.

Dr. Stockmann.   And what have you to say to it?

Peter Stockmann (with a sidelong glance).   Hm!——

Mrs. Stockmann.   Come along, Petra.

[*She and* Petra *go into the room on the left.*

Peter Stockmann (after a pause).   Was it necessary to make all these investigations behind my back?

Dr. Stockmann.   Yes, because until I was absolutely certain about it——

Peter Stockmann.   Then you mean that you are absolutely certain now?

Dr. Stockmann.   Surely you are convinced of that.

Peter Stockmann.   Is it your intention to bring this document before the Baths Committee as a sort of official communication?

Dr. Stockmann.   Certainly. Something must be done in the matter—and that quickly.

Peter Stockmann.   As usual, you employ violent expressions in your report. You say, amongst other things, that what we offer visitors in our Baths is a permanent supply of poison.

Dr. Stockmann.   Well, can you describe it any other way, Peter? Just think—water that is poisonous, whether you drink it or bathe in it! And this we offer to the poor sick folk who come to us trustfully and pay us at an exorbitant rate to be made well again!

Peter Stockmann.   And your reasoning leads you to this conclusion, that we must build a sewer to draw off the alleged impurities from Mölledal and must relay the water-conduits.

Dr. Stockmann. Yes. Do you see any other way out of it? I don't.

Peter Stockmann. I made a pretext this morning to go and see the town engineer, and, as if only half seriously, broached the subject of these proposals as a thing we might perhaps have to take under consideration some time later on.

Dr. Stockmann. Some time later on!

Peter Stockmann. He smiled at what he considered to be my extravagance, naturally. Have you taken the trouble to consider what your proposed alterations would cost? According to the information I obtained, the expenses would probably mount up to fifteen or twenty thousand pounds.

Dr. Stockmann. Would it cost so much?

Peter Stockmann. Yes; and the worst part of it would be that the work would take at least two years.

Dr. Stockmann. Two years? Two whole years?

Peter Stockmann. At least. And what are we to do with the Baths in the meantime? Close them? Indeed we should be obliged to. And do you suppose any one would come near the place after it had got about that the water was dangerous?

Dr. Stockmann. Yes, but, Peter, that is what it is.

Peter Stockmann. And all this at this juncture—just as the Baths are beginning to be known. There are other towns in the neighbourhood with qualifications to attract visitors for bathing purposes. Don't you suppose they would immediately strain every nerve to divert the entire stream of strangers to themselves? Unquestionably they would; and then where should we be? We should probably have to abandon the whole thing, which has cost us so much money—and then you would have ruined your native town.

Dr. Stockmann. I—should have ruined——!

Peter Stockmann. It is simply and solely through the

Baths that the town has before it any future worth mentioning. You know that just as well as I.

Dr. Stockmann. But what do you think ought to be done, then?

Peter Stockmann. Your report has not convinced me that the condition of the water at the Baths is as bad as you represent it to be.

Dr. Stockmann. I tell you it is even worse!—or at all events it will be in summer, when the warm weather comes.

Peter Stockmann. As I said, I believe you exaggerate the matter considerably. A capable physician ought to know what measures to take—he ought to be capable of preventing injurious influences or of remedying them if they become obviously persistent.

Dr. Stockmann. Well? What more?

Peter Stockmann. The water-supply for the Baths is now an established fact, and in consequence must be treated as such. But probably the Committee, at its discretion, will not be disinclined to consider the question of how far it might be possible to introduce certain improvements consistently with a reasonable expenditure.

Dr. Stockmann. And do you suppose that I will have anything to do with such a piece of trickery as that?

Peter Stockmann. Trickery!!

Dr. Stockmann. Yes, it would be a trick—a fraud, a lie, a downright crime towards the public, towards the whole community!

Peter Stockmann. I have not, as I remarked before, been able to convince myself that there is actually any imminent danger.

Dr. Stockmann. You have! It is impossible that you should not be convinced. I know I have represented the facts absolutely truthfully and fairly. And you know it very well, Peter, only you won't acknowledge it. It was owing to your action that both the Baths and the water-conduits were built where they are; and that is what you won't acknowledge—that damnable blunder of yours. Pooh!—do you suppose I don't see through you?

Peter Stockmann. And even if that were true? If I perhaps guard my reputation somewhat anxiously, it is in the interests of the town. Without moral authority I am powerless to direct public affairs as seems, to my judgment, to be best for the common good. And on that account—and for various other reasons, too—it appears to me to be a matter of importance that your report should not be delivered to the Committee. In the interests of the public, you must withhold it. Then, later on, I will raise the question and we will do our best, privately; but nothing of this unfortunate affair—not a single word of it—must come to the ears of the public.

Dr. Stockmann. I am afraid you will not be able to prevent that now, my dear Peter.

Peter Stockmann. It must and shall be prevented.

Dr. Stockmann. It is no use, I tell you. There are too many people that know about it.

Peter Stockmann. That know about it? Who? Surely you don't mean those fellows on the "People's Messenger"?

Dr. Stockmann. Yes, they know. The liberal-minded independent press is going to see that you do your duty.

Peter Stockmann (after a short pause). You are an extraordinarily independent man, Thomas. Have you given no thought to the consequences this may have for yourself?

Dr. Stockmann. Consequences?—for me?

Peter Stockmann. For you and yours, yes.

Dr. Stockmann. What the deuce do you mean?

Peter Stockmann. I believe I have always behaved in a brotherly way to you—have always been ready to oblige or to help you?

Dr. Stockmann. Yes, you have, and I am grateful to you for it.

Peter Stockmann. There is no need. Indeed, to some

extent I was forced to do so—for my own sake. I always hoped that, if I helped to improve your financial position, I should be able to keep some check on you.

Dr. Stockmann. What!! Then it was only for your own sake——!

Peter Stockmann. Up to a certain point, yes. It is painful for a man in an official position to have his nearest relative compromising himself time after time.

Dr. Stockmann. And do you consider that I do that?

Peter Stockmann. Yes, unfortunately, you do, without even being aware of it. You have a restless, pugnacious, rebellious disposition. And then there is that disastrous propensity of yours to want to write about every sort of possible and impossible thing. The moment an idea comes into your head, you must needs go and write a newspaper article or a whole pamphlet about it.

Dr. Stockmann. Well, but is it not the duty of a citizen to let the public share in any new ideas he may have?

Peter Stockmann. Oh, the public doesn't require any new ideas. The public is best served by the good, old-established ideas it already has.

Dr. Stockmann. And that is your honest opinion?

Peter Stockmann. Yes, and for once I must talk frankly to you. Hitherto I have tried to avoid doing so, because I know how irritable you are; but now I must tell you the truth, Thomas. You have no conception what an amount of harm you do yourself by your impetuosity. You complain of the authorities, you even complain of the government—you are always pulling them to pieces; you insist that you have been neglected and persecuted. But what else can such a cantankerous man as you expect?

Dr. Stockmann. What next! Cantankerous, am I?

Peter Stockmann. Yes, Thomas, you are an extremely cantankerous man to work with—I know that to my cost. You disregard everything that you ought to have consideration for. You seem completely to forget that it is me you have to thank for your appointment here as medical officer to the Baths——

Dr. Stockmann. I was entitled to it as a matter of course!—I and nobody else! I was the first person to see that the town could be made into a flourishing watering-place, and I was the only one who saw it at that time. I had to fight single-handed in support of the idea for many years; and I wrote and wrote——

Peter Stockmann. Undoubtedly. But things were not ripe for the scheme then—though, of course, you could not judge of that in your out-of-the-way corner up north. But as soon as the opportune moment came I—and the others—took the matter into our hands——

Dr. Stockmann. Yes, and made this mess of all my beautiful plan. It is pretty obvious now what clever fellows you were!

Peter Stockmann. To my mind the whole thing only seems to mean that you are seeking another outlet for your combativeness. You want to pick a quarrel with your superiors—an old habit of yours. You cannot put up with any authority over you. You look askance at anyone who occupies a superior official position; you regard him as a personal enemy, and then any stick is good enough to beat him with. But now I have called your attention to the fact that the town's interests are at stake—and, incidentally, my own too. And therefore I must tell you, Thomas, that you will find me inexorable with regard to what I am about to require you to do.

Dr. Stockmann. And what is that?

Peter Stockmann. As you have been so indiscreet as to speak of this delicate matter to outsiders, despite the fact that you ought to have treated it as entirely official and confidential, it is obviously impossible to hush it up now. All sorts of rumours will get about directly, and everybody who has a grudge against us will take care to embellish these rumours.   So it will be necessary for you to refute them publicly.

Dr. Stockmann.   I!   How?   I don't understand.

Peter Stockmann.   What we shall expect is that, after making further investigations, you will come to the conclusion that the matter is not by any means as dangerous or as critical as you imagined in the first instance.

Dr. Stockmann.   Oho!—so that is what you expect!

Peter Stockmann.   And, what is more, we shall expect you to make public profession of your confidence in the Committee and in their readiness to consider fully and conscientiously what steps may be necessary to remedy any possible defects.

Dr. Stockmann.   But you will never be able to do that by patching and tinkering at it—never!   Take my word for it, Peter; I mean what I say, as deliberately and emphatically as possible.

Peter Stockmann.   As an officer under the Committee, you have no right to any individual opinion.

Dr. Stockmann (amazed).   No right?

Peter Stockmann.   In your official capacity, no.   As a private person, it is quite another matter.   But as a subordinate member of the staff of the Baths, you have no right to express any opinion which runs contrary to that of your superiors.

Dr. Stockmann.   This is too much!   I, a doctor, a man of science, have no right to——!

Peter Stockmann.   The matter in hand is not simply a scientific one.   It is a complicated matter, and has its economic as well as its technical side.

Dr. Stockmann.   I don't care what it is!   I intend to be free to express my opinion on any subject under the sun.

Peter Stockmann.   As you please—but not on any subject concerning the Baths.   That we forbid.

Dr. Stockmann (shouting).   You forbid——!   You!   A pack of——

Peter Stockmann. I forbid it—I, your chief; and if I forbid it, you have to obey.

Dr. Stockmann (controlling himself). Peter—if you were not my brother——

Petra (throwing open the door). Father, you shan't stand this!

Mrs. Stockmann (coming in after her). Petra, Petra!

Peter Stockmann. Oh, so you have been eavesdropping.

Mrs. Stockmann. You were talking so loud, we couldn't help——

Petra. Yes, I was listening.

Peter Stockmann. Well, after all, I am very glad——

Dr. Stockmann (going up to him). You were saying something about forbidding and obeying?

Peter Stockmann. You obliged me to take that tone with you.

Dr. Stockmann. And so I am to give myself the lie, publicly?

Peter Stockmann. We consider it absolutely necessary that you should make some such public statement as I have asked for.

Dr. Stockmann. And if I do not—obey?

Peter Stockmann. Then we shall publish a statement ourselves to reassure the public.

Dr. Stockmann. Very well; but in that case I shall use my pen against you. I stick to what I have said; I will show that I am right and that you are wrong. And what will you do then?

Peter Stockmann. Then I shall not be able to prevent your being dismissed.

Dr. Stockmann. What——?

Petra. Father—dismissed!

Mrs. Stockmann. Dismissed!

Peter Stockmann. Dismissed from the staff of the Baths. I shall be obliged to propose that you shall immediately be

given notice, and shall not be allowed any further participa-
tion in the Baths' affairs.

Dr. Stockmann. You would dare to do that!

Peter Stockmann. It is you that are playing the daring
game.

Petra. Uncle, that is a shameful way to treat a man like
father!

Mrs. Stockmann. Do hold your tongue, Petra!

Peter Stockmann (looking at PETRA*).* Oh, so we volun-
teer our opinions already, do we? Of course. *(To* MRS.
STOCKMANN.*)* Katherine, I imagine you are the most sensible person in this house. Use any influence you may have
over your husband, and make him see what this will entail
for his family as well as——

Dr. Stockmann. My family is my own concern and nobody else's!

Peter Stockmann. ——for his own family, as I was saying, as well as for the town he lives in.

Dr. Stockmann. It is I who have the real good of the
town at heart! I want to lay bare the defects that sooner
or later must come to the light of day. I will show whether
I love my native town.

Peter Stockmann. You, who in your blind obstinacy
want to cut off the most important source of the town's welfare?

Dr. Stockmann. The source is poisoned, man! Are you
mad? We are making our living by retailing filth and corruption! The whole of our flourishing municipal life de-
rives its sustenance from a lie!

Peter Stockmann. All imagination—or something even
worse. The man who can throw out such offensive insinua-
tions about his native town must be an enemy of our community.

Dr. Stockmann (going up to him). Do you dare to——!

Mrs. Stockmann (throwing herself between them).
Thomas!

Petra (catching her father by the arm). Don't lose your temper, father!

Peter Stockmann. I will not expose myself to violence. Now you have had a warning; so reflect on what you owe to yourself and your family. Good-bye.   [*Goes out.*

Dr. Stockmann (walking up and down). Am I to put up with such treatment as this? In my own house, Katherine! What do you think of that!

Mrs. Stockmann. Indeed it is both shameful and absurd, Thomas——

Petra. If only I could give uncle a piece of my mind——

Dr. Stockmann. It is my own fault. I ought to have flown out at him long ago!—shown my teeth!—bitten! To hear him call me an enemy to our community! Me! I shall not take that lying down, upon my soul!

Mrs. Stockmann. But, dear Thomas, your brother has power on his side——

Dr. Stockmann. Yes, but I have right on mine, I tell you.

Mrs. Stockmann. Oh yes, right—right. What is the use of having right on your side if you have not got might?

Petra. Oh, mother!—how can you say such a thing!

Dr. Stockmann. Do you imagine that in a free country it is no use having right on your side? You are absurd, Katherine. Besides, haven't I got the liberal-minded, independent press to lead the way, and the compact majority behind me? That is might enough, I should think!

Mrs. Stockmann. But, good heavens, Thomas, you don't mean to——?

Dr. Stockmann. Don't mean to what?

Mrs. Stockmann. To set yourself up in opposition to your brother.

Dr. Stockmann. In God's name, what else do you suppose I should do but take my stand on right and truth?

Petra. Yes, I was just going to say that.

Mrs. Stockmann. But it won't do you any earthly good. If they won't do it, they won't.

Dr. Stockmann. Oho, Katherine! Just give me time, and you will see how I will carry the war into their camp.

Mrs. Stockmann. Yes, you carry the war into their camp, and you get your dismissal—that is what you will do.

Dr. Stockmann. In any case I shall have done my duty towards the public—towards the community. I, who am called its enemy!

Mrs. Stockmann. But towards your family, Thomas? Towards your own home! Do you think that is doing your duty towards those you have to provide for?

Petra. Ah, don't think always first of us, mother.

Mrs. Stockmann. Oh, it is easy for you to talk; you are able to shift for yourself, if need be. But remember the boys, Thomas; and think a little, too, of yourself, and of me——

Dr. Stockmann. I think you are out of your senses, Katherine! If I were to be such a miserable coward as to go on my knees to Peter and his damned crew, do you suppose I should ever know an hour's peace of mind all my life afterwards?

Mrs. Stockmann. I don't know anything about that; but God preserve us from the peace of mind we shall have, all the same, if you go on defying him! You will find yourself again without the means of subsistence, with no income to count upon. I should think we had had enough of that in the old days. Remember that, Thomas; think what that means.

Dr. Stockmann (collecting himself with a struggle and clenching his fists). And this is what this slavery can bring upon a free, honourable man! Isn't it horrible, Katherine?

Mrs. Stockmann. Yes, it is sinful to treat you so, it is perfectly true. But, good heavens, one has to put up with so much injustice in this world.—There are the boys.

Thomas! Look at them! What is to become of them? Oh, no, no, you can never have the heart——.

       [EJLIF *and* MORTEN *have come in while she was speaking, with their school books in their hands.*

Dr. Stockmann. The boys——! (*Recovers himself suddenly.*) No, even if the whole world goes to pieces, I will never bow my neck to this yoke!

       [*Goes towards his room.*

Mrs. Stockmann (*following him*). Thomas—what are you going to do!

Dr. Stockmann (*at his door*). I mean to have the right to look my sons in the face when they are grown men.

       [*Goes into his room.*

Mrs. Stockmann (*bursting into tears*). God help us all!

Petra. Father is splendid! He will not give in.

       [*The boys look on in amazement;* PETRA *signs to them not to speak.*

ACT III

Scene.—*The editorial office of the "People's Messenger."*
*The entrance door is on the left-hand side of the back
wall; on the right-hand side is another door with glass
panels through which the printing-room can be seen.
Another door in the right-hand wall. In the middle of
the room is a large table covered with papers, newspapers and books. In the foreground on the left a window, before which stand a desk and a high stool. There
are a couple of easy chairs by the table, and other chairs
standing along the wall. The room is dingy and uncomfortable; the furniture is old, the chairs stained and
torn. In the printing-room the compositors are seen at
work, and a printer is working a hand-press. Hovstad
is sitting at the desk, writing. Billing comes in from
the right with Dr. Stockmann's manuscript in his
hand.*

Billing. Well, I must say!

Hovstad (still writing). Have you read it through?

Billing (laying the MS. on the desk). Yes, indeed I have

Hovstad. Don't you think the Doctor hits them pretty
hard?

Billing. Hard? Bless my soul, he's crushing! Every
word falls like—how shall I put it?—like the blow of a
sledgehammer.

Hovstad. Yes, but they are not the people to throw up
the sponge at the first blow.

Billing. That is true; and for that reason we must strike
blow upon blow until the whole of this aristocracy tumbles

to pieces.   As I sat in there reading this, I almost seemed to see a revolution in being.

Hovstad (turning round).   Hush!—Speak so that Aslaksen cannot hear you.

Billing (lowering his voice).   Aslaksen is a chicken-hearted chap, a coward; there is nothing of the man in him. But this time you will insist on your own way, won't you? You will put the Doctor's article in?

Hovstad.   Yes, and if the Mayor doesn't like it——

Billing.   That will be the devil of a nuisance.

Hovstad.   Well, fortunately we can turn the situation to good account, whatever happens. If the Mayor will not fall in with the Doctor's project, he will have all the small tradesmen down on him—the whole of the Householders' Association and the rest of them.   And if he does fall in with it, he will fall out with the whole crowd of large shareholders in the Baths, who up to now have been his most valuable supporters——

Billing.   Yes, because they will certainly have to fork out a pretty penny——

Hovstad.   Yes, you may be sure they will.   And in this way the ring will be broken up, you see, and then in every issue of the paper we will enlighten the public on the Mayor's incapability on one point and another, and make it clear that all the positions of trust in the town, the whole control of municipal affairs, ought to be put in the hands of the Liberals.

Billing.   That is perfectly true!   I see it coming—I see it coming; we are on the threshold of a revolution!

[*A knock is heard at the door.*

Hovstad.   Hush!   *(Calls out.)*   Come in!   (DR. STOCKMANN *comes in by the street door.*   HOVSTAD *goes to meet him.)*   Ah, it is you, Doctor!   Well?

Dr. Stockmann.   You may set to work and print it, Mr. Hovstad!

Hovstad.   Has it come to that, then?

Billing. Hurrah!

Dr. Stockmann. Yes, print away. Undoubtedly it has come to that. Now they must take what they get. There is going to be a fight in the town, Mr. Billing!

Billing. War to the knife, I hope! We will get our knives to their throats, Doctor!

Dr. Stockmann. This article is only a beginning. I have already got four or five more sketched out in my head. Where is Aslaksen?

Billing (calls into the printing-room). Aslaksen, just come here for a minute!

Hovstad. Four or five more articles, did you say? On the same subject?

Dr. Stockmann. No—far from it, my dear fellow. No, they are about quite another matter. But they all spring from the question of the water-supply and the drainage. One thing leads to another, you know. It is like beginning to pull down an old house, exactly.

Billing. Upon my soul, it's true; you find you are not done till you have pulled all the old rubbish down.

Aslaksen (coming in). Pulled down? You are not thinking of pulling down the Baths surely, Doctor?

Hovstad. Far from it, don't be afraid.

Dr. Stockmann. No, we meant something quite different. Well, what do you think of my article, Mr. Hovstad?

Hovstad. I think it is simply a masterpiece——

Dr. Stockmann. Do you really think so? Well, I am very pleased, very pleased.

Hovstad. It is so clear and intelligible. One need have no special knowledge to understand the bearing of it. You will have every enlightened man on your side.

Aslaksen. And every prudent man too, I hope?

Billing. The prudent and the imprudent—almost the whole town.

Aslaksen. In that case we may venture to print it.

Dr. Stockmann. I should think so!

Hovstad. We will put it in to-morrow morning.

Dr. Stockmann. Of course—you must not lose a single day. What I wanted to ask you, Mr. Aslaksen, was if you would supervise the printing of it yourself.

Aslaksen. With pleasure.

Dr. Stockmann. Take care of it as if it were a treasure! No misprints—every word is important. I will look in again a little later; perhaps you will be able to let me see a proof. I can't tell you how eager I am to see it in print, and see it burst upon the public——

Billing. Burst upon them—yes, like a flash of lightning!

Dr. Stockmann. ——and to have it submitted to the judgment of my intelligent fellow-townsmen. You cannot imagine what I have gone through to-day. I have been threatened first with one thing and then with another; they have tried to rob me of my most elementary rights as a man——

Billing. What! Your rights as a man!

Dr. Stockmann. ——they have tried to degrade me, to make a coward of me, to force me to put personal interests before my most sacred convictions——

Billing. That is too much—I'm damned if it isn't.

Hovstad. Oh, you mustn't be surprised at anything from that quarter.

Dr. Stockmann. Well, they will get the worst of it with me; they may assure themselves of that. I shall consider the "People's Messenger" my sheet-anchor now, and every single day I will bombard them with one article after another, like bomb-shells——

Aslaksen. Yes, but——

Billing. Hurrah!—it is war, it is war!

Dr. Stockmann. I shall smite them to the ground—I shall crush them—I shall break down all their defences, before the eyes of the honest public! That is what I shall do!

Aslaksen. Yes, but in moderation, Doctor—proceed with moderation——

Billing.   Not a bit of it, not a bit of it!   Don't spare the dynamite!

Dr. Stockmann.   Because it is not merely a question of water-supply and drains now, you know.   No—it is the whole of our social life that we have got to purify and disinfect——

Billing.   Spoken like a deliverer!

Dr. Stockmann.   All the incapables must be turned out, you understand—and that in every walk of life!   Endless vistas have opened themselves to my mind's eye to-day.   I cannot see it all quite clearly yet, but I shall in time. Young and vigorous standard-bearers—those are what we need and must seek, my friends; we must have new men in command at all our outposts.

Billing.   Hear, hear!

Dr. Stockmann.   We only need to stand by one another, and it will all be perfectly easy.   The revolution will be launched like a ship that runs smoothly off the stocks. Don't you think so?

Hovstad.   For my part I think we have now a prospect of getting the municipal authority into the hands where it should lie.

Aslaksen.   And if only we proceed with moderation, I cannot imagine that there will be any risk.

Dr. Stockmann.   Who the devil cares whether there is any risk or not!   What I am doing, I am doing in the name of truth and for the sake of my conscience.

Hovstad.   You are a man who deserves to be supported, Doctor.

Aslaksen.   Yes, there is no denying that the Doctor is a true friend to the town—a real friend to the community, that he is.

Billing.   Take my word for it, Aslaksen, Dr. Stockmann is a friend of the people.

Aslaksen.   I fancy the Householders' Association will make use of that expression before long.

Dr. Stockmann (affected, grasps their hands). Thank you, thank you, my dear staunch friends. It is very refreshing to me to hear you say that; my brother called me something quite different. By Jove, he shall have it back, with interest! But now I must be off to see a poor devil ——. I will come back, as I said. Keep a very careful eye on the manuscript, Aslaksen, and don't for worlds leave out any of my notes of exclamation! Rather put one or two more in! Capital, capital! Well, good-bye for the present—good-bye, good-bye!

[*They show him to the door, and bow him out.*

Hovstad. He may prove an invaluably useful man to us.

Aslaksen. Yes, so long as he confines himself to this matter of the Baths. But if he goes farther afield, I don't think it would be advisable to follow him.

Hovstad. Hm!—that all depends——

Billing. You are so infernally timid, Aslaksen!

Aslaksen. Timid? Yes, when it is a question of the local authorities, I am timid, Mr. Billing; it is a lesson I have learnt in the school of experience, let me tell you. But try me in higher politics, in matters that concern the government itself, and then see if I am timid.

Billing. No, you aren't, I admit. But this is simply contradicting yourself.

Aslaksen. I am a man with a conscience, and that is the whole matter. If you attack the government, you don't do the community any harm, anyway; those fellows pay no attention to attacks, you see—they go on just as they are, in spite of them. But *local* authorities are different; they *can* be turned out, and then perhaps you may get an ignorant lot into office who may do irreparable harm to the householders and everybody else.

Hovstad. But what of the education of citizens by self-government—don't you attach any importance to that?

Aslaksen. When a man has interests of his own to protect, he cannot think of everything, Mr. Hovstad.

Hovstad. Then I hope I shall never have interests of my own to protect!

Billing. Hear, hear!

Aslaksen (with a smile). Hm! *(Points to the desk.)* Mr. Sheriff Stensgaard was your predecessor at that editorial desk.

Billing (spitting). Bah! That turncoat.

Hovstad. I am not a weathercock—and never will be.

Aslaksen. A politician should never be too certain of anything, Mr. Hovstad. And as for you, Mr. Billing, I should think it is time for you to be taking in a reef or two in your sails, seeing that you are applying for the post of secretary to the Bench.

Billing. I——!

Hovstad. Are you, Billing?

Billing. Well, yes—but you must clearly understand I am doing it only to annoy the bigwigs.

Aslaksen. Anyhow, it is no business of mine. But if I am to be accused of timidity and of inconsistency in my principles, this is what I want to point out: my political past is an open book. I have never changed, except perhaps to become a little more moderate, you see. My heart is still with the people; but I don't deny that my reason has a certain bias towards the authorities—the local ones, I mean.

[*Goes into the printing-room.*

Billing. Oughtn't we to try and get rid of him, Hovstad?

Hovstad. Do you know anyone else who will advance the money for our paper and printing bill?

Billing. It is an infernal nuisance that we don't possess some capital to trade on.

Hovstad (sitting down at his desk). Yes, if we only had that, then——

Billing. Suppose you were to apply to Dr. Stockmann?

Hovstad (turning over some papers). What is the use? He has got nothing.

Billing. No, but he has got a warm man in the back·

ground, old Morten Kiil—"the Badger," as they call him.

Hovstad (writing). Are you so sure *he* has got anything?

Billing. Good Lord, of course he has! And some of it must come to the Stockmanns. Most probably he will do something for the children, at all events.

Hovstad (turning half round). Are you counting on that?

Billing. Counting on it? Of course I am not counting on anything.

Hovstad. That is right. And I should not count on the secretaryship to the Bench either, if I were you; for I can assure you—you won't get it.

Billing. Do you think I am not quite aware of that? My object is precisely *not* to get it. A slight of that kind stimulates a man's fighting power—it is like getting a supply of fresh bile—and I am sure one needs that badly enough in a hole-and-corner place like this, where it is so seldom anything happens to stir one up.

Hovstad (writing). Quite so, quite so.

Billing. Ah, I shall be heard of yet!—Now I shall go and write the appeal to the Householders' Association.

[*Goes into the room on the right.*

Hovstad (sitting at his desk, biting his penholder, says slowly). Hm!—that's it, is it? *(A knock is heard.)* Come in! *(PETRA comes in by the outer door.* HOVSTAD *gets up.)* What, you!—here?

Petra. Yes, you must forgive me——

Hovstad (pulling a chair forward). Won't you sit down?

Petra. No, thank you; I must go again in a moment.

Hovstad. Have you come with a message from your father, by any chance?

Petra. No, I have come on my own account. *(Takes a book out of her coat pocket.)* Here is the English story.

Hovstad. Why have you brought it back?

Petra. Because I am not going to translate it.

Hovstad. But you promised me faithfully——

Petra. Yes, but then I had not read it. I don't suppose you have read it either?

Hovstad. No, you know quite well I don't understand English; but——

Petra. Quite so. That is why I wanted to tell you that you must find something else. *(Lays the book on the table.)* You can't use this for the "People's Messenger."

Hovstad. Why not?

Petra. Because it conflicts with all your opinions.

Hovstad. Oh, for that matter——

Petra. You don't understand me. The burden of this story is that there is a supernatural power that looks after the so-called good people in this world and makes everything happen for the best in their case—while all the so-called bad people are punished.

Hovstad. Well, but that is all right. That is just what our readers want.

Petra. And are you going to be the one to give it to them? For myself, I do not believe a word of it. You know quite well that things do not happen so in reality.

Hovstad. You are perfectly right; but an editor cannot always act as he would prefer. He is often obliged to bow to the wishes of the public in unimportant matters. Politics are the most important thing in life—for a newspaper, anyway; and if I want to carry my public with me on the path that leads to liberty and progress, I must not frighten them away. If they find a moral tale of this sort in the serial at the bottom of the page, they will be all the more ready to read what is printed above it; they feel more secure, as it were.

Petra. For shame! You would never go and set a snare like that for your readers; you are not a spider!

Hovstad (smiling). Thank you for having such a good opinion of me. No; as a matter of fact that is Billing's idea and not mine.

Petra. Billing's!

Hovstad. Yes; anyway he propounded that theory here one day. And it is Billing who is so anxious to have that story in the paper; I don't know anything about the book.

Petra. But how can Billing, with his emancipated views——

Hovstad. Oh, Billing is a many-sided man. He is applying for the post of secretary to the Bench, too, I hear.

Petra. I don't believe it, Mr. Hovstad. How could he possibly bring himself to do such a thing?

Hovstad. Ah, you must ask him that.

Petra. I should never have thought it of him.

Hovstad (looking more closely at her). No? Does it really surprise you so much?

Petra. Yes. Or perhaps not altogether. Really, I don't quite know——

Hovstad. We journalists are not much worth, Miss Stockmann.

Petra. Do you really mean that?

Hovstad. I think so sometimes.

Petra. Yes, in the ordinary affairs of everyday life, perhaps; I can understand that. But now, when you have taken a weighty matter in hand——

Hovstad. This matter of your father's, you mean?

Petra. Exactly. It seems to me that now you must feel you are a man worth more than most.

Hovstad. Yes, to-day I do feel something of that sort.

Petra. Of course you do, don't you? It is a splendid vocation you have chosen—to smooth the way for the march of unappreciated truths, and new and courageous lines of thought. If it were nothing more than because you stand fearlessly in the open and take up the cause of an injured man——

Hovstad. Especially when that injured man is—ahem! —I don't rightly know how to——

Petra. When that man is so upright and so honest, you mean?

Hovstad (more gently). Especially when he is your father, I meant.

Petra (suddenly checked). That?

Hovstad. Yes, Petra—Miss Petra.

Petra. Is it *that,* that is first and foremost with you? Not the matter itself? Not the truth?—not my father's big generous heart?

Hovstad. Certainly—of course—that too.

Petra. No, thank you; you have betrayed yourself, Mr. Hovstad, and now I shall never trust you again in anything.

Hovstad. Can you really take it so amiss in me that it is mostly for your sake——?

Petra. What I am angry with you for, is for not having been honest with my father. You talked to him as if the truth and the good of the community were what lay nearest to your heart. You have made fools of both my father and me. You are not the man you made yourself out to be. And that I shall never forgive you—never!

Hovstad. You ought not to speak so bitterly, Miss Petra —least of all now.

Petra. Why not now, especially?

Hovstad. Because your father cannot do without my help.

Petra (looking him up and down). Are you that sort of man too? For shame!

Hovstad. No, no, I am not. This came upon me so unexpectedly—you must believe that.

Petra. I know what to believe. Good-bye.

Aslaksen (coming from the printing-room, hurriedly and with an air of mystery). Damnation, Hovstad!—*(Sees* Petra.*)* Oh, this is awkward——

Petra. There is the book; you must give it to some one else.   [*Goes towards the door.*

Hovstad (following her). But, Miss Stockmann——

Petra. Good-bye.   [*Goes out.*

Aslaksen. I say—Mr. Hovstad——

Hovstad. Well, well!—what is it?

Aslaksen. The Mayor is outside in the printing-room.

Hovstad. The Mayor, did you say?

Aslaksen. Yes, he wants to speak to you. He came in by the back door—didn't want to be seen, you understand.

Hovstad. What can he want? Wait a bit—I will go myself. [*Goes to the door of the printing-room, opens it, bows and invites* PETER STOCKMANN *in.)* Just see, Aslaksen, that no one——

Aslaksen. Quite so.   [*Goes into the printing-room.*

Peter Stockmann. You did not expect to see me here, Mr. Hovstad?

Hovstad. No, I confess I did not.

Peter Stockmann (looking round). You are very snug in here—very nice indeed.

Hovstad. Oh——

Peter Stockmann. And here I come, without any notice, to take up your time!

Hovstad. By all means, Mr. Mayor. I am at your service. But let me relieve you of your—— *(takes* STOCKMANN'S *hat and stick and puts them on a chair).* Won't you sit down?

Peter Stockmann (sitting down by the table). Thank you. (HOVSTAD *sits down.)* I have had an extremely annoying experience to-day, Mr. Hovstad.

Hovstad. Really? Ah well, I expect with all the various business you have to attend to——

Peter Stockmann. The Medical Officer of the Baths is responsible for what happened to-day.

Hovstad. Indeed? The Doctor?

Peter Stockmann. He has addressed a kind of report to the Baths Committee on the subject of certain supposed defects in the Baths.

Hovstad. Has he indeed?

Peter Stockmann. Yes—has he not told you? I thought he said——

Hovstad. Ah, yes—it is true he did mention something about——

Aslaksen (coming from the printing-room). I ought to have that copy——

Hovstad (angrily). Ahem!—there it is on the desk.

Aslaksen (taking it). Right.

Peter Stockmann. But look there—that is the thing I was speaking of!

Aslaksen. Yes, that is the Doctor's article, Mr. Mayor.

Hovstad. Oh, is *that* what you were speaking about?

Peter Stockmann. Yes, that is it. What do you think of it?

Hovstad. Oh, I am only a layman—and I have only taken a very cursory glance at it.

Peter Stockmann. But you are going to print it?

Hovstad. I cannot very well refuse a distinguished man——

Aslaksen. I have nothing to do with editing the paper, Mr. Mayor——

Peter Stockmann. I understand.

Aslaksen. I merely print what is put into my hands.

Peter Stockmann. Quite so.

Aslaksen. And so I must——

[*Moves off towards the printing-room.*

Peter Stockmann. No, but wait a moment, Mr. Aslaksen. You will allow me, Mr. Hovstad?

Hovstad. If you please, Mr. Mayor.

Peter Stockmann. You are a discreet and thoughtful man, Mr. Aslaksen.

Aslaksen. I am delighted to hear you think so, sir.

Peter Stockmann. And a man of very considerable influence.

Aslaksen. Chiefly among the small tradesmen, sir.

Peter Stockmann. The small tax-payers are the majority —here as everywhere else.

Aslaksen. That is true.

Peter Stockmann. And I have no doubt you know the general trend of opinion among them, don't you?

Aslaksen. Yes, I think I may say I do, Mr. Mayor.

Peter Stockmann. Yes. Well, since there is such a praiseworthy spirit of self-sacrifice among the less wealthy citizens of our town——

Aslaksen. What?

Hovstad. Self-sacrifice?

Peter Stockmann. It is pleasing evidence of a public-spirited feeling, extremely pleasing evidence. I might almost say I hardly expected it. But you have a closer knowledge of public opinion than I.

Aslaksen. But, Mr. Mayor——

Peter Stockmann. And indeed it is no small sacrifice that the town is going to make.

Hovstad. The town?

Aslaksen. But I don't understand. Is it the Baths——?

Peter Stockmann. At a provisional estimate, the alterations that the Medical Officer asserts to be desirable will cost somewhere about twenty thousand pounds.

Aslaksen. That is a lot of money, but——

Peter Stockmann. Of course it will be necessary to raise a municipal loan.

Hovstad (getting up). Surely you never mean that the town must pay——?

Aslaksen. Do you mean that it must come out of the municipal funds?—out of the ill-filled pockets of the small tradesmen?

Peter Stockmann. Well, my dear Mr. Aslaksen, where else is the money to come from?

Aslaksen. The gentlemen who own the Baths ought to provide that.

Peter Stockmann. The proprietors of the Baths are not in a position to incur any further expense.

Aslaksen. Is that absolutely certain, Mr. Mayor?

Peter Stockmann. I have satisfied myself that it is so. If the town wants these very extensive alterations, it will have to pay for them.

Aslaksen. But, damn it all—I beg your pardon—this is quite another matter, Mr. Hovstad!

Hovstad. It is, indeed.

Peter Stockmann. The most fatal part of it is that we shall be obliged to shut the Baths for a couple of years.

Hovstad. Shut them? Shut them altogether?

Aslaksen. For two years?

Peter Stockmann. Yes, the work will take as long as that —at least.

Aslaksen. I'm damned if we will stand that, Mr. Mayor! What are we householders to live upon in the meantime?

Peter Stockmann. Unfortunately, that is an extremely difficult question to answer, Mr. Aslaksen. But what would you have us do? Do you suppose we shall have a single visitor in the town, if we go about proclaiming that our water is polluted, that we are living over a plague spot, that the entire town——

Aslaksen. And the whole thing is merely imagination?

Peter Stockmann. With the best will in the world, I have not been able to come to any other conclusion.

Aslaksen. Well then I must say it is absolutely unjustifiable of Dr. Stockmann—I beg your pardon, Mr. Mayor——

Peter Stockmann. What you say is lamentably true, Mr. Aslaksen. My brother has, unfortunately, always been a headstrong man.

Aslaksen. After this, do you mean to give him your support, Mr. Hovstad?

Hovstad. Can you suppose for a moment that I——?

Peter Stockmann. I have drawn up a short *résumé* of the situation as it appears from a reasonable man's point of view. In it I have indicated how certain possible defects might suitably be remedied without outrunning the resources of the Baths Committee.

Hovstad. Have you got it with you, Mr. Mayor?

Peter Stockmann (fumbling in his pocket). Yes, I brought it with me in case you should——

Aslaksen. Good Lord, there he is!

Peter Stockmann. Who? My brother?

Hovstad. Where? Where?

Aslaksen. He has just gone through the printing-room.

Peter Stockmann. How unlucky! I don't want to meet him here, and I had still several things to speak to you about.

Hovstad (pointing to the door on the right). Go in there for the present.

Peter Stockmann. But——?

Hovstad. You will only find Billing in there.

Aslaksen. Quick, quick, Mr. Mayor—he is just coming.

Peter Stockmann. Yes, very well; but see that you get rid of him quickly.

> [*Goes out through the door on the right, which* ASLAKSEN *opens for him and shuts after him.*

Hovstad. Pretend to be doing something, Aslaksen.

> [*Sits down and writes.* ASLAKSEN *begins foraging among a heap of newspapers that are lying on a chair.*

Dr. Stockmann (coming in from the printing-room). Here I am again. [*Puts down his hat and stick.*

Hovstad (writing). Already, Doctor? Hurry up with what we were speaking about, Aslaksen. We are very pressed for time to-day.

Dr. Stockmann (to ASLAKSEN*).* No proof for me to see yet, I hear.

Aslaksen (without turning round). You couldn't expect it yet, Doctor.

Dr. Stockmann. No, no; but I am impatient, as you can understand. I shall not know a moment's peace of mind till I see it in print.

Hovstad. Hm!—it will take a good while yet, won't it, Aslaksen?

Aslaksen. Yes, I am almost afraid it will.

Dr. Stockmann. All right, my dear friends; I will come back. I do not mind coming back twice if necessary. A matter of such great importance—the welfare of the town at stake—it is no time to shirk trouble. *(Is just going, but stops and comes back.)* Look here—there is one thing more I want to speak to you about.

Hovstad. Excuse me, but could it not wait till some other time?

Dr. Stockmann. I can tell you in half a dozen words. It is only this. When my article is read to-morrow and it is realised that I have been quietly working the whole winter for the welfare of the town——

Hovstad. Yes, but, Doctor——

Dr. Stockmann. I know what you are going to say. You don't see how on earth it was any more than my duty —my obvious duty as a citizen. Of course it wasn't; I know that as well as you. But my fellow-citizens, you know——! Good Lord, think of all the good souls who think so highly of me——!

Aslaksen. Yes, our townsfolk have had a very high opinion of you so far, Doctor.

Dr. Stockmann. Yes, and that is just why I am afraid they——. Well, this is the point; when this reaches them, especially the poorer classes, and sounds in their ears like a summons to take the town's affairs into their own hands for the future——

Hovstad (getting up). Ahem! Doctor, I won't conceal from you the fact——

Dr. Stockmann. Ah!—I knew there was something in

the wind! . But I won't hear a word of it. If anything of that sort is being set on foot——

Hovstad. Of what sort?

Dr. Stockmann. Well, whatever it is—whether it is a demonstration in my honour, or a banquet, or a subscription list for some presentation to me—whatever it is, you must promise me solemnly and faithfully to put a stop to it. You too, Mr. Aslaksen; do you understand?

Hovstad. You must forgive me, Doctor, but sooner or later we must tell you the plain truth——

[*He is interrupted by the entrance of* MRS. STOCK-MANN, *who comes in from the street door.*

Mrs. Stockmann (seeing her husband). Just as I thought!

Hovstad (going towards her). You too, Mrs. Stockmann?

Dr. Stockmann. What on earth do *you* want here, Katherine?

Mrs. Stockmann. I should think you know very well what I want.

Hovstad. Won't you sit down? Or perhaps——

Mrs. Stockmann. No, thank you; don't trouble. And you must not be offended at my coming to fetch my husband; I am the mother of three children, you know.

Dr. Stockmann. Nonsense!—we know all about that.

Mrs. Stockmann. Well, one would not give you credit for much thought for your wife and children to-day; if you had had that, you would not have gone and dragged us all into misfortune.

Dr. Stockmann. Are you out of your senses, Katherine! Because a man has a wife and children, is he not to be allowed to proclaim the truth—is he not to be allowed to be an actively useful citizen—is he not to be allowed to do a service to his native town!

Mrs. Stockmann. Yes, Thomas—in reason.

Aslaksen. Just what I say. Moderation is everything.

Mrs. Stockmann. And that is why you wrong us, Mr. Hovstad, in enticing my husband away from his home and making a dupe of him in all this.

Hovstad. I certainly am making a dupe of no one——

Dr. Stockmann. Making a dupe of me! Do you suppose *I* should allow myself to be duped!

Mrs. Stockmann. It is just what you do. I know quite well you have more brains than anyone in the town, but you are extremely easily duped, Thomas. *(To* Hovstad.*)* Please to realise that he loses his post at the Baths if you print what he has written——

Aslaksen. What!

Hovstad. Look here, Doctor——

Dr. Stockmann (laughing). Ha—ha!—just let them try! No, no—they will take good care not to. I have got the compact majority behind me, let me tell you!

Mrs. Stockmann. Yes, that is just the worst of it—your having any such horrid thing behind you.

Dr. Stockmann. Rubbish, Katherine!—Go home and look after your house and leave me to look after the community. How can you be so afraid, when I am so confident and happy? *(Walks up and down, rubbing his hands.)* Truth and the People will win the fight, you may be certain! I see the whole of the broad-minded middle class marching like a victorious army——! *(Stops beside a chair.)* What the deuce is that lying there?

Aslaksen. Good Lord!

Hovstad. Ahem!

Dr. Stockmann. Here we have the topmost pinnacle of authority!

   [*Takes the Mayor's official hat carefully between
    his finger-tips and holds it up in the air.*

Mrs. Stockmann. The Mayor's hat!

Dr. Stockmann. And here is the staff of office too. How in the name of all that's wonderful——?

Hovstad. Well, you see——

Dr. Stockmann. Oh, I understand. He has been here trying to talk you over. Ha—ha!—he made rather a mistake there! And as soon as he caught sight of me in the printing-room——. *(Bursts out laughing.)* Did he run away. Mr. Aslaksen?

Aslaksen (hurriedly). Yes, he ran away, Doctor.

Dr. Stockmann. Ran away without his stick or his——. Fiddlesticks! Peter doesn't run away and leave his belongings behind him. But what the deuce have you done with him? Ah!—in there, of course. Now you shall see, Katherine.

Mrs. Stockmann. Thomas—please don't——!

Aslaksen. Don't be rash, Doctor.

> [DR. STOCKMANN *has put on the Mayor's hat and taken his stick in his hand. He goes up to the door, opens it and stands with his hand to his hat at the salute.* PETER STOCKMANN *comes in, red with anger.* BILLING *follows him.*

Peter Stockmann. What does this tomfoolery mean?

Dr. Stockmann. Be respectful, my good Peter. I am the chief authority in the town now.   [*Walks up and down.*

Mrs. Stockmann (almost in tears). Really, Thomas!

Peter Stockmann (following him about). Give me my hat and stick.

Dr. Stockmann (in the same tone as before). If you are chief constable, let me tell you that I am the Mayor—I am the master of the whole town, please understand!

Peter Stockmann. Take off my hat, I tell you. Remember it is part of an official uniform.

Dr. Stockmann. Pooh! Do you think the newly awakened lion-hearted people are going to be frightened by an official hat? There is going to be a revolution in the town to-morrow, let me tell you. You thought you could turn me out; but now I shall turn you out—turn you out of all your various offices. Do you think I cannot? Listen to me. I have triumphant social forces behind me. Hovstad and Billing will thunder in the "People's Messenger," and Aslaksen will take the field at the head of the whole House-holders' Association——

Aslaksen. That I won't, Doctor.

Dr. Stockmann. Of course you will——

Peter Stockmann. Ah!—may I ask then if Mr. Hovstad intends to join this agitation?

Hovstad. No, Mr. Mayor.

Aslaksen. No, Mr. Hovstad is not such a fool as to go and ruin his paper and himself for the sake of an imaginary grievance.

Dr. Stockmann (looking round him). What does this mean?

Hovstad. You have represented your case in a false light, Doctor, and therefore I am unable to give you my support.

Billing. And after what the Mayor was so kind as to tell me just now, I——

Dr. Stockmann. A false light! Leave that part of it to me. Only print my article; I am quite capable of de-fending it.

Hovstad. I am not going to print it. I cannot and will not and dare not print it.

Dr. Stockmann. You dare not? What nonsense!—you are the editor; and an editor controls his paper, I suppose!

Aslaksen. No, it is the subscribers, Doctor.

Peter Stockmann. Fortunately, yes.

Aslaksen. It is public opinion—the enlightened public—householders and people of that kind; they control the news-papers.

Dr. Stockmann (composedly). And I have all these in-fluences against me?

Aslaksen. Yes, you have. It would mean the absolute ruin of the community if your article were to appear.

Dr. Stockmann. Indeed.

Peter Stockmann. My hat and stick, if you please. (DR. STOCKMANN *takes off the hat and lays it on the table with the stick.* PETER STOCKMANN *takes them up.*) Your authority as mayor has come to an untimely end.

Dr. Stockmann. We have not got to the end yet. (*To* HOVSTAD.) Then it is quite impossible for you to print my article in the "People's Messenger"?

Hovstad. Quite impossible—out of regard for your family as well.

Mrs. Stockmann. You need not concern yourself about his family, thank you, Mr. Hovstad.

Peter Stockmann (taking a paper from his pocket). It will be sufficient, for the guidance of the public, if this appears. It is an official statement. May I trouble you?

Hovstad (taking the paper). Certainly; I will see that it is printed.

Dr. Stockmann. But not mine. Do you imagine that you can silence me and stifle the truth! You will not find it so easy as you suppose. Mr. Aslaksen, kindly take my manuscript at once and print it as a pamphlet—at my expense. I will have four hundred copies—no, five—six hundred.

Aslaksen. If you offered me its weight in gold, I could not lend my press for any such purpose, Doctor. It would be flying in the face of public opinion. You will not get it printed anywhere in the town.

Dr. Stockmann. Then give it me back.

Hovstad (giving him the MS.) Here it is.

Dr. Stockmann (taking his hat and stick). It shall be made public all the same. I will read it out at a mass meeting of the townspeople. All my fellow-citizens shall hear the voice of truth!

Peter Stockmann. You will not find any public body in the town that will give you the use of their hall for such a purpose.

Aslaksen. Not a single one, I am certain.

Billing. No, I'm damned if you will find one.

Mrs. Stockmann. But this is too shameful! Why should every one turn against you like that?

Dr. Stockmann (angrily). I will tell you why. It is because all the men in this town are old women—like you; they all think of nothing but their families, and never of the community.

Mrs. Stockmann (putting her arm into his). Then I will show them that an—an old woman can be a man for once. I am going to stand by you, Thomas!

Dr. Stockmann. Bravely said, Katherine! It shall be made public—as I am a living soul! If I can't hire a hall, I shall hire a drum, and parade the town with it and read it at every street-corner.

Peter Stockmann. You are surely not such an arrant fool as that!

Dr. Stockmann. Yes, I am.

Aslaksen. You won't find a single man in the whole town to go with you.

Billing. No, I'm damned if you will.

Mrs. Stockmann. Don't give in, Thomas. I will tell the boys to go with you.

Dr. Stockmann. That is a splendid idea!

Mrs. Stockmann. Morten will be delighted; and Ejlif will do whatever he does.

Dr. Stockmann. Yes, and Petra!—and you two, Katherine!

Mrs. Stockmann. No, I won't do that; but I will stand at the window and watch you, that's what I will do.

Dr. Stockmann (puts his arms round her and kisses her). Thank you, my dear! Now you and I are going to try a fall, my fine gentlemen! I am going to see whether a pack of cowards can succeed in gagging a patriot who wants to purify society!

[*He and his wife go out by the street door.*
Peter Stockmann (shaking his head seriously).   Now he
has sent *her* out of her senses, too.

ACT IV

Scene. *A big old-fashioned room in* Captain Horster's *house. At the back folding-doors, which are standing open, lead to an ante-room. Three windows in the left-hand wall. In the middle of the opposite wall a platform has been erected. On this is a small table with two candles, a water-bottle and glass, and a bell. The room is lit by lamps placed between the windows. In the foreground on the left there is a table with candles and a chair. To the right is a door and some chairs standing near it. The room is nearly filled with a crowd of townspeople of all sorts, a few women and schoolboys being amongst them. People are still streaming in from the back, and the room is soon filled.*

1st *Citizen (meeting another).* Hullo, Lamstad! You here too?

2nd *Citizen.* I go to every public meeting, I do.

3rd *Citizen.* Brought your whistle too, I expect!

2nd *Citizen.* I should think so. Haven't you?

3rd *Citizen.* Rather! And old Evensen said he was going to bring a cow-horn, he did.

2nd *Citizen.* Good old Evensen!

[*Laughter among the crowd.*

4th *Citizen (coming up to them).* I say, tell me what is going on here to-night.

2nd *Citizen.* Dr. Stockmann is going to deliver an address attacking the Mayor.

4th *Citizen.* But the Mayor is his brother.

1st Citizen. That doesn't matter; Dr. Stockmann's not the chap to be afraid.

3rd Citizen. But he is in the wrong; it said so in the "People's Messenger."

2nd Citizen. Yes, I expect he must be in the wrong this time, because neither the Householders' Association nor the Citizens' Club would lend him their hall for his meeting.

1st Citizen. He couldn't even get the loan of the hall at the Baths.

2nd Citizen. No, I should think not.

A Man in another part of the crowd. I say—who are we to back up in this?

Another Man, beside him. Watch Aslaksen, and do as he does.

Billing (pushing his way through the crowd, with a writing-case under his arm). Excuse me, gentlemen—do you mind letting me through? I am reporting for the "People's Messenger." Thank you very much!

[*He sits down at the table on the left.*

A Workman. Who was that?

Second Workman. Don't you know him? It's Billing, who writes for Aslaksen's paper.

[CAPTAIN HORSTER *brings in* MRS. STOCKMANN *and* PETRA *through the door on the right.* EJLIF *and* MORTEN *follow them in.*

Horster. I thought you might all sit here; you can slip out easily from here, if things get too lively.

Mrs. Stockmann. Do you think there will be a disturbance?

Horster. One can never tell—with such a crowd. But sit down, and don't be uneasy.

Mrs. Stockmann (sitting down). It was extremely kind of you to offer my husband the room.

Horster. Well, if nobody else would——

Petra (who has sat down beside her mother). And it was a plucky thing to do, Captain Horster.

Horster. Oh, it is not such a great matter as all that.

　　　　[HOVSTAD *and* ASLAKSEN *make their way through
　　　　the crowd.*

Aslaksen (going up to HORSTER*).* Has the Doctor not
come yet?

Horster. He is waiting in the next room.

　　　　[*Movement in the crowd by the door at the back.*

Hovstad. Look—here comes the Mayor!

Billing. Yes, I'm damned if he hasn't come after all!

　　　　[PETER STOCKMANN *makes his way gradually
　　　　through the crowd, bows courteously and takes
　　　　up a position by the wall on the left. Shortly
　　　　afterwards* DR. STOCKMANN *comes in by the
　　　　right-hand door. He is dressed in a black frock-
　　　　coat, with a white tie. There is a little feeble
　　　　applause, which is hushed down. Silence is ob-
　　　　tained.*

Dr. Stockmann (in an undertone). How do you feel,
Katherine?

Mrs. Stockmann. All right, thank you. *(Lowering her
voice.)* Be sure not to lose your temper, Thomas.

Dr. Stockmann. Oh, I know how to control myself
(Looks at his watch, steps on to the platform and bows.)
It is a quarter past—so I will begin.

　　　　　　　　[*Takes his M.S. out of his pocket*

Aslaksen. I think we ought to elect a chairman first.

Dr. Stockmann. No, it is quite unnecessary.

Some of the Crowd. Yes—yes!

Peter Stockmann. I certainly think, too, that we ought to
have a chairman.

Dr. Stockmann. But I have called this meeting to deliver a lecture, Peter.

Peter Stockmann. Dr. Stockmann's lecture may possibly
lead to a considerable conflict of opinion.

Voices in the Crowd. A chairman! A chairman!

Hovstad. The general wish of the meeting seems to be that a chairman should be elected.

Dr. Stockmann (restraining himself). Very well—let the meeting have its way.

Aslaksen. Will the Mayor be good enough to undertake the task?

Three Men (clapping their hands). Bravo! Bravo!

Peter Stockmann. For various reasons, which you will easily understand, I must beg to be excused. But fortunately we have amongst us a man who I think will be acceptable to you all. I refer to the President of the Householders' Association, Mr. Aslaksen.

Several Voices. Yes—Aslaksen! Bravo Aslaksen!

> [DR. STOCKMANN *takes up his MS. and walks up and down the platform.*

Aslaksen. Since my fellow-citizens choose to entrust me with this duty, I cannot refuse.

> [*Loud applause.* ASLAKSEN *mounts the platform.*

Billing (writing). "Mr. Aslaksen was elected with enthusiasm."

Aslaksen. And now, as I am in this position, I should like to say a few brief words. I am a quiet and peaceable man, who believes in discreet moderation, and—and—in moderate discretion. All my friends can bear witness to that.

Several Voices. That's right! That's right, Aslaksen!

Aslaksen. I have learnt in the school of life and experience that moderation is the most valuable virtue a citizen can possess——

Peter Stockmann. Hear, hear!

Aslaksen. ——And moreover that discretion and moderation are what enable a man to be of most service to the community. I would therefore suggest to our esteemed fellow-citizen, who has called this meeting, that he should strive to keep strictly within the bounds of moderation.

A Man by the door. Three cheers for the Moderation Society!

A Voice. Shame!

Several Voices. Sh!—Sh!

Aslaksen. No interruptions, gentlemen, please! Does anyone wish to make any remarks?

Peter Stockmann. Mr. Chairman.

Aslaksen. The Mayor will address the meeting.

Peter Stockmann. In consideration of the close relationship in which, as you all know, I stand to the present Medical Officer of the Baths, I should have preferred not to speak this evening. But my official position with regard to the Baths and my solicitude for the vital interests of the town compel me to bring forward a motion. I venture to presume that there is not a single one of our citizens present who considers it desirable that unreliable and exaggerated accounts of the sanitary condition of the Baths and the town should be spread abroad.

Several Voices. No, no! Certainly not! We protest against it!

Peter Stockmann. Therefore I should like to propose that the meeting should not permit the Medical Officer either to read or to comment on his proposed lecture.

Dr. Stockmann (impatiently). Not permit——! What the devil——!

Mrs. Stockmann (coughing). Ahem!—ahem!

Dr. Stockmann (collecting himself). Very well. Go ahead!

Peter Stockmann. In my communication to the "People's Messenger," I have put the essential facts before the public in such a way that every fair-minded citizen can easily form his own opinion. From it you will see that the main result of the Medical Officer's proposals—apart from their constituting a vote of censure on the leading men of the town— would be to saddle the ratepayers with an unnecessary expenditure of at least some thousands of pounds.

[Sounds of disapproval among the audience, and some cat-calls.

Aslaksen (ringing his bell). Silence, please, gentlemen! I beg to support the Mayor's motion. I quite agree with him that there is something behind this agitation started by the Doctor. He talks about the Baths; but it is a revolution he is aiming at—he wants to get the administration of the town put into new hands. No one doubts the honesty of the Doctor's intentions—no one will suggest that there can be any two opinions as to that. I myself am a believer in self-government for the people, provided it does not fall too heavily on the ratepayers. But that would be the case here; and that is why I will see Dr. Stockmann damned—I beg your pardon—before I go with him in the matter. You can pay too dearly for a thing sometimes; that is my opinion.

[Loud applause on all sides.

Hovstad. I, too, feel called upon to explain my position. Dr. Stockmann's agitation appeared to be gaining a certain amount of sympathy at first, so I supported it as impartially as I could. But presently we had reason to suspect that we had allowed ourselves to be misled by misrepresentation of the state of affairs——

Dr. Stockmann. Misrepresentation——!

Hovstad. Well, let us say a not entirely trustworthy representation. The Mayor's statement has proved that I hope no one here has any doubt as to my liberal principles; the attitude of the "People's Messenger" towards important political questions is well known to every one. But the advice of experienced and thoughtful men has convinced me that in purely local matters a newspaper ought to proceed with a certain caution.

Aslaksen. I entirely agree with the speaker.

Hovstad. And, in the matter before us, it is now an undoubted fact that Dr. Stockmann has public opinion against him. Now, what is an editor's first and most obvious duty, gentlemen? Is it not to work in harmony with his readers?

Has he not received a sort of tacit mandate to work persistently and assiduously for the welfare of those whose opinions he represents?   Or is it possible I am mistaken in that?

Voices from the crowd.   No, no!   You are quite right!

Hovstad.   It has cost me a severe struggle to break with a man in whose house I have been lately a frequent guest— a man who till to-day has been able to pride himself on the undivided goodwill of his fellow-citizens—a man whose only, or at all events whose essential, failing is that he is swayed by his heart rather than his head.

A few scattered voices.   That is true!   Bravo, Stockmann!

Hovstad.   But my duty to the community obliged me to break with him.   And there is another consideration that impels me to oppose him, and, as far as possible, to arrest him on the perilous course he has adopted; that is, consideration for his family——

Dr. Stockmann.   Please stick to the water-supply and drainage!

Hovstad.   ——consideration, I repeat, for his wife and his children for whom he has made no provision.

Morten.   Is that us, mother?

Mrs. Stockmann.   Hush!

Aslaksen.   I will now put the Mayor's proposition to the vote.

Dr. Stockmann.   There is no necessity!   To-night I have no intention of dealing with all that filth down at the Baths. No; I have something quite different to say to you.

Peter Stockmann (aside).   What is coming now?

A Drunken Man (by the entrance door).   I am a ratepayer!   And therefore I have a right to speak too!   And my entire—firm—inconceivable opinion is——

A number of voices.   Be quiet, at the back there!

Others.   He is drunk!   Turn him out!

[*They turn him out.*

Dr. Stockmann. Am I allowed to speak?

Aslaksen (ringing his bell). Dr. Stockmann will address the meeting.

Dr. Stockmann. I should like to have seen anyone, a few days ago, dare to attempt to silence me as has been done to-night! I would have defended my sacred rights as a man, like a lion! But now it is all one to me; I have something of even weightier importance to say to you.

> [*The crowd presses nearer to him,* MORTEN KIIL *conspicuous among them.*

Dr. Stockmann (continuing). I have thought and pondered a great deal, these last few days—pondered over such a variety of things that in the end my head seemed too full to hold them——

Peter Stockmann (with a cough). Ahem!

Dr. Stockmann. ——but I got them clear in my mind at last, and then I saw the whole situation lucidly. And that is why I am standing here to-night. I have a great revelation to make to you, my fellow-citizens! I will impart to you a discovery of a far wider scope than the trifling matter that our water-supply is poisoned and our medicinal Baths are standing on pestiferous soil.

A number of voices (shouting). Don't talk about the Baths! We won't hear you! None of that!

Dr. Stockmann. I have already told you that what I want to speak about is the great discovery I have made lately —the discovery that all the sources of our *moral* life are poisoned and that the whole fabric of our civic community is founded on the pestiferous soil of falsehood.

Voices of disconcerted Citizens. What is that he says?

Peter Stockmann. Such an insinuation——!

Aslaksen (with his hand on his bell). I call upon the speaker to moderate his language.

Dr. Stockmann. I have always loved my native town as a man only can love the home of his youthful days. I was not old when I went away from here; and exile, longing and memories cast, as it were, an additional halo over both the town and its inhabitants. *(Some clapping and applause.)* And there I stayed, for many years, in a horrible hole far away up north. When I came into contact with some of the people that lived scattered about among the rocks, I often thought it would of been more service to the poor half-starved creatures if a veterinary doctor had been sent up there, instead of a man like me.

[Murmurs among the crowd.

Billing (laying down his pen). I'm damned if I have ever heard——!

Hovstad. It is an insult to a respectable population!

Dr. Stockmann. Wait a bit! I do not think anyone will charge me with having forgotten my native town up there. I was like one of the eider-ducks brooding on its nest, and what I hatched was—the plans for these Baths. *(Applause and protests.)* And then when fate at last decreed for me the great happiness of coming home again—I assure you, gentlemen, I thought I had nothing more in the world to wish for. Or rather, there was one thing I wished for— eagerly, untiringly, ardently—and that was to be able to be of service to my native town and the good of the community.

Peter Stockmann (looking at the ceiling). You chose a strange way of doing it—ahem!

Dr. Stockmann. And so, with my eyes blinded to the real facts, I revelled in happiness. But yesterday morning—no, to be precise, it was yesterday afternoon—the eyes of my mind were opened wide, and the first thing I realised was the colossal stupidity of the authorities——.

[Uproar, shouts and laughter. MRS. STOCKMANN *coughs persistently.*

Peter Stockmann. Mr. Chairman!

Aslaksen (ringing his bell). By virtue of my authority——!

Dr. Stockmann. It is a petty thing to catch me up on a word, Mr. Aslaksen. What I mean is only that I got scent of the unbelievable piggishness our leading men had been responsible for down at the Baths. I can't stand leading men at any price!—I have had enough of such people in my time. They are like billy-goats in a young plantation; they do mischief everywhere. They stand in a free man's way, whichever way he turns, and what I should like best would be to see them exterminated like any other vermin——.

[*Uproar.*

Peter Stockmann. Mr. Chairman, can we allow such expressions to pass?

Aslaksen (with his hand on his bell). Doctor——!

Dr. Stockmann. I cannot understand how it is that I have only now acquired a clear conception of what these gentry are, when I had almost daily before my eyes in this town such an excellent specimen of them—my brother Peter —slow-witted and hide-bound in prejudice——.

[*Laughter, uproar and hisses.* MRS. STOCKMANN *sits coughing assiduously.* ASLAKSEN *rings his bell violently.*

The Drunken Man (who has got in again). Is it me he is talking about? My name's Petersen, all right—but devil take me if I——

Angry Voices. Turn out that drunken man! Turn him out. [*He is turned out again.*

Peter Stockmann. Who was that person?

1st Citizen. I don't know who he is, Mr. Mayor.

2nd Citizen. He doesn't belong here.

3rd Citizen. I expect he is a navvy from over at (*the rest is inaudible*).

Aslaksen. He had obviously had too much beer.—Proceed, Doctor; but please strive to be moderate in your language.

Dr. Stockmann. Very well, gentlemen, I will say no more about our leading men. And if anyone imagines, from what I have just said, that my object is to attack these people this evening, he is wrong—absolutely wide of the mark.

For I cherish the comforting conviction that these parasites —all these venerable relics of a dying school of thought— are most admirably paving the way for their own extinction; they need no doctor's help to hasten their end.   Nor is it folk of that kind who constitute the most pressing danger to the community.   It is not they who are most instrumental in poisoning the sources of our moral life and infecting the ground on which we stand.   It is not they who are the most dangerous enemies of truth and freedom amongst us.

Shouts from all sides.   Who then?   Who is it?   Name! Name!

Dr. Stockmann.   You may depend upon it I shall name them!   That is precisely the great discovery I made yesterday.   *(Raises his voice.)*   The most dangerous enemy of truth and freedom amongst us is the compact majority—yes, the damned compact Liberal majority—that is it!   Now you know!

> [*Tremendous uproar. Most of the crowd are shouting, stamping and hissing. Some of the older men among them exchange stolen glances and seem to be enjoying themselves.* MRS. STOCKMANN *gets up, looking anxious.* EJLIF *and* MORTEN *advance threateningly upon some schoolboys who are playing pranks.* ASLAKSEN *rings his bell and begs for silence.* HOVSTAD *and* BILLING *both talk at once, but are inaudible. At last quiet is restored.*

Aslaksen.   As chairman, I call upon the speaker to withdraw the ill-considered expressions he has just used.

Dr. Stockmann.   Never, Mr. Aslaksen!   It is the majority in our community that denies me my freedom and seeks to prevent my speaking the truth.

Hovstad.   The majority always has right on its side.

Billing.   And truth too, by God!

Dr. Stockmann.   The majority *never* has right on its side. Never, I say!   That is one of these social lies against which an independent, intelligent man must wage war. Who is it that constitute the majority of the population in a country? Is it the clever folk or the stupid? I don't imagine you will dispute the fact that at present the stupid people are in an absolutely overwhelming majority all the world over. But, good Lord!—you can never pretend that it is right that the stupid folk should govern the clever ones! *(Uproar and cries.)* Oh, yes—you can shout me down, I know! but you cannot answer me. The majority has *might* on its side— unfortunately; but *right* it has *not*. I am in the right—I and a few other scattered individuals. The minority is always in the right. [*Renewed uproar.*

Hovstad. Aha!—so Dr. Stockmann has become an aristocrat since the day before yesterday!

Dr. Stockmann. I have already said that I don't intend to waste a word on the puny, narrow-chested, short-winded crew whom we are leaving astern. Pulsating life no longer concerns itself with them. I am thinking of the few, the scattered few amongst us, who have absorbed new and vigorous truths. Such men stand, as it were, at the outposts, so far ahead that the compact majority has not yet been able to come up with them; and there they are fighting for truths that are too newly-born into the world of consciousness to have any considerable number of people on their side as yet.

Hovstad. So the Doctor is a revolutionary now!

Dr. Stockmann. Good heavens—of course I am, Mr. Hovstad! I propose to raise a revolution against the lie that the majority has the monopoly of the truth. What sort of truths are they that the majority usually supports? They are truths that are of such advanced age that they are beginning to break up. And if a truth is as old as that, it is also in a fair way to become a lie, gentlemen. *(Laughter and mocking cries.)* Yes, believe me or not, as you like; but truths are by no means as long-lived as Methuselah—as some folk imagine. A normally constituted truth lives, let us say, as a rule seventeen or eighteen, or at most twenty

years; seldom longer. But truths as aged as that are always
worn frightfully thin, and nevertheless it is only then that
the majority recognises them and recommends them to the
community as wholesome moral nourishment. There is no
great nutritive value in that sort of fare, I can assure you;
and, as a doctor, I ought to know. These "majority truths"
are like last year's cured meat—like rancid, tainted ham;
and they are the origin of the moral scurvy that is rampant
in our communities.

Aslaksen. It appears to me that the speaker is wandering
a long way from his subject.

Peter Stockmann. I quite agree with the Chairman.

Dr. Stockmann. Have you gone clean out of your senses,
Peter? I am sticking as closely to my subject as I can; for
my subject is precisely this, that it is the masses, the majority—this infernal compact majority—that poisons the
sources of our moral life and infects the ground we stand on.

Hovstad. And all this because the great, broad-minded
majority of the people is prudent enough to show deference
only to well-ascertained and well-approved truths?

Dr. Stockmann. Ah, my good Mr. Hovstad, don't talk
nonsense about well-ascertained truths! The truths of
which the masses now approve are the very truths that the
fighters at the outposts held to in the days of our grand-
fathers. We fighters at the outposts nowadays no longer
approve of them; and I do not believe there is any other
well-ascertained truth except this, that no community can
live a healthy life if it is nourished only on such old marrowless truths.

Hovstad. But instead of standing there using vague gen-
eralities, it would be interesting if you would tell us what
these old marrowless truths are, that we are nourished on.

[*Applause from many quarters.*

Dr. Stockmann. Oh, I could give you a whole string of
such abominations; but to begin with I will confine myself
to one well-approved truth, which at bottom is a foul lie,

but upon which nevertheless Mr. Hovstad and the "People's Messenger" and all the "Messenger's" supporters are nourished.

Hovstad. And that is——?

Dr. Stockmann. That is, the doctrine you have inherited from your forefathers and proclaim thoughtlessly far and wide—the doctrine that the public, the crowd, the masses are the essential part of the population—that they constitute the People—that the common folk, the ignorant and incomplete element in the community, have the same right to pronounce judgment and to approve, to direct and to govern, as the isolated, intellectually superior personalities in it.

Billing. Well, damn me if ever I——

Hovstad (at the same time, shouting out). Fellow-citizens, take good note of that!

A number of voices (angrily). Oho!—we are not the People! Only the superior folks are to govern, are they!

A Workman. Turn the fellow out, for talking such rubbish!

Another. Out with him!

Another (calling out). Blow your horn, Evensen!

> [*A horn is blown loudly, amidst hisses and an angry uproar.*

Dr. Stockmann (when the noise has somewhat abated). Be reasonable! Can't you stand hearing the voice of truth for once? I don't in the least expect you to agree with me all at once; but I must say I did expect Mr. Hovstad to admit I was right, when he had recovered his composure a little. He claims to be a freethinker——

Voices (in murmurs of astonishment). Freethinker, did he say? Is Hovstad a freethinker?

Hovstad (shouting). Prove it, Dr. Stockmann! When have I said so in print?

Dr. Stockmann (reflecting). No, confound it, you are right!—you have never had the courage to. Well, I won't

put you in a hole, Mr. Hovstad. Let us say it is I that am
the freethinker, then. I am going to prove to you, scien-
tifically, that the "People's Messenger" leads you by the
nose in a shameful manner when it tells you that you—that
the common people, the crowd, the masses are the real es-
sence of the People. That is only a newspaper lie, I tell
you! The common people are nothing more than the raw
material of which a People is made. *(Groans, laughter and
uproar.)* Well, isn't that the case? Isn't there an enor-
mous difference between a well-bred and an ill-bred strain of
animals? Take, for instance, a common barn-door hen.
What sort of eating do you get from a shrivelled up old scrag
of a fowl like that? Not much, do you! And what sort of
eggs does it lay? A fairly good crow or a raven can lay
pretty nearly as good an egg. But take a well-bred Spanish
or Japanese hen, or a good pheasant or a turkey—then you
will see the difference. Or take the case of dogs, with whom
we humans are on such intimate terms. Think first of an
ordinary common cur—I mean one of the horrible, coarse-
haired, low-bred curs that do nothing but run about the
streets and befoul the walls of the houses. Compare one
of these curs with a poodle whose sires for many generations have been bred in a gentleman's house, where they
have had the best of food and had the opportunity of hearing soft voices and music. Do you not think that the
poodle's brain is developed to quite a different degree from
that of the cur? Of course it is. It is puppies of well-bred
poodles like that, that showmen train to do incredibly clever
tricks—things that a common cur could never learn to do
even if it stood on its head. [*Uproar and mocking cries.*

A Citizen (calls out). Are you going to make out we are
dogs, now?

Another Citizen. We are not animals, Doctor!

Dr. Stockmann. Yes, but, bless my soul, we *are*, my
friend! It is true we are the finest animals anyone could
wish for; but, even amongst us, exceptionally fine animals

are rare. There is a tremendous difference between poodle-men and cur-men. And the amusing part of it is, that Mr. Hovstad quite agrees with me as long as it is a question of four-footed animals——

Hovstad. Yes, it is true enough as far as they are concerned.

Dr. Stockmann. Very well. But as soon as I extend the principle and apply it to two-legged animals, Mr. Hovstad stops short. He no longer dares to think independently, or to pursue his ideas to their logical conclusion; so he turns the whole theory upside down and proclaims in the "People's Messenger" that it is the barn-door hens and street curs that are the finest specimens in the menagerie. But that is always the way, as long as a man retains the traces of common origin and has not worked his way up to intellectual distinction.

Hovstad. I lay no claim to any sort of distinction. I am the son of humble countryfolk, and I am proud that the stock I come from is rooted deep among the common people he insults.

Voices. Bravo, Hovstad! Bravo! Bravo!

Dr. Stockmann. The kind of common people I mean are not only to be found low down in the social scale; they crawl and swarm all around us—even in the highest social positions. You have only to look at your own fine, distinguished Mayor! My brother Peter is every bit as plebeian as anyone that walks in two shoes——

[*Laughter and hisses.*

Peter Stockmann. I protest against personal allusions of this kind.

Dr. Stockmann (imperturbably). ——and that, not because he is, like myself, descended from some old rascal of a pirate from Pomerania or thereabouts—because that is who we are descended from——

Peter Stockmann. An absurd legend. I deny it!

Dr. Stockmann. ——but because he thinks what his superiors think and holds the same opinions as they. People who do that are, intellectually speaking, common people; and that is why my magnificent brother Peter is in reality so very far from any distinction—and consequently also so far from being liberal-minded.

Peter Stockmann. Mr. Chairman——!

Hovstad. So it is only the distinguished men that are liberal-minded in this country? We are learning something quite new!   [*Laughter.*

Dr. Stockmann. Yes, that is part of my new discovery too. And another part of it is that broad-mindedness is almost precisely the same thing as morality. That is why I maintain that it is absolutely inexcusable in the "People's Messenger" to proclaim, day in and day out, the false doctrine that it is the masses, the crowd, the compact majority that have the monopoly of broad-mindedness and morality—and that vice and corruption and every kind of intellectual depravity are the result of culture, just as all the filth that is draining into our Baths is the result of the tanneries up at Mölledal! *(Uproar and interruptions.* DR. STOCKMANN *is undisturbed, and goes on, carried away by his ardour, with a smile.)* And yet this same "People's Messenger" can go on preaching that the masses ought to be elevated to higher conditions of life! But, bless my soul, if the "Messenger's" teaching is to be depended upon, this very raising up the masses would mean nothing more or less than setting them straightway upon the paths of depravity! Happily the theory that culture demoralises is only an old falsehood that our forefathers believed in and we have inherited. No, it is ignorance, poverty, ugly conditions of life that do the devil's work! In a house which does not get aired and swept every day—my wife Katherine maintains that the floor ought to be scrubbed as well, but that is a debatable question—in such a house, let me tell you, people will lose within two or three years the power of thinking or acting in a moral man-ner. Lack of oxygen weakens the conscience. And there must be a plentiful lack of oxygen in very many houses in this town, I should think, judging from the fact that the whole compact majority can be unconscientious enough to wish to build the town's prosperity on a quagmire of falsehood and deceit.

Aslaksen. We cannot allow such a grave accusation to be flung at a citizen community.

A Citizen. I move that the Chairman direct the speaker to sit down.

Voices (angrily). Hear, hear! Quite right! Make him sit down!

Dr. Stockmann (losing his self-control). Then I will go and shout the truth at every street corner! I will write it in other towns' newspapers! The whole country shall know what is going on here!

Hovstad. It almost seems as if Dr. Stockmann's intention were to ruin the town.

Dr. Stockmann. Yes, my native town is so dear to me that I would rather ruin it than see it flourishing upon a lie.

Aslaksen. This is really serious.

> [*Uproar and cat-calls.* MRS. STOCKMANN *coughs, but to no purpose; her husband does not listen to her any longer.*

Hovstad (shouting above the din). A man must be a public enemy to wish to ruin a whole community!

Dr. Stockmann (with growing fervour). What does the destruction of a community matter, if it lives on lies! It ought to be razed to the ground, I tell you! All who live by lies ought to be exterminated like vermin! You will end by infecting the whole country; you will bring about such a state of things that the whole country will deserve to be ruined. And if things come to that pass, I shall say from the bottom of my heart: Let the whole country perish, let all these people be exterminated!

Voices from the crowd. That is talking like an out-and-out enemy of the people!

Billing. There sounded the voice of the people, by all that's holy!

The whole crowd (shouting). Yes, yes! He is an enemy of the people! He hates his country! He hates his own people!

Aslaksen. Both as a citizen and as an individual, I am profoundly disturbed by what we have had to listen to. Dr. Stockmann has shown himself in a light I should never have dreamed of. I am unhappily obliged to subscribe to the opinion which I have just heard my estimable fellow-citizens utter; and I propose that we should give expression to that opinion in a resolution. I propose a resolution as follows: "This meeting declares that it considers Dr. Thomas Stockmann, Medical Officer of the Baths, to be an enemy of the people."

> [*A storm of cheers and applause. A number of men surround the* DOCTOR *and hiss him.* MRS. STOCKMANN *and* PETRA *have got up from their seats.* MORTEN *and* EJLIF *are fighting the other schoolboys for hissing; some of their elders separate them.*

Dr. Stockmann (to the men who are hissing him). Oh, you fools! I tell you that——

Aslaksen (ringing his bell). We cannot hear you now, Doctor. A formal vote is about to be taken; but, out of regard for personal feelings, it shall be by ballot and not verbal. Have you any clean paper, Mr. Billings?

Billing. I have both blue and white here.

Aslaksen (going to him). That will do nicely; we shall get on more quickly that way. Cut it up into small strips— yes, that's it. *(To the meeting.)* Blue means no; white means yes. I will come round myself and collect votes.

> [PETER STOCKMANN *leaves the hall.* ASLAKSEN *and one or two others go round the room with the slips of paper in their hats.*

1st Citizen (to Hovstad*).* I say, what has come to the Doctor? What are we to think of it?

Hovstad. Oh, you know how headstrong he is.

2nd Citizen (to Billing*).* Billing, you go to their house —have you ever noticed if the fellow drinks?

Billings. Well I'm hanged if I know what to say. There are always spirits on the table when you go.

3rd Citizen. I rather think he goes quite off his head sometimes.

1st Citizen. I wonder if there is any madness in his family?

Billing. I shouldn't wonder if there were.

4th Citizen. No, it is nothing more than sheer malice; he wants to get even with somebody for something or other.

Billing. Well certainly he suggested a rise in his salary on one occasion lately, and did not get it.

The Citizens (together). Ah!—then it is easy to understand how it is!

The Drunken Man (who has got amongst the audience again). I want a blue one, I do! And I want a white one too!

Voices. It's that drunken chap again! Turn him out!

Morten Kiil (going up to Dr. Stockmann*).* Well, Stockmann, do you see what these monkey tricks of yours lead to?

Dr. Stockmann. I have done my duty.

Morten Kiil. What was that you said about the tanneries at Mölledal?

Dr. Stockmann. You heard well enough. I said they were the source of all the filth.

Morten Kiil. My tannery too?

Dr. Stockmann. Unfortunately your tannery is by far the worst.

Morten Kiil. Are you going to put that in the papers?

Dr. Stockmann. I shall conceal nothing.

Morten Kiil. That may cost you dear, Stockmann.

[*Goes out.*

A Stout Man (going up to CAPTAIN HORSTER, *without taking any notice of the ladies).* Well, Captain, so you lend your house to enemies of the people?

Horster. I imagine I can do what I like with my own possessions, Mr. Vik.

The Stout Man. Then you can have no objection to my doing the same with mine.

Horster. What do you mean, sir?

The Stout Man. You shall hear from me in the morning.

[*Turns his back on him and moves off.*

Petra. Was that not your owner, Captain Horster?

Horster. Yes, that was Mr. Vik the ship-owner.

Aslaksen (with the voting-papers in his hands, gets up on to the platform and rings his bell). Gentlemen, allow me to announce the result. By the votes of every one here except one person——

A Young Man. That is the drunk chap!

Aslaksen. By the votes of every one here except a tipsy man, this meeting of citizens declares Dr. Thomas Stockmann to be an enemy of the people. *(Shouts and applause.)* Three cheers for our ancient and honourable citizen community! *(Renewed applause.)* Three cheers for our able and energetic Mayor, who has so loyally suppressed the promptings of family feeling! *(Cheers.)* The meeting is dissolved. [*Gets down.*

Billing. Three cheers for the Chairman!

The whole crowd. Three cheers for Aslaksen! Hurrah!

Dr. Stockmann. My hat and coat, Petra! Captain, have you room on your ship for passengers to the New World?

Horster. For you and yours we will make room, Doctor.

Dr. Stockmann (as PETRA *helps him into his coat).* Good. Come, Katherine! Come, boys!

Mrs. Stockmann (in an undertone). Thomas, dear, let us go out by the back way.

Dr. Stockmann. No back ways for me, Katherine. *(Raising his voice.)* You will hear more of this enemy of the people, before he shakes the dust off his shoes upon you! I am not so forgiving as a certain Person; I do not say: "I forgive you, for ye know not what ye do."

Aslaksen (shouting). That is a blasphemous comparison, Dr. Stockmann!

Billing. It is, by God! It's dreadful for an earnest man to listen to.

A Coarse Voice. Threatens us now, does he!

Other Voices (excitedly). Let's go and break his windows! Duck him in the fjord!

Another Voice. Blow your horn, Evensen! Pip, pip!

> [*Horn-blowing, hisses and wild cries.* Dr. Stockmann *goes out through the hall with his family,* Horster *elbowing a way for them.*

The Whole Crowd (howling after them as they go). Enemy of the People! Enemy of the People!

Billing (as he puts his papers together). Well, I'm damned if I go and drink toddy with the Stockmanns to-night!

> [*The crowd press towards the exit. The uproar continues outside; shouts of "Enemy of the People!" are heard from without.*

ACT V

SCENE.—DR. STOCKMANN'S *study. Bookcases, and cabi-nets containing specimens, line the walls. At the back is a door leading to the hall; in the foreground on the left, a door leading to the sitting-room. In the right-hand wall are two windows, of which all the panes are broken. The* DOCTOR'S *desk, littered with books and papers, stands in the middle of the room, which is in disorder. It is morning.* DR. STOCKMANN *in dressing-gown, slippers and a smoking-cap, is bending down and raking with an umbrella under one of the cabinets After a little while he rakes out a stone.*

Dr. Stockmann (calling through the open sitting-room door). Katherine, I have found another one.

Mrs. Stockmann (from the sitting-room). Oh, you will find a lot more yet, I expect.

Dr. Stockmann (adding the stone to a heap of others on the table). I shall treasure these stones as relics. Ejlif and Morten shall look at them every day, and when they are grown up they shall inherit them as heirlooms. *(Rakes about under a bookcase.)* Hasn't—what the deuce is her name?—the girl, you know—hasn't she been to fetch the glazier yet?

Mrs. Stockmann (coming in). Yes, but he said he didn't know if he would be able to come to-day.

Dr. Stockmann. You will see he won't dare to come.

Mrs. Stockmann. Well, that is just what Randine thought—that he didn't dare to, on account of the neigh-bours. *(Calls into the sitting-room.)* What is it you want,

267

Randine? Give it to me. *(Goes in, and comes out again directly.)* Here is a letter for you, Thomas.

Dr. Stockmann. Let me see it. *(Opens and reads it.)* Ah!—of course.

Mrs. Stockmann. Who is it from?

Dr. Stockmann. From the landlord. Notice to quit.

Mrs. Stockmann. Is it possible? Such a nice man——

Dr. Stockmann (looking at the letter). Does not dare do otherwise, he says. Doesn't like doing it, but dare not do otherwise—on account of his fellow-citizens—out of regard for public opinion. Is in a dependent position—dare not offend certain influential men——

Mrs. Stockmann. There, you see, Thomas!

Dr. Stockmann. Yes, yes, I see well enough; the whole lot of them in the town are cowards; not a man among them dares do anything for fear of the others. *(Throws the letter on to the table.)* But it doesn't matter to us, Katherine. We are going to sail away to the New World, and——

Mrs. Stockmann. But, Thomas, are you sure we are well advised to take this step?

Dr. Stockmann. Are you suggesting that I should stay here, where they have pilloried me as an enemy of the people—branded me—broken my windows! And just look here, Katherine—they have torn a great rent in my black trousers too!

Mrs. Stockmann. Oh, dear!—and they are the best pair you have got!

Dr. Stockmann. You should never wear your best trousers when you go out to fight for freedom and truth. It is not that I care so much about the trousers, you know; you can always sew them up again for me. But that the common herd should dare to make this attack on me, as if they were my equals—that is what I cannot, for the life of me, swallow!

Mrs. Stockmann. There is no doubt they have behaved very ill to you, Thomas; but is that sufficient reason for our leaving our native country for good and all?

Dr. Stockmann. If we went to another town, do you suppose we should not find the common people just as inso- lent as they are here? Depend upon it, there is not much to choose between them. Oh, well, let the curs snap—that is not the worst part of it. The worst is that, from one end of this country to the other, every man is the slave of his Party. Although, as far as that goes, I daresay it is not much better in the free West either; the compact majority, and liberal public opinion, and all that infernal old bag of tricks are probably rampant there too. But there things are done on a larger scale, you see. They may kill you, but they won't put you to death by slow torture. They don't squeeze a free man's soul in a vice, as they do here. And, if need be, one can live in solitude. *(Walks up and down.)* If only I knew where there was a virgin forest or a small South Sea island for sale, cheap——

Mrs. Stockmann. But think of the boys, Thomas.

Dr. Stockmann (standing still). What a strange woman you are, Katherine! Would you prefer to have the boys grow up in a society like this? You saw for yourself last night that half the population are out of their minds; and if the other half have not lost their senses, it is because they are mere brutes, with no sense to lose.

Mrs. Stockmann. But, Thomas dear, the imprudent things you said had something to do with it, you know.

Dr. Stockmann. Well, isn't what I said perfectly true? Don't they turn every idea topsy-turvy? Don't they make a regular hotch-potch of right and wrong? Don't they say that the things I know are true, are lies? The craziest part of it all is the fact of these "liberals," men of full age, going about in crowds imagining that they are the broad-minded party! Did you ever hear anything like it, Katherine!

Mrs. Stockmann. Yes, yes, it's mad enough of them, certainly; but—— (PETRA *comes in from the sitting-room*). Back from school already?

Petra. Yes. I have been given notice of dismissal.

Mrs. Stockmann. Dismissal?

Dr. Stockmann. You too?

Petra. Mrs. Busk gave me my notice; so I thought it was best to go at once.

Dr. Stockmann. You were perfectly right, too!

Mrs. Stockmann. Who would have thought Mrs. Busk was a woman like that!

Petra. Mrs. Busk isn't a bit like that, mother; I saw quite plainly how it hurt her to do it. But she didn't dare do otherwise, she said; and so I got my notice.

Dr. Stockmann (laughing and rubbing his hands). She didn't dare do otherwise, either! It's delicious!

Mrs. Stockmann. Well, after the dreadful scenes last night——

Petra. It was not only that. Just listen to this, father!

Dr. Stockmann. Well?

Petra. Mrs. Busk showed me no less than three letters she received this morning——

Dr. Stockmann. Anonymous, I suppose?

Petra. Yes.

Dr. Stockmann. Yes, because they didn't dare to risk signing their names, Katherine!

Petra. And two of them were to the effect that a man, who has been our guest here, was declaring last night at the Club that my views on various subjects are extremely emancipated——

Dr. Stockmann. You did not deny that, I hope?

Petra. No, you know I wouldn't. Mrs. Busk's own views are tolerably emancipated, when we are alone together; but now that this report about me is being spread, she dare not keep me on any longer.

Mrs Stockmann. And some one who had been a guest of

ours! That shows you the return you get for your hospitality, Thomas!

Dr. Stockmann. We won't live in such a disgusting hole any longer. Pack up as quickly as you can, Katherine; the sooner we can get away, the better.

Mrs. Stockmann. Be quiet—I think I hear some one in the hall. See who it is, Petra.

Petra (opening the door). Oh, it's you, Captain Horster! Do come in.

Horster (coming in). Good morning. I thought I would just come in and see how you were.

Dr. Stockmann (shaking his hand). Thanks—that is really kind of you.

Mrs. Stockmann. And thank you, too, for helping us through the crowd, Captain Horster.

Petra. How did you manage to get home again?

Horster. Oh, somehow or other. I am fairly strong and there is more sound than fury about these folk.

Dr. Stockmann. Yes, isn't their swinish cowardice astonishing? Look here, I will show you something! There are all the stones they have thrown through my windows. Just look at them! I'm hanged if there are more than two decently large bits of hardstone in the whole heap; the rest are nothing but gravel—wretched little things. And yet they stood out there bawling and swearing that they would do me some violence; but as for *doing* anything—you don't see much of that in this town.

Horster. Just as well for you this time, doctor!

Dr. Stockmann. True enough. But it makes one angry all the same; because if some day it should be a question of a national fight in real earnest, you will see that public opinion will be in favour of taking to one's heels, and the compact majority will turn tail like a flock of sheep, Captain Horster. That is what is so mournful to think of; it gives me so much concern, that——. No, devil take it, it is ridiculous to care about it! They have called me an enemy of the people, so an enemy of the people let me be!

Mrs. Stockmann. You will never be that, Thomas.

Dr. Stockmann. Don't swear to that, Katherine. To be called an ugly name may have the same effect as a pin-scratch in the lung. And that hateful name—I can't get quit of it. It is sticking here in the pit of my stomach, eating into me like a corrosive acid. And no magnesia will remove it.

Petra. Bah!—you should only laugh at them, father.

Horster. They will change their minds some day, Doctor.

Mrs. Stockmann. Yes, Thomas, as sure as you are standing here.

Dr. Stockmann. Perhaps, when it is too late. Much good may it do them! They may wallow in their filth then and rue the day when they drove a patriot into exile. When do you sail, Captain Horster?

Horster. Hm!—that was just what I had come to speak about——

Dr. Stockmann. Why, has anything gone wrong with the ship?

Horster. No; but what has happened is that I am not to sail in it.

Petra. Do you mean that you have been dismissed from your command?

Horster (smiling). Yes, that's just it.

Petra. You too.

Mrs. Stockmann. There, you see, Thomas!

Dr. Stockmann. And that for the truth's sake! Oh, if I had thought such a thing possible——

Horster. You mustn't take it to heart; I shall be sure to find a job with some ship-owner or other, elsewhere.

Dr Stockmann. And that is this man Vik—a wealthy man, independent of every one and everything——! Shame on him!

Horster. He is quite an excellent fellow otherwise; he

told me himself he would willingly have kept me on, if only he had dared——

Dr. Stockmann. But he didn't dare? No, of course not.

Horster. It is not such an easy matter, he said, for a party man——

Dr. Stockmann. The worthy man spoke the truth. A party is like a sausage machine; it mashes up all sorts of heads together into the same mincemeat—fatheads and blockheads, all in one mash!

Mrs. Stockmann. Come, come, Thomas dear!

Petra (to HORSTER*).* If only you had not come home with us, things might not have come to this pass.

Horster. I do not regret it.

Petra (holding out her hand to him). Thank you for that!

Horster (to DR. STOCKMANN*).* And so what I came to say was that if you are determined to go away, I have thought of another plan——

Dr. Stockmann. That's splendid!—if only we can get away at once.

Mrs. Stockmann. Hush!—wasn't that some one knocking?

Petra. That is uncle, surely.

Dr. Stockmann. Aha! *(Calls out.)* Come in!

Mrs. Stockmanr. Dear Thomas, promise me definitely——

[PETER STOCKMANN *comes in from the hall.*

Peter Stockmann. Oh, you are engaged. In that case, I will——

Dr. Stockmann. No, no, come in.

Peter Stockmann. But I wanted to speak to you alone.

Mrs. Stockmann. We will go into the sitting-room in the meanwhile.

Horster. And I will look in again later.

Dr. Stockmann. No, go in there with them, Captain Horster; I want to hear more about——.

Horster. Very well, I will wait, then.

      [*He follows* Mrs. Stockmann *and* Petra *into the
sitting-room.*

Dr. Stockmann. I daresay you find it rather draughty
here to-day. Put your hat on.

Peter Stockmann. Thank you, if I may. *(Does so.)*
I think I caught cold last night; I stood and shivered——

Dr. Stockmann. Really? I found it warm enough.

Peter Stockmann. I regret that it was not in my power
to prevent those excesses last night.

Dr. Stockmann. Have you anything particular to say to
me besides that?

Peter Stockmann (taking a big letter from his pocket).
I have this document for you, from the Baths Committee.

Dr. Stockmann. My dismissal?

Peter Stockmann. Yes, dating from to-day. *(Lays the
letter on the table.)* It gives us pain to do it; but, to speak
frankly, we dared not do otherwise on account of public
opinion.

Dr. Stockmann (smiling). Dared not? I seem to have
heard that word before, to-day.

Peter Stockmann. I must beg you to understand your
position clearly. For the future you must not count on any
practice whatever in the town.

Dr. Stockmann. Devil take the practice! But why are
you so sure of that?

Peter Stockmann. The Householders' Association is cir-
culating a list from house to house. All right-minded citizens are being called upon to give up employing you; and
I can assure you that not a single head of a family will risk
refusing his signature. They simply dare not.

Dr. Stockmann. No, no; I don't doubt it. But what
then?

Peter Stockmann. If I might advise you, it would be best
to leave the place for a little while——

Dr. Stockmann. Yes, the propriety of leaving the place *has* occurred to me.

Peter Stockmann. Good. And then, when you have had six months to think things over, if, after mature considera-tion, you can persuade yourself to write a few words of re-gret, acknowledging your error——

Dr. Stockmann. I might have my appointment restored to me, do you mean?

Peter Stockmann. Perhaps. It is not at all impossible.

Dr. Stockmann. But what about public opinion, then? Surely you would not dare to do it on account of public feeling.

Peter Stockmann. Public opinion is an extremely muta-ble thing. And, to be quite candid with you, it is a matter of great importance to us to have some admission of that sort from you in writing.

Dr. Stockmann. Oh, that's what you are after, is it! I will just trouble you to remember what I said to you lately about foxy tricks of that sort!

Peter Stockmann. Your position was quite different then. At that time you had reason to suppose you had the whole town at your back——

Dr. Stockmann. Yes, and now I feel I have the whole town *on* my back—(*flaring up*) I would not do it if I had the devil and his dam on my back——! Never—never, I tell you!

Peter Stockmann. A man with a family has no right to behave as you do. You have no right to do it, Thomas.

Dr. Stockmann. I have no right! There is only one single thing in the world a free man has no right to do. Do you know what that is?

Peter Stockmann. No.

Dr. Stockmann. Of course you don't, but I will tell you. A free man has no right to soil himself with filth; he has no right to behave in a way that would justify his spitting in his own face.

Peter Stockmann. This sort of thing sounds extremely plausible, of course; and if there were no other explanation for your obstinacy——. But as it happens that there is.

Dr. Stockmann. What do you mean?

Peter Stockmann. You understand very well what I mean. But, as your brother and as a man of discretion, I advise you not to build too much upon expectations and prospects that may so very easily fail you.

Dr. Stockmann. What in the world is all this about?

Peter Stockmann. Do you really ask me to believe that you are ignorant of the terms of Mr. Kiil's will?

Dr. Stockmann. I know that the small amount he possesses is to go to an institution for indigent old workpeople. How does that concern me?

Peter Stockmann. In the first place, it is by no means a small amount that is in question. Mr. Kiil is a fairly wealthy man.

Dr. Stockmann. I had no notion of that!

Peter Stockmann. Hm!—hadn't you really? Then I suppose you had no notion, either, that a considerable portion of his wealth will come to your children, you and your wife having a life-rent of the capital. Has he never told you so?

Dr. Stockmann. Never, on my honour! Quite the reverse; he has consistently done nothing but fume at being so unconscionably heavily taxed. But are you perfectly certain of this, Peter?

Peter Stockmann. I have it from an absolutely reliable source.

Dr. Stockmann. Then, thank God, Katherine is provided for—and the children too! I must tell her this at once— *(calls out)* Katherine, Katherine!

Peter Stockmann (restraining him). Hush, don't say a word yet!

Mrs. Stockmann (opening the door). What is the matter?

Dr. Stockmann. Oh, nothing, nothing; you can go back. *(She shuts the door.* DR. STOCKMANN *walks up and down in his excitement.)* Provided for!——Just think of it, we are all provided for! And for life! What a blessed feeling it is to know one is provided for!

Peter Stockmann. Yes, but that is just exactly what you are not. Mr. Kiil can alter his will any day he likes.

Dr. Stockmann. But he won't do that, my dear Peter. The "Badger" is much too delighted at my attack on you and your wise friends.

Peter Stockmann (starts and looks intently at him). Ah, that throws a light on various things.

Dr. Stockmann. What things?

Peter Stockmann. I see that the whole thing was a combined manœuvre on your part and his. These violent, reckless attacks that you have made against the leading men of the town, under the pretence that it was in the name of truth——

Dr. Stockmann. What about them?

Peter Stockmann. I see that they were nothing else than the stipulated price for that vindictive old man's will.

Dr. Stockmann (almost speechless). Peter—you are the most disgusting plebeian I have ever met in all my life.

Peter Stockmann. All is over between us. Your dismissal is irrevocable—we have a weapon against you now.

[*Goes out.*

Dr. Stockmann. For shame! For shame! *(Calls out.)* Katherine, you must have the floor scrubbed after him! Let—what's her name—devil take it, the girl who has always got soot on her nose——

Mrs. Stockmann (in the sitting-room). Hush, Thomas, be quiet!

Petra (coming to the door). Father, grandfather is here, asking if he may speak to you alone.

Dr. Stockmann. Certainly he may. *(Going to the door.)* Come in, Mr. Kiil. *(*MORTEN KIIL *comes in.* DR.

Stockmann *shuts the door after him.)* What can I do for you? Won't you sit down?

Morten Kiil. I won't sit. *(Looks around.)* You look very comfortable here to-day, Thomas.

Dr. Stockmann. Yes, don't we!

Morten Kiil. Very comfortable—plenty of fresh air. I should think you have got enough to-day of that oxygen you were talking about yesterday. Your conscience must be in splendid order to-day, I should think.

Dr. Stockmann. It is.

Morten Kiil. So I should think. *(Taps his chest.)* Do you know what I have got here?

Dr. Stockmann. A good conscience, too, I hope.

Morten Kiil. Bah!—No, it is something better than that.

> [*He takes a thick pocket-book from his breast-pocket, opens it, and displays a packet of papers.*

Dr. Stockmann (looking at him in astonishment). Shares in the Baths?

Morten Kiil. They were not difficult to get to-day.

Dr. Stockmann. And you have been buying——?

Morten Kiil. As many as I could pay for.

Dr. Stockmann. But, my dear Mr. Kiil—consider the state of the Baths' affairs!

Morten Kiil. If you behave like a reasonable man, you can soon set the Baths on their feet again.

Dr. Stockmann. Well, you can see for yourself that I have done all I can, but——. They are all mad in this town!

Morten Kiil. You said yesterday that the worst of this pollution came from my tannery. If that is true, then my grandfather and my father before me, and I myself, for many years past, have been poisoning the town like three destroying angels. Do you think I am going to sit quiet under that reproach?

Dr. Stockmann. Unfortunately, I am afraid you will have to.

Morten Kiil. No, thank you. I am jealous of my name and reputation. They call me "the Badger," I am told. A badger is a kind of pig, I believe; but I am not going to give them the right to call me that. I mean to live and die a clean man.

Dr. Stockmann. And how are you going to set about it?

Morten Kiil. You shall cleanse me, Thomas.

Dr. Stockmann. I!

Morten Kiil. Do you know what money I have bought these shares with? No, of course you can't know—but I will tell you. It is the money that Katherine and Petra and the boys will have when I am gone. Because I have been able to save a little bit after all, you know.

Dr. Stockmann (flaring up). And you have gone and taken Katherine's money for *this!*

Morten Kiil. Yes, the whole of the money is invested in the Baths now. And now I just want to see whether you are quite stark, staring mad, Thomas! If you still make out that these animals and other nasty things of that sort come from my tannery, it will be exactly as if you were to flay broad strips of skin from Katherine's body, and Petra's, and the boys'; and no decent man would do that—unless he were mad.

Dr. Stockmann (walking up and down). Yes, but I *am* mad; I *am* mad!

Morten Kiil. You cannot be so absurdly mad as all that, when it is a question of your wife and children.

Dr. Stockmann (standing still in front of him). Why couldn't you consult me about it, before you went and bought all that trash?

Morten Kiil. What is done cannot be undone.

Dr. Stockmann (walks about uneasily). If only I were not so certain about it——! But I am absolutely convinced that I am right.

Morten Kiil (weighing the pocket-book in his hand).

If you stick to your mad idea, this won't be worth much, you know. *(Puts the pocket-book in his pocket.)*

Dr. Stockmann. But, hang it all! it might be possible for science to discover some prophylactic, I should think— or some antidote of some kind——

Morten Kiil. To kill these animals, do you mean?

Dr. Stockmann. Yes, or to make them innocuous.

Morten Kiil. Couldn't you try some rat's-bane?

Dr. Stockmann. Don't talk nonsense! They all say it is only imagination, you know. Well, let it go at that! Let them have their own way about it! Haven't the ignorant, narrow-minded curs reviled me as an enemy of the people? —and haven't they been ready to tear the clothes off my back too?

Morten Kiil. And broken all your windows to pieces!

Dr. Stockmann. And then there is my duty to my family. I must talk it over with Katherine; she is great on those things.

Morten Kiil. That is right; be guided by a reasonable woman's advice.

Dr. Stockmann (advancing towards him). To think you could do such a preposterous thing! Risking Katherine's money in this way, and putting me in such a horribly painful dilemma! When I look at you, I think I see the devil himself——.

Morten Kiil. Then I had better go. But I must have an answer from you before two o'clock—yes or no. If it is no, the shares go to a charity, and that this very day.

Dr. Stockmann. And what does Katherine get?

Morten Kiil. Not a halfpenny. *(The door leading to the hall opens, and* HOVSTAD *and* ASLAKSEN *make their appearance.)* Look at those two!

Dr. Stockmann (staring at them). What the devil!— have *you* actually the face to come into my house?

Hovstad. Certainly.

Aslaksen.   We have something to say to you, you see.

Morten Kiil (in a whisper).   Yes or no—before two o'clock.

Aslaksen (glancing at Hovstad*).*   Aha!

[Morten Kiil *goes out.*

Dr. Stockmann.   Well, what do you want with me?   Be brief.

Hovstad.   I can quite understand that you are annoyed with us for our attitude at the meeting yesterday——

Dr. Stockmann.   Attitude, do you call it?   Yes, it was a charming attitude!   I call it weak, womanish—damnably shameful!

Hovstad.   Call it what you like, we could not do otherwise.

Dr. Stockmann.   You *dared* not do otherwise—isn't that it?

Hovstad.   Well, if you like to put it that way.

Aslaksen.   But why did you not let us have word of it beforehand?—just a hint to Mr. Hovstad or to me?

Dr. Stockmann.   A hint?   Of what?

Aslaksen.   Of what was behind it all.

Dr. Stockmann.   I don't understand you in the least.

Aslaksen (with a confidential nod).   Oh, yes, you do, Dr. Stockmann.

Hovstad.   It is no good making a mystery of it any longer.

Dr. Stockmann (looking first at one of them and then at the other).   What the devil do you both mean?

Aslaksen.   May I ask if your father-in-law is not going round the town buying up all the shares in the Baths?

Dr. Stockmann.   Yes, he has been buying Baths' shares to-day; but——

Aslaksen.   It would have been more prudent to get some one else to do it—some one less nearly related to you.

Hovstad.   And you should not have let your name appear

in the affair. There was no need for anyone to know that the attack on the Baths came from you. You ought to have consulted me, Dr. Stockmann.

Dr. Stockmann (looks in front of him; then a light seems to dawn on him and he says in amazement:) Are such things conceivable? Are such things possible?

Aslaksen (with a smile). Evidently they are. But it is better to use a little *finesse,* you know.

Hovstad. And it is much better to have several persons in a thing of that sort; because the responsibility of each individual is lessened, when there are others with him.

Dr. Stockmann (composedly). Come to the point, gentlemen. What do you want?

Aslaksen. Perhaps Mr. Hovstad had better——

Hovstad. No, you tell him, Aslaksen.

Aslaksen. Well, the fact is that, now we know the bearings of the whole affair, we think we might venture to put the "People's Messenger" at your disposal.

Dr. Stockmann. Do you dare do that now? What about public opinion? Are you not afraid of a storm breaking upon our heads?

Hovstad. We will try to weather it.

Aslaksen. And you must be ready to go off quickly on a new tack, Doctor. As soon as your invective has done its work——

Dr. Stockmann. Do you mean, as soon as my father-in-law and I have got hold of the shares at a low figure?

Hovstad. Your reasons for wishing to get the control of the Baths are mainly scientific, I take it.

Dr. Stockmann. Of course; it was for scientific reasons that I persuaded the old "Badger" to stand in with me in the matter. So we will tinker at the conduit-pipes a little, and dig up a little bit of the shore, and it shan't cost the town a sixpence. That will be all right—eh?

Hovstad. I think so—if you have the "People's Messenger" behind you.

Aslaksen. The Press is a power in a free community, Doctor.

Dr. Stockmann. Quite so. And so is public opinion. And you, Mr. Aslaksen—I suppose you will be answerable for the Householders' Association?

Aslaksen. Yes, and for the Temperance Society. You may rely on that.

Dr. Stockmann. But, gentlemen—I really am ashamed to ask the question—but, what return do you——?

Hovstad. We should prefer to help you without any return whatever, believe me. But the "People's Messenger" is in rather a shaky condition; it doesn't go really well; and I should be very unwilling to suspend the paper now, when there is so much work to do here in the political way.

Dr. Stockmann. Quite so; that would be a great trial to such a friend of the people as you are. *(Flares up.)* But I am an enemy of the people, remember! *(Walks about the room.)* Where have I put my stick? Where the devil is my stick?

Hovstad. What's that?

Aslaksen. Surely you never mean——?

Dr. Stockmann (standing still). And suppose I don't give you a single penny of all I get out of it? Money is not very easy to get out of us rich folk, please to remember!

Hovstad. And you please to remember that this affair of the shares can be represented in two ways!

Dr. Stockmann. Yes, and you are just the man to do it. If I don't come to the rescue of the "People's Messenger," you will certainly take an evil view of the affair; you will hunt me down, I can well imagine—pursue me—try to throttle me as a dog does a hare.

Hovstad. It is a natural law; every animal must fight for its own livelihood.

Aslaksen. And get its food where it can, you know.

Dr. Stockmann (walking about the room). Then you go and look for yours in the gutter; because I am going to show you which is the strongest animal of us three! *(Finds an umbrella and brandishes it above his head.)* Ah, now——!

Hovstad. You are surely not going to use violence!

Aslaksen. Take care what you are doing with that umbrella.

Dr. Stockmann. Out of the window with you, Mr. Hovstad!

Hovstad (edging to the door). Are you quite mad!

Dr. Stockmann. Out of the window, Mr. Aslaksen! Jump, I tell you! You will have to do it, sooner or later.

Aslaksen (running round the writing-table). Moderation, Doctor—I am a delicate man—I can stand so little— *(calls out.)* help, help!

> [MRS. STOCKMANN, PETRA *and* HORSTER *come in from the sitting-room.*

Mrs. Stockmann. Good gracious, Thomas! What is happening?

Dr. Stockmann (brandishing the umbrella). Jump out, I tell you! Out into the gutter!

Hovstad. An assault on an unoffending man! I call you to witness, Captain Horster.

> [*Hurries out through the hall.*

Aslaksen (irresolutely). If only I knew the way about here——. [*Steals out through the sitting-room.*

Mrs. Stockmann (holding her husband back). Control yourself, Thomas!

Dr. Stockmann (throwing down the umbrella). Upon my soul, they have escaped after all.

Mrs. Stockmann. What did they want you to do?

Dr. Stockmann. I will tell you later on; I have something else to think about now. *(Goes to the table and writes something on a calling-card.)* Look there, Katherine; what is written there?

Mrs. Stockmann. Three big No's; what does that mean?

Dr. Stockmann. I will tell you that too, later on. *(Holds out the card to* PETRA.*)* There, Petra; tell sooty-face to run over to the "Badger's" with that, as quickly as she can. Hurry up!

[PETRA *takes the card and goes out to the hall.*

Dr. Stockmann. Well, I think I have had a visit from every one of the devil's messengers to-day! But now I am going to sharpen my pen till they can feel its point; I shall dip it in venom and gall; I shall hurl my ink-pot at their heads!

Mrs. Stockmann. Yes, but we are going away, you know, Thomas.

[PETRA *comes back.*

Dr. Stockmann. Well?

Petra. She has gone with it.

Dr. Stockmann. Good.——Going away, did you say? No, I'll be hanged if we are going away! We are going to stay where we are, Katherine!

Petra. Stay here?

Mrs. Stockmann. Here, in the town?

Dr. Stockmann. Yes, here. This is the field of battle— this is where the fight will be. This is where I shall triumph! As soon as I have had my trousers sewn up I shall go out and look for another house. We must have a roof over our heads for the winter.

Horster. That you shall have in my house.

Dr. Stockmann. Can I?

Horster. Yes, quite well. I have plenty of room, and I am almost never at home.

Mrs. Stockmann. How good of you, Captain Horster!

Petra. Thank you!

Dr. Stockmann (grasping his hand). Thank you, thank you! That is one trouble over! Now I can set to work in earnest at once. There is an endless amount of things to look through here, Katherine! Luckily I shall have all my time at my disposal; because I have been dismissed from the Baths, you know.

Mrs. Stockmann (with a sigh). Oh, yes, I expected that

Dr. Stockmann. And they want to take my practice away from me, too. Let them! I have got the poor people to fall back upon, anyway—those that don't pay anything; and, after all, they need me most, too. But, by Jove, they will have to listen to me; I shall preach to them in season and out of season, as it says somewhere.

Mrs. Stockmann. But, dear Thomas, I should have thought events had showed you what use it is to preach.

Dr. Stockmann. You are really ridiculous, Katherine. Do you want me to let myself be beaten off the field by public opinion and the compact majority and all that devilry? No, thank you! And what I want to do is so simple and clear and straightforward. I only want to drum into the heads of these curs the fact that the liberals are the most insidious enemies of freedom—that party programmes strangle every young and vigorous truth—that considerations of expediency turn morality and justice upside down—and that they will end by making life here unbearable. Don't you think, Captain Horster, that I ought to be able to make people understand that?

Horster. Very likely; I don't know much about such things myself.

Dr. Stockmann. Well, look here—I will explain! It is the party leaders that must be exterminated A party leader is like a wolf, you see—like a voracious wolf. He requires a certain number of smaller victims to prey upon every year, if he is to live. Just look at Hovstad and Aslaksen! How many smaller victims have they not put an end to—or at any rate maimed and mangled until they are fit for nothing except to be householders or subscribers to the "People's Messenger"! *(Sits down on the edge of the table.)* Come here, Katherine—look how beautifully the sun shines to-day! And this lovely spring air I am drinking in!

Mrs. Stockmann. Yes, if only we could live on sunshine and spring air, Thomas.

Dr. Stockmann. Oh, you will have to pinch and save a bit—then we shall get along. That gives me very little concern. What is much worse is that I know of no one who is liberal-minded and high-minded enough to venture to take up my work after me.

Petra. Don't think about that, father; you have plenty of time before you.——Hullo, here are the boys already!

> [EJLIF *and* MORTEN *come in from the sitting-room.*

Mrs. Stockmann. Have you got a holiday?

Morten. No; but we were fighting with the other boys between lessons——

Ejlif. That isn't true; it was the other boys were fighting with us.

Morten. Well, and then Mr. Rörlund said we had better stay at home for a day or two.

Dr. Stockmann (snapping his fingers and getting up from the table). I have it! I have it, by Jove! You shall never set foot in the school again!

The Boys. No more school!

Mrs. Stockmann. But, Thomas——

Dr. Stockmann. Never, I say. I will educate you myself; that is to say, you shan't learn a blessed thing——

Morten. Hooray!

Dr. Stockmann. ——but I will make liberal-minded and high-minded men of you. You must help me with that, Petra.

Petra. Yes, father, you may be sure I will.

Dr. Stockmann. And my school shall be in the room where they insulted me and called me an enemy of the people. But we are too few as we are; I must have at least twelve boys to begin with.

Mrs. Stockmann. You will certainly never get them in this town.

Dr. Stockmann. We shall. *(To the boys.)* Don't you know any street urchins—regular ragamuffins——?

Morten.   Yes, father, I know lots!

Dr. Stockmann.   That's capital!   Bring me some specimens of them.   I am going to experiment with curs, just for
once; there may be some exceptional heads amongst them.

Morten.   And what are we going to do, when you have
made liberal-minded and high-minded men of us?

Dr. Stockmann.   Then you shall drive all the wolves out
of the country, my boys!

       [EJLIF *looks rather doubtful about it;* MORTEN
           jumps about crying "Hurrah!"

Mrs. Stockmann.   Let us hope it won't be the wolves that
will drive you out of the country, Thomas.

Dr. Stockmann.   Are you out of your mind, Katherine?
Drive me out!   Now—when I am the strongest man in the
town!

Mrs. Stockmann.   The strongest—now?

Dr. Stockmann.   Yes, and I will go so far as to say that
now I am the strongest man in the whole world.

Morten.   I say!

Dr. Stockmann (lowering his voice).   Hush!   You
mustn't say anything about it yet; but I have made a great
discovery.

Mrs. Stockmann.   Another one?

Dr. Stockmann.   Yes. *(Gathers them round him, and
says confidentially:)* It is this, let me tell you—that the
strongest man in the world is he who stands most alone.

Mrs. Stockmann (smiling and shaking her head).   Oh,
Thomas, Thomas!

Petra (encouragingly, as she grasps her father's hands).
Father!

THE MASTER BUILDER
(1892)

CHARACTERS

HALVARD SOLNESS, *Master Builder*.
ALINE SOLNESS, *his wife*.
DOCTOR HERDAL, *physician*.
KNUT BROVIK, *formerly an architect, now in* SOLNESS'S *employment*.
RAGNER BROVIK, *his son, draughtsman*.
KAIA FOSLI, *his niece, book-keeper*.
MISS HILDA WANGEL.
Some Ladies.
A Crowd in the street.

The action passes in and about SOLNESS'S *house*.

THE MASTER BUILDER

ACT I

A plainly furnished work-room in the house of HALVARD
SOLNESS. *Folding doors on the left lead out to the hall.
On the right is the door leading to the inner rooms of
the house. At the back is an open door into the
draughtsmen's office. In front, on the left, a desk with
books, papers and writing materials. Further back
than the folding-door, a stove. In the right-hand corner, a sofa, a table and one or two chairs. On the
table a water-bottle and glass. A smaller table, with a
rocking-chair and arm-chair, in front on the right.
Lighted lamps, with shades, on the table in the draughtsmen's office, on the table in the corner and on the desk.*
In the draughtsmen's office sit KNUT BROVIK *and his son*
RAGNAR, *occupied with plans and calculations. At the
desk in the outer office stands* KAIA FOSLI, *writing in
the ledger.* KNUT BROVIK *is a spare old man with
white hair and beard. He wears a rather threadbare
but well-brushed black coat, spectacles and a somewhat
discoloured white neckcloth.* RAGNAR BROVIK *is a
well-dressed, light-haired man in his thirties, with a
slight stoop.* KAIA FOSLI *is a slightly built girl, a little
over twenty, carefully dressed and delicate-looking
She has a green shade over her eyes.——All three go on
working for some time in silence.*

Knut Brovik *(rises suddenly, as if in distress, from the*

table; breathes heavily and laboriously as he comes forward into the doorway). No, I can't bear it much longer!

Kaia (going up to him). You are feeling very ill this evening, are you not, uncle?

Brovik. Oh, I seem to get worse every day.

Ragnar (has risen and advances). You ought to go home, father. Try to get a little sleep——

Brovik (impatiently). Go to bed, I suppose? Would you have me stifled outright?

Kaia. Then take a little walk.

Ragnar. Yes, do. I will come with you.

Brovik (with warmth). I will not go till he comes! I am determined to have it out this evening with—*(in a tone of suppressed bitterness)*—with him—with the chief.

Kaia (anxiously). Oh no, uncle—do wait awhile before doing that.

Ragnar. Yes, better wait, father!

Brovik (draws his breath laboriously). Ha—ha——! I haven't much time for waiting.

Kaia (listening). Hush! I hear him on the stairs.

    [*All three go back to their work. A short silence.*

    [HALVARD SOLNESS *comes in through the hall door. He is a man no longer young, but healthy and vigorous, with close-cut curly hair, dark moustache and dark thick eyebrows. He wears a greyish-green buttoned jacket with an upstanding collar and broad lapels. On his head he wears a soft grey felt hat, and he has one or two light portfolios under his arm.*

Solness (near the door, points towards the draughtsmen's office, and asks in a whisper:) Are they gone?

Kaia (softly, shaking her head). No.

    [*She takes the shade off her eyes.* SOLNESS *crosses the room, throws his hat on a chair, places the portfolios on the table by the sofa and ap-*

proaches the desk again. KAIA *goes on writing without intermission, but seems nervous and un-easy.*

Solness (aloud). What is that you are entering, Miss Fosli?

Kaia (starts). Oh, it is only something that——

Solness. Let me look at it, Miss Fosli. *(Bends over her, pretends to be looking into the ledger, and whispers:)* Kaia!

Kaia (softly, still writing). Well?

Solness. Why do you always take that shade off when I come?

Kaia (as before). I look so ugly with it on.

Solness (smiling). Then you don't like to look ugly, Kaia?

Kaia (half glancing up at him.) Not for all the world. Not in your eyes.

Solness (stroking her hair gently). Poor, poor little Kaia——

Kaia (bending her head). Hush—they can hear you.

[SOLNESS *strolls across the room to the right, turns and pauses at the door of the draughtsmen's office.*

Solness. Has any one been here for me?

Ragnar (rising). Yes, the young couple who want a villa built, out at Lövstrand.

Solness (growling). Oh, those two! They must wait. I am not quite clear about the plans yet.

Ragnar (advancing, with some hesitation). They were very anxious to have the drawings at once.

Solness (as before). Yes, of course—so they all are.

Brovik (looks up). They say they are longing so to get into a house of their own.

Solness. Yes, yes—we know all that! And so they are content to take whatever is offered them. They get a—a

roof over their heads—an address—but nothing to call a
home. No thank you! In that case, let them apply to
somebody else. Tell them that, the next time they call.

*Brovik (pushes his glasses up on to his forehead and looks
in astonishment at him.)* To somebody else? Are you
prepared to give up the commission?

Solness (impatiently). Yes, yes, yes, devil take it! If
that is to be the way of it——. Rather that, than build
away at random. *(Vehemently.)* Besides, I know very
little about these people as yet.

Brovik. The people are safe enough. Ragnar knows
them. He is a friend of the family. Perfectly safe people.

Solness. Oh, safe—safe enough! That is not at all what
I mean. Good Lord—don't you understand me either?
(Angrily.) I won't have anything to do with these strangers. They may apply to whom they please, so far as I am
concerned.

Brovik (rising). Do you really mean that?

Solness (sulkily). Yes I do,—For once in a way.

> [*He comes forward.*
>> [Brovik *exchanges a glance with* Ragnar, *who
>> makes a warning gesture. Then* Brovik *comes
>> into the front room.*

Brovik. May I have a few words with you?

Solness. Certainly.

Brovik (to Kaia*).* Just go in there for a moment, Kaia.

Kaia (uneasily). Oh, but uncle——

Brovik. Do as I say, child. And shut the door after
you.

> [Kaia *goes reluctantly into the draughtsmen's of-
> fice, glances anxiously and imploringly at* Sol-
> ness, *and shuts the door.*

Brovik (lowering his voice a little). I don't want the
poor children to know how ill I am.

Solness. Yes, you have been looking very poorly of late.

Brovik. It will soon be all over with me. My strength is ebbing—from day to day.

Solness. Won't you sit down?

Brovik. Thanks—may I?

Solness (placing the arm-chair more conveniently). Here —take this chair.—And now?

Brovik (has seated himself with difficulty). Well, you see, it's about Ragnar. That is what weighs most upon me. What is to become of him?

Solness. Of course your son will stay with me as long as ever he likes.

Brovik. But that is just what he does not like. He feels that he cannot stay here any longer.

Solness. Why, I should say he was very well off here. But if he wants more money, I should not mind——

Brovik. No, no! It is not that. *(Impatiently.)* But sooner or later he, too, must have a chance of doing something on his own account.

Solness (without looking at him). Do you think that Ragnar has quite talent enough to stand alone?

Brovik. No, that is just the heartbreaking part of it—I have begun to have my doubts about the boy. For you have never said so much as—as one encouraging word about him. And yet I cannot but think there must be something in him—he can't be without talent.

Solness. Well, but he has learnt nothing—nothing thoroughly, I mean. Except, of course, to draw.

Brovik (looks at him with covert hatred and says hoarsely). You had learned little enough of the business when you were in my employment. But that did not prevent you from setting to work—*(breathing with difficulty)*—and pushing your way up and taking the wind out of my sails— mine, and so many other people's.

Solness. Yes, you see—circumstances favoured me.

Brovik. You are right there. Everything favoured you.

But then how can you have the heart to let me go to my grave—without having seen what Ragnar is fit for? And of course I am anxious to see them married, too—before I go.

Solness (sharply). Is it she who wishes it?

Brovik. Not Kaia so much as Ragnar—he talks about it every day. *(Appealingly.)* You must—you must help him to get some independent work now! I must see something that the lad has done. Do you hear?

Solness (peevishly). Hang it, man, you can't expect me to drag commissions down from the moon for him!

Brovik. He has the chance of a capital commission at this very moment. A big bit of work.

Solness (uneasily, startled). Has he?

Brovik. If you would give your consent.

Solness. What sort of work do you mean?

Brovik (with some hesitation). He can have the building of that villa out at Lövstrand.

Solness. That! Why, I am going to build that myself.

Brovik. Oh, you don't much care about doing it.

Solness (flaring up). Don't care! I? Who dares to say that?

Brovik. You said so yourself just now.

Solness. Oh, never mind what I say.—Would they give Ragnar the building of that villa?

Brovik. Yes. You see, he knows the family. And then —just for the fun of the thing—he has made drawings and estimates and so forth——

Solness. Are they pleased with the drawings? The people who will have to live in the house?

Brovik. Yes. If you would only look through them and approve of them.

Solness. Then they would let Ragnar build their home for them?

Brovik. They were immensely pleased with his idea. They thought it exceedingly original, they said.

Solness. Oho! Original! Not the old-fashioned stuff that *I* am in the habit of turning out!

Brovik. It seemed to them different.

Solness (with suppressed irritation). So it was to see Ragnar that they came here—whilst I was out!

Brovik. They came to call upon you—and at the same time to ask whether you would mind retiring——

Solness (angrily). Retire? I?

Brovik. In case you thought that Ragnar's drawings——

Solness. I? Retire in favour of your son!

Brovik. Retire from the agreement, they meant.

Solness. Oh, it comes to the same thing. *(Laughs angrily.)* So that is it, is it? Halvard Solness is to see about retiring now! To make room for younger men! For the very youngest, perhaps! He must make room! Room! Room!

Brovik. Why, good heavens! there is surely room for more than one single man——

Solness. Oh, there's not so very much room to spare either. But, be that as it may—I will never retire! I will never give way to anybody! Never of my own free will. Never in this world will I do that!

Brovik (rises with difficulty). Then I am to pass out of life without any certainty? Without a gleam of happiness? Without any faith or trust in Ragnar? Without having seen a single piece of work of his doing? Is that to be the way of it?

Solness (turns half aside and mutters). H'm—don't ask more just now.

Brovik. I must have an answer to this one question. Am I to pass out of life in such utter poverty?

Solness (seems to struggle with himself; finally he says, in a low but firm voice:) You must pass out of life as best you can.

Brovik. Then be it so.   [*He goes up the room.*

Solness (following him, half in desperation). Don't you understand that I cannot help it? I am what I am, and I cannot change my nature!

Brovik. No, no; I suppose you can't. *(Reels and supports himself against the sofa-table.)* May I have a glass of water?

Solness. By all means.

[*Fills a glass and hands it to him.*

Brovik. Thanks.

[*Drinks and puts the glass down again.*
[SOLNESS *goes up and opens the door of the draughtsmen's office.*

Solness. Ragnar—you must come and take your father home.

[RAGNAR *rises quickly. He and* KAIA *come into the work-room.*

Ragnar. What is the matter, father?

Brovik. Give me your arm. Now let us go.

Ragnar. Very well. You had better put your things on, too, Kaia.

Solness. Miss Fosli must stay—just for a moment. There is a letter I want written.

Brovik (looks at SOLNESS*).* Good night. Sleep well—if you can.

Solness. Good night.

[BROVIK *and* RAGNAR *go out by the hall door.* KAIA *goes to the desk.* SOLNESS *stands with bent head, to the right, by the armchair.*

Kaia (dubiously). Is there any letter——?

Solness (curtly). No, of course not. *(Looks sternly at her.)* Kaia!

Kaia (anxiously, in a low voice). Yes!

Solness (points imperatively to a spot on the floor). Come here! At once!

Kaia (hesitatingly). Yes.

Solness (as before). Nearer!

Kaia (obeying).   What do you want with me?

Solness (looks at her for a while).   Is it you I have to thank for all this?

Kaia.   No, no, don't think that!

Solness.   But confess now—you want to get married!

Kaia (softly).   Ragnar and I have been engaged for four or five years, and so——

Solness.   And so you think it time there were an end to it.   Is not that so?

Kaia.   Ragnar and Uncle say I must.   So I suppose I shall have to give in.

Solness (more gently).   Kaia, don't you really care a little bit for Ragnar, too?

Kaia.   I cared very much for Ragnar once—before I came here to you.

Solness.   But you don't now?   Not in the least?

Kaia (passionately, clasping her hands and holding them out towards him).   Oh, you know very well there is only one person I care for now!   One, and one only, in all the world!   I shall never care for any one else.

Solness.   Yes, you say that.   And yet you go away from me—leave me alone here with everything on my hands.

Kaia.   But could I not stay with you, even if Ragnar ——?

Solness (repudiating the idea).   No, no, that is quite impossible.   If Ragnar leaves me and starts work on his own account, then of course he will need you himself.

Kaia (wringing her hands).   Oh, I feel as if I could not be separated from you!   It's quite, quite impossible!

Solness.   Then be sure you get those foolish notions out of Ragnar's head.   Marry him as much as you please— *(alters his tone.)*—I mean—don't let him throw up his good situation with me.   For then I can keep you, too, my dear Kaia.

Kaia.   Oh yes, how lovely that would be, if it could only be managed!

Solness (clasps her head with his two hands and whispers). For I cannot get on without you, you see. I must have you with me every single day.

Kaia (in nervous exaltation). My God! My God!

Solness (kisses her hair). Kaia—Kaia!

Kaia (sinks down before him). Oh, how good you are to me! How unspeakably good you are!

Solness (vehemently). Get up! For goodness' sake get up! I think I hear some one!

> [*He helps her to rise. She staggers over to the desk.*
>
> [MRS. SOLNESS *enters by the door on the right. She looks thin and wasted with grief, but shows traces of bygone beauty. Blonde ringlets. Dressed with good taste, wholly in black. Speaks somewhat slowly and in a plaintive voice.*

Mrs. Solness (in the doorway). Halvard!

Solness (turns). Oh, are you there, my dear——?

Mrs. Solness (with a glance at KAIA*).* I am afraid I am disturbing you.

Solness. Not in the least. Miss Fosli has only a short letter to write.

Mrs. Solness. Yes, so I see.

Solness. What do you want with me, Aline?

Mrs. Solness. I merely wanted to tell you that Dr. Herdal is in the drawing-room. Won't you come and see him, Halvard?

Solness (looks suspiciously at her). H'm—is the doctor so very anxious to talk to me?

Mrs. Solness. Well, not exactly anxious. He really came to see me; but he would like to say how-do-you-do to you at the same time.

Solness (laughs to himself). Yes, I daresay. Well, you must ask him to wait a little.

Mrs. Solness. Then you will come in presently?

Solness. Perhaps I will. Presently, presently, dear. In a little while.

Mrs. Solness (glancing again at KAIA*).* Well, now, don't forget, Halvard.

[*Withdraws and closes the door behind her.*

Kaia (softly). Oh dear, oh dear—I am sure Mrs. Solness thinks ill of me in some way!

Solness. Oh, not in the least. Not more than usual, at any rate. But all the same, you had better go now, Kaia.

Kaia. Yes, yes, now I must go.

Solness (severely). And mind you get that matter settled for me. Do you hear?

Kaia. Oh, if it only depended on me——

Solness. I will have it settled, I say! And to-morrow too—not a day later!

Kaia (terrified). If there's nothing else for it, I am quite willing to break off the engagement.

Solness (angrily). Break it off? Are you mad? Would you think of breaking it off?

Kaia (distracted). Yes, if necessary. For I must—I must stay here with you! I can't leave you! That is utterly—utterly impossible!

Solness (with a sudden outburst). But deuce take it—how about Ragnar then! It's Ragnar that I——

Kaia (looks at him with terrified eyes). It is chiefly on Ragnar's account, that—that you——

Solness (collecting himself). No, no, of course not! You don't understand me either. (*Gently and softly.*) Of course it is you I want to keep—you above everything, Kaia. But for that very reason, you must prevent Ragnar, too, from throwing up his situation. There, there,—now go home.

Kaia. Yes, yes—good-night, then.

Solness. Good-night. (*As she is going.*) Oh, stop a moment! Are Ragnar's drawings in there?

Kaia. I did not see him take them with him.

Solness. Then just go and find them for me. I might perhaps glance over them, after all.

Kaia (happy). Oh yes, please do!

Solness. For your sake, Kaia dear. Now, let me have them at once, please.

> [KAIA *hurries into the draughtsmen's office, searches anxiously in the table-drawer, finds a portfolio and brings it with her.*

Kaia. Here are all the drawings.

Solness. Good. Put them down there on the table.

Kaia (putting down the portfolio). Good-night, then. (*Beseechingly.*) And please, please think kindly of me.

Solness. Oh, that I always do. Good-night, my dear little Kaia. *(Glances to the right.)* Go, go now!

> [MRS. SOLNESS *and* DR. HERDAL *enter by the door on the right. He is a stoutish, elderly man, with a round, good-humoured face, clean shaven, with thin, light hair, and gold spectacles.*

Mrs. Solness (still in the doorway). Halvard, I cannot keep the doctor any longer.

Solness. Well then, come in here.

Mrs. Solness (to KAIA, *who is turning down the desk-lamp).* Have you finished the letter already, Miss Fosli?

Kaia (in confusion). The letter——?

Solness. Yes, it was quite a short one.

Mrs. Solness. It must have been very short.

Solness. You may go now, Miss Fosli. And please come in good time to-morrow morning.

Kaia. I will be sure to. Good-night, Mrs. Solness.

> [*She goes out by the hall door.*

Mrs. Solness. She must be quite an acquisition to you, Halvard, this Miss Fosli.

Solness. Yes, indeed. She is useful in all sorts of ways.

Mrs. Solness. So it seems.

Dr. Herdal. Is she good at book-keeping too?

Solness. Well—of course she has had a good deal of practice during these two years. And then she is so nice and willing to do whatever one asks of her.

Mrs. Solness. Yes, that must be very delightful——

Solness. It is. Especially when one is not too much accustomed to that sort of thing.

Mrs. Solness (in a tone of gentle remonstrance). Can you say that, Halvard?

Solness. Oh, no, no, my dear Aline; I beg your pardon.

Mrs. Solness. There's no occasion.—Well then, doctor, you will come back later on and have a cup of tea with us?

Dr. Herdal. I have only that one patient to see and then I'll come back.

Mrs. Solness. Thank you.

                    [*She goes out by the door on the right*

Solness. Are you in a hurry, doctor?

Dr. Herdal. No, not at all.

Solness. May I have a little chat with you?

Dr. Herdal. With the greatest of pleasure.

Solness. Then let us sit down. *(He motions the doctor to take the rocking-chair and sits down himself in the armchair. Looks searchingly at him.)* Tell me—did you notice anything odd about Aline?

Dr. Herdal. Do you mean just now, when she was here?

Solness. Yes, in her manner to me. Did you notice anything?

Dr. Herdal (smiling). Well, I admit—one couldn't well avoid noticing that your wife—h'm——

Solness. Well?

Dr. Herdal. ——that your wife is not particularly fond of this Miss Fosli.

Solness. Is that all? I have noticed that myself.

Dr. Herdal. And I must say I am scarcely surprised at it.

Solness. At what?

Dr. Herdal. That she should not exactly approve of your seeing so much of another woman, all day and every day.

Solness. No, no, I suppose you are right there—and Aline too. But it's impossible to make any change.

Dr. Herdal. Could you not engage a clerk?

Solness. The first man that came to hand? No, thank you—that would never do for me.

Dr. Herdal. But now, if your wife——? Suppose, with her delicate health, all this tries her too much?

Solness. Even then—I might almost say—it can make no difference. I must keep Kaia Fosli. No one else could fill her place.

Dr. Herdal. No one else?

Solness (curtly). No, no one.

Dr. Herdal (drawing his chair closer). Now listen to me, my dear Mr. Solness. May I ask you a question, quite between ourselves?

Solness. By all means.

Dr. Herdal. Women, you see—in certain matters, they have a deucedly keen intuition——

Solness. They have, indeed. There is not the least doubt of that. But——?

Dr. Herdal. Well, tell me now—if your wife can't endure this Kaia Fosli——?

Solness. Well, what then?

Dr. Herdal. ——may she not have just—just the least little bit of reason for this instinctive dislike?

Solness (looks at him and rises). Oho!

Dr. Herdal. Now don't be offended—but hasn't she?

Solness (with curt decision). No.

Dr. Herdal. No reason of any sort?

Solness. No other reason than her own suspicious nature.

Dr. Herdal. I know you have known a good many women in your time.

Solness. Yes, I have.

Dr. Herdal. And have been a good deal taken with some of them, too.

Solness. Oh, yes, I don't deny it.

Dr. Herdal. But as regards Miss Fosli, then? There is nothing of that sort in the case?

Solness. No; nothing at all—on my side.

Dr. Herdal. But on her side?

Solness. I don't think you have any right to ask that question, doctor.

Dr. Herdal. Well, you know, we were discussing your wife's intuition.

Solness. So we were. And for that matter—*(lowers his voice)*—Aline's intuition, as you call it—in a certain sense, it has not been so far astray.

Dr. Herdal. Aha! there we have it!

Solness (sits down). Doctor Herdal—I am going to tell you a strange story—if you care to listen to it.

Dr. Herdal. I like listening to strange stories.

Solness. Very well then. I daresay you recollect that I took Knut Brovik and his son into my employment—after the old man's business had gone to the dogs.

Dr. Herdal. Yes, so I have understood.

Solness. You see, they really are clever fellows, these two. Each of them has talent in his own way. But then the son took it into his head to get engaged; and the next thing, of course, was that he wanted to get married—and begin to build on his own account. That is the way with all these young people.

Dr. Herdal (laughing). Yes, they have a bad habit of wanting to marry.

Solness. Just so. But of course that did not suit my plans; for I needed Ragnar myself—and the old man, too. He is exceedingly good at calculating bearing-strains and cubic contents—and all that sort of devilry, you know.

Dr. Herdal. Oh, yes, no doubt that's indispensable.

Solness. Yes, it is. But Ragnar was absolutely bent on setting to work for himself. He would hear of nothing else.

Dr. Herdal. But he has stayed with you all the same.

Solness. Yes, I'll tell you how that came about. One

day this girl, Kaia Fosli, came to see them on some errand
or other.   She had never been here before.   And when I
saw how utterly infatuated they were with each other, the
thought occurred to me: if I could only get her into the
office here, then perhaps Ragnar, too, would stay where he is.

Dr. Herdal.   That was not at all a bad idea.

Solness.   Yes, but at the time I did not breathe a word of
what was in my mind.   I merely stood and looked at her—
and kept on wishing intently that I could have her here.
Then I talked to her a little, in a friendly way—about one
thing and another.   And then she went away.

Dr. Herdal.   Well?

Solness.   Well, then, next day, pretty late in the evening,
when old Brovik and Ragnar had gone home, she came here
again and behaved as if I had made an arrangement with
her.

Dr. Herdal.   An arrangement?   What about?

Solness.   About the very thing my mind had been fixed
on.   But I hadn't said one single word about it.

Dr. Herdal.   That was most extraordinary.

Solness.   Yes, was it not?   And now she wanted to know
what she was to do here—whether she could begin the very
next morning, and so forth.

Dr. Herdal.   Don't you think she did it in order to be
with her sweetheart?

Solness.   That was what occurred to me at first.   But
no, that was not it.   She seemed to drift quite away from
him—when once she had come here to me.

Dr. Herdal.   She drifted over to you, then?

Solness.   Yes, entirely.   If I happen to look at her when
her back is turned, I can tell that she feels it.   She quivers
and trembles the moment I come near her.   What do you
think of that?

Dr. Herdal.   H'm—that's not very hard to explain.

Solness.   Well, but what about the other thing?   That
she believed I had said to her what I had only wished and

willed—silently—inwardly—to myself? What do you say to that? Can you explain that, Dr. Herdal?

Dr. Herdal. No, I won't undertake to do that.

Solness. I felt sure you would not; and so I have never cared to talk about it till now. But it's a cursed nuisance to me in the long run, you understand. Here I have to go on day after day pretending——. And it's a shame to treat her so, too, poor girl. *(Vehemently.)* But I cannot do anything else. For if she runs away from me—then Ragnar will be off too.

Dr. Herdal. And you have not told your wife the rights of the story?

Solness. No.

Dr. Herdal. Then why on earth don't you?

Solness (looks fixedly at him, and says in a low voice:) Because I seem to find a sort of—of salutary self-torture in allowing Aline to do me an injustice.

Dr. Herdal (shakes his head). I don't in the least understand what you mean.

Solness. Well, you see—it is like paying off a little bit of a huge, immeasurable debt——

Dr. Herdal. To your wife?

Solness. Yes; and that always helps to relieve one's mind a little. One can breathe more freely for a while, you understand.

Dr. Herdal. No, goodness knows, I don't understand at all——

Solness (breaking off, rises again). Well, well, well—then we won't talk any more about it. *(He saunters across the room, returns and stops beside the table. Looks at the doctor with a sly smile.)* I suppose you think you have drawn me out nicely now, doctor?

Dr. Herdal (with some irritation). Drawn you out? Again I have not the faintest notion what you mean, Mr. Solness.

Solness. Oh come, out with it; I have seen it quite clearly, you know.

Dr. Herdal. What have you seen?

Solness (in a low voice, slowly). That you have been quietly keeping on eye upon me.

Dr. Herdal. That *I* have! And why in all the world should I do that?

Solness. Because you think that I—— *(Passionately.)* Well, devil take it—you think the same of me as Aline does.

Dr. Herdal. And what does she think about you?

Solness (having recovered his self-control). She has begun to think that I am—that I am—ill.

Dr. Herdal. Ill! You! She has never hinted such a thing to me. Why, what can she think is the matter with you?

Solness (leans over the back of the chair and whispers). Aline has made up her mind that I am mad. That is what she thinks.

Dr. Herdal (rising). Why, my dear good fellow——!

Solness. Yes, on my soul she does! I tell you it is so. And she has got you to think the same! Oh, I can assure you, doctor, I see it in your face as clearly as possible. You don't take me in so easily, I can tell you.

Dr. Herdal (looks at him in amazement). Never, Mr. Solness—never has such a thought entered my mind.

Solness (with an incredulous smile). Really? Has it not?

Dr. Herdal. No, never! Nor your wife's mind either, I am convinced. I could almost swear to that.

Solness. Well, I wouldn't advise you to. For, in a certain sense, you see, perhaps—perhaps she is not so far wrong in thinking something of the kind.

Dr. Herdal. Come now, I really must say——

Solness (interrupting, with a sweep of his hand). Well, well, my dear doctor—don't let us discuss this any further.

We had better agree to differ. *(Changes to a tone of quiet amusement.)* But look here now, doctor—h'm——

Dr. Herdal. Well?

Solness. Since you don't believe that I am—ill—and crazy, and mad, and so forth——

Dr. Herdal. What then?

Solness. Then I daresay you fancy that I am an extremely happy man.

Dr. Herdal. Is that mere fancy?

Solness (laughs). No, no—of course not! Heaven forbid! Only think—to be Solness the master builder! Halvard Solness! What could be more delightful?

Dr. Herdal. Yes, I must say it seems to me you have had the luck on your side to an astounding degree.

Solness (suppresses a gloomy smile). So I have, I can't complain on that score.

Dr. Herdal. First of all that grim old robbers' castle was burnt down for you. And that was certainly a great piece of luck.

Solness (seriously). It was the home of Aline's family. Remember that.

Dr. Herdal. Yes, it must have been a great grief to her.

Solness. She has not got over it to this day—not in all these twelve or thirteen years.

Dr. Herdal. Ah, but what followed must have been the worst blow for her.

Solness. The one thing with the other.

Dr. Herdal. But you—yourself—you rose upon the ruins. You began as a poor boy from a country village—and now you are at the head of your profession. Ah, yes, Mr. Solness, you have undoubtedly had the luck on your side.

Solness (looking at him with embarrassment). Yes, but that is just what makes me so horribly afraid.

Dr. Herdal. Afraid? Because you have the luck on your side!

Solness. It terrifies me—terrifies me every hour of the day. For sooner or later the luck must turn, you see.

Dr. Herdal. Oh nonsense! What should make the luck turn?

Solness (with firm assurance). The younger generation.

Dr. Herdal. Pooh! The younger generation! You are not laid on the shelf yet, I should hope. Oh no—your position here is probably firmer now than it has ever been.

Solness. The luck will turn. I know it—I feel the day approaching. Some one or other will take it into his head to say: Give me a chance! And then all the rest will come clamouring after him, and shake their fists at me and shout: Make room—make room—make room! Yes, just you see, doctor—presently the younger generation will come knock at my door——

Dr. Herdal (laughing). Well, and what if they do?

Solness. What if they do? Then there's an end of Halvard Solness.

[*There is a knock at the door on the left.*

Solness (starts). What's that? Did you not hear something?

Dr. Herdal. Some one is knocking at the door.

Solness (loudly). Come in.

[HILDA WANGEL *enters by the hall door. She is of middle height, supple and delicately built. Somewhat sunburnt. Dressed in a tourist costume, with skirt caught up for walking, a sailor's collar open at the throat and a small sailor hat on her head. Knapsack on back, plaid in strap, and alpenstock.*

Hilda (goes straight up to SOLNESS, *her eyes sparkling with happiness).* Good evening!

Solness (looks doubtfully at her). Good evening——

Hilda (laughs). I almost believe you don't recognise me!

Solness. No—I must admit that—just for the moment

Dr. Herdal (approaching). But I recognise you, my dear young lady——

Hilda (pleased). Oh, is it you that——

Dr. Herdal. Of course it is. *(To* SOLNESS.*)* We met at one of the mountain stations this summer. *(To* HILDA.*)* What became of the other ladies?

Hilda. Oh, they went westward.

Dr. Herdal. They didn't much like all the fun we used to have in the evenings.

Hilda. No, I believe they didn't.

Dr. Herdal (holds up his finger at her). And I am afraid it can't be denied that you flirted a little with us.

Hilda. Well that was better fun than to sit there knitting stockings with all those old women.

Dr. Herdal (laughs). There I entirely agree with you.

Solness. Have you come to town this evening?

Hilda. Yes, I have just arrived.

Dr. Herdal. Quite alone, Miss Wangel?

Hilda. Oh, yes!

Solness. Wangel? Is your name Wangel?

Hilda (looks in amused surprise at him). Yes, of course it is.

Solness. Then you must be a daughter of the district doctor up at Lysanger?

Hilda (as before). Yes, who else's daughter should I be?

Solness. Oh, then I suppose we met up there, that summer when I was building a tower on the old church.

Hilda (more seriously). Yes, of course it was then we met.

Solness. Well, that is a long time ago.

Hilda (looks hard at him). It is exactly ten years.

Solness. You must have been a mere child then, I should think.

Hilda (carelessly). Well, I was twelve or thirteen.

Dr. Herdal. Is this the first time you have ever been up to town, Miss Wangel?

Hilda. Yes, it is indeed.

Solness. And don't you know any one here?

Hilda. Nobody but you. And of course, your wife.

Solness. So you know her, too?

Hilda. Only a little. We spent a few days together at the sanatorium.

Solness. Ah, up there?

Hilda. She said I might come and pay her a visit if ever I came up to town. *(Smiles.)* Not that that was necessary.

Solness. Odd that she should never have mentioned it.

> [HILDA *puts her stick down by the stove, takes off the knapsack and lays it and the plaid on the sofa.* DR. HERDAL *offers to help her.* SOLNESS *stands and gazes at her.*

Hilda (going towards him). Well, now I must ask you to let me stay the night here.

Solness. I am sure there will be no difficulty about that.

Hilda. For I have no other clothes than those I stand in, except a change of linen in my knapsack. And that has to go to the wash, for it's very dirty.

Solness. Oh, yes, that can be managed. Now I'll just let my wife know——

Dr. Herdal. Meanwhile I will go and see my patient.

Solness. Yes, do; and come again later on.

Dr. Herdal (playfully, with a glance at HILDA*).* Oh, that I will, you may be very certain! *(Laughs.)* So your prediction has come true, Mr. Solness!

Solness. How so?

Dr. Herdal. The younger generation did come knocking at your door.

Solness (cheerfully). Yes, but in a very different way from what I meant.

Dr. Herdal. Very different, yes. That's undeniable.

> [*He goes out by the hall door.* SOLNESS *opens the door on the right and speaks into the side room.*

Solness. Aline! Will you come in here, please. Here is a friend of yours—Miss Wangel.

Mrs. Solness (appears in the doorway). Who do you say it is? *(Sees* HILDA.*)* Oh, is it you, Miss Wangel? *(Goes up to her and offers her hand.)* So you have come to town after all.

Solness. Miss Wangel has this moment arrived; and she would like to stay the night here.

Mrs. Solness. Here with us? Oh yes, certainly.

Solness. Till she can get her things a little in order, you know.

Mrs. Solness. I will do the best I can for you. It's no more than my duty. I suppose your trunk is coming on later?

Hilda. I have no trunk.

Mrs. Solness. Well, it will be all right, I daresay. In the meantime, you must excuse my leaving you here with my husband, until I can get a room made a little comfortable for you.

Solness. Can we not give her one of the nurseries? They are all ready as it is.

Mrs. Solness. Oh, yes. There we have room and to spare. *(To* HILDA.*)* Sit down now, and rest a little.

[*She goes out to the right*

[HILDA, *with her hands behind her back, strolls about the room and looks at various objects.* SOLNESS *stands in front, beside the table, also with his hands behind his back, and follows her with his eyes.*

Hilda (stops and looks at him). Have you several nurseries?

Solness. There are three nurseries in the house.

Hilda. That's a lot. Then I suppose you have a great many children?

Solness. No. We have no child. But now you can be the child here, for the time being.

Hilda. For to-night, yes. I shall not cry. I mean to sleep as sound as a stone.

Solness. Yes, you must be very tired, I should think.

Hilda. Oh, no! But all the same—— It's so delicious to lie and dream.

Solness. Do you dream much of nights?

Hilda. Oh, yes! Almost always.

Solness. What do you dream about most?

Hilda. I shan't tell you to-night. Another time, perhaps.

> [*She again strolls about the room, stops at the desk and turns over the books and papers a little.*

Solness (approaching). Are you searching for anything?

Hilda. No, I am merely looking at all these things. (*Turns.*) Perhaps I mustn't?

Solness. Oh, by all means.

Hilda. Is it you that write in this great ledger?

Solness. No, it's my book-keeper.

Hilda. Is it a woman?

Solness (smiles). Yes.

Hilda. One you employ here, in your office?

Solness. Yes.

Hilda. Is she married?

Solness. No, she is single.

Hilda. Oh, indeed!

Solness. But I believe she is soon going to be married.

Hilda. That's a good thing for her.

Solness. But not such a good thing for me. For then I shall have nobody to help me.

Hilda. Can't you get hold of some one else who will do just as well?

Solness. Perhaps you would stay here and write in the ledger?

Hilda (measures him with a glance). Yes, I daresay! No, thank you—nothing of that sort for me.

[*She again strolls across the room and sits down in the rocking-chair.* SOLNESS, *too, goes to the table.*

Hilda (continuing). For there must surely be plenty of other things to be done here. *(Looks smiling at him.)* Don't you think so, too?

Solness. Of course. First of all, I suppose, you want to make a round of the shops and get yourself up in the height of fashion.

Hilda (amused). No, I think I shall let that alone!

Solness. Indeed.

Hilda. For you must know I have run through all my money.

Solness (laughs). Neither trunk nor money, then.

Hilda. Neither one nor the other. But never mind—it doesn't matter now.

Solness. Come now, I like you for that.

Hilda. Only for that?

Solness. For that among other things. *(Sits in the arm-chair.)* Is your father alive still?

Hilda. Yes, father's alive.

Solness. Perhaps you are thinking of studying here?

Hilda. No, that hadn't occurred to me.

Solness. But I suppose you will be staying for some time?

Hilda. That must depend upon circumstances.

[*She sits awhile rocking herself and looking at him, half seriously, half with a suppressed smile. Then she takes off her hat and puts it on the table in front of her.*

Hilda. Mr. Solness!

Solness. Well?

Hilda. Have you a very bad memory?

Solness. A bad memory? No, not that I am aware of.

Hilda. Then have you nothing to say to me about what happened up there?

Solness (in momentary surprise). Up at Lysanger? *(Indifferently.)* Why, it was nothing much to talk about, it seems to me.

Hilda (looks reproachfully at him). How can you sit there and say such things?

Solness. Well, then, you talk to me about it.

Hilda. When the tower was finished, we had grand doings in the town.

Solness. Yes, I shall not easily forget that day.

Hilda (smiles). Will you not? That comes well from you.

Solness. Comes well?

Hilda. There was music in the churchyard—and many, many hundreds of people. We school-girls were dressed in white; and we all carried flags.

Solness. Ah yes, those flags—I can tell you I remember them!

Hilda. Then you climbed right up the scaffolding, straight to the very top; and you had a great wreath with you; and you hung that wreath right away up on the weather-vane.

Solness (curtly interrupting). I always did that in those days. It was an old custom.

Hilda. It was so wonderfully thrilling to stand below and look up at you. Fancy, if he should fall over! He—the master builder himself!

Solness (as if to divert her from the subject). Yes, yes, yes, that might very well have happened, too. For one of those white-frocked little devils,—she went on in such a way, and screamed up at me so——

Hilda (sparkling with pleasure). "Hurrah for Master Builder Solness!" Yes!

Solness. ——and waved and flourished with her flag, so that I—so that it almost made me giddy to look at it.

Hilda (in a lower voice, seriously). That little devil—that was *I*.

Solness (fixes his eyes steadily upon her). I am sure of that now. It must have been you.

Hilda (lively again). Oh, it was so gloriously thrilling! I could not have believed there was a builder in the whole world that could build such a tremendously high tower. And then, that you yourself should stand at the very top of it, as large as life! And that you should not be the least bit dizzy! It was that above everything that made one—made one dizzy to think of.

Solness. How could you be so certain that I was not ——?

Hilda (scouting the idea). No indeed! Oh, no! I knew that instinctively. For if you had been, you could never have stood up there and sung.

Solness (looks at her in astonishment). Sung? Did *I* sing?

Hilda. Yes, I should think you did.

Solness (shakes his head). I have never sung a note in my life.

Hilda. Yes indeed, you sang then. It sounded like harps in the air.

Solness (thoughtfully). This is very strange—all this.

Hilda (is silent awhile, looks at him and says in a low voice:) But then,—it was after that—and the real thing happened.

Solness. The real thing?

Hilda (sparkling with vivacity). Yes, I surely don't need to remind you of that?

Solness. Oh, yes, do remind me a little of that, too.

Hilda. Don't you remember that a great dinner was given in your honour at the Club?

Solness. Yes, to be sure. It must have been the same afternoon, for I left the place next morning.

Hilda. And from the Club you were invited to come round to our house to supper.

Solness. Quite right, Miss Wangel. It is wonderful how

all these trifles have impressed themselves on your mind.

Hilda. Trifles! I like that! Perhaps it was a trifle, too, that I was alone in the room when you came in?

Solness. Were you alone?

Hilda (without answering him). You didn't call me a little devil then?

Solness. No, I suppose I did not.

Hilda. You said I was lovely in my white dress, and that I looked like a little princess.

Solness. I have no doubt you did, Miss Wangel.—And besides—I was feeling so buoyant and free that day——

Hilda. And then you said that when I grew up I should be your princess.

Solness (laughing a little). Dear, dear—did I say that, too?

Hilda. Yes, you did. And when I asked how long I should have to wait, you said that you would come again in ten years—like a troll and carry me off—to Spain or some such place. And you promised you would buy me a kingdom there.

Solness (as before). Yes, after a good dinner one doesn't haggle about the halfpence. But did I really say all that?

Hilda (laughs to herself). Yes. And you told me, too, what the kingdom was to be called.

Solness. Well, what was it?

Hilda. It was to be called the kingdom of Orangia,* you said.

Solness. Well, that was an appetising name.

Hilda. No, I didn't like it a bit; for it seemed as though you wanted to make game of me.

Solness. I am sure that cannot have been my intention.

Hilda. No, I should hope not—considering what you did next——

Solness. What in the world did I do next?

* In the original "Appelsinia," "appelsin" meaning "orange."

Hilda. Well, that's the finishing touch, if you have forgotten that, too. I should have thought no one could help remembering such a thing as that.

Solness. Yes, yes, just give me a hint, and then perhaps —— Well——

Hilda (looks fixedly at him). You came and kissed me, Mr. Solness.

Solness (open-mouthed, rising from his chair). I did!

Hilda. Yes, indeed you did. You took me in both your arms, and bent my head back and kissed me—many times.

Solness. Now really, my dear Miss Wangel——!

Hilda (rises). You surely cannot mean to deny it?

Solness. Yes, I do. I deny it altogether!

Hilda (looks scornfully at him). Oh, indeed!

> [*She turns and goes slowly close up to the stove, where she remains standing motionless, her face averted from him, her hands behind her back Short pause.*

Solness (goes cautiously up behind her). Miss Wangel ——!

Hilda (is silent and does not move).

Solness. Don't stand there like a statue. You must have dreamt all this. *(Lays his hand on her arm.)* Now just listen——

Hilda (makes an impatient movement with her arm).

Solness (as a thought flashes upon him). Or——! Wait a moment! There is something under all this, you may depend!

Hilda (does not move).

Solness (in a low voice, but with emphasis). I must have thought all that. I must have wished it—have willed it—have longed to do it. And then——. May not that be the explanation?

Hilda (is still silent).

Solness (impatiently). Oh very well, deuce take it all—then I did it, I suppose.

Hilda (turns her head a little, but without looking at him). Then you admit it now?

Solness. Yes—whatever you like.

Hilda. You came and put your arms around me?

Solness. Oh, yes!

Hilda. And bent my head back?

Solness. Very far back.

Hilda. And kissed me?

Solness. Yes, I did.

Hilda. Many times?

Solness. As many as ever you like.

Hilda (turns quickly towards him and has once more the sparkling expression of gladness in her eyes). Well, you see, I got it out of you at last!

Solness (with a slight smile). Yes—just think of my forgetting such a thing as that.

Hilda (again a little sulky, retreats from him). Oh, you have kissed so many people in your time, I suppose.

Solness. No, you mustn't think that of me. (HILDA *seats herself in the armchair.* SOLNESS *stands and leans against the rocking-chair. Looks observantly at her.)* Miss Wangel!

Hilda. Yes!

Solness. How was it now? What came of all this—between us two?

Hilda. Why, nothing more came of it. You know that quite well. For then the other guests came in, and then—bah!

Solness. Quite so! The others came in. To think of my forgetting that, too!

Hilda. Oh, you haven't really forgotten anything: you are only a little ashamed of it all. I am sure one doesn't forget things of that kind.

Solness. No, one would suppose not.

Hilda (lively again, looks at him). Perhaps you have even forgotten what day it was?

Solness. What day——?

Hilda. Yes, on what day did you hang the wreath on the tower? Well? Tell me at once!

Solness. H'm—I confess I have forgotten the particular day. I only knew it was ten years ago. Sometime in the autumn.

Hilda (nods her head slowly several times). It was ten years ago—on the 19th of September.

Solness. Yes, it must have been about that time. Fancy your remembering that, too! *(Stops.)* But wait a moment ——! Yes—it's the 19th of September to-day.

Hilda. Yes, it is; and the ten years are gone. And you didn't come—as you promised me.

Solness. Promised you? Threatened, I suppose you mean?

Hilda. I don't think there was any sort of threat in that.

Solness. Well then, a little bit of fun.

Hilda. Was that all you wanted? To make fun of me?

Solness. Well, or to have a little joke with you. Upon my soul, I don't recollect. But it must have been some-thing of that kind; for you were a mere child then.

Hilda. Oh, perhaps I wasn't quite such a child either. Not such a mere chit as you imagine.

Solness (looks searchingly at her). Did you really and seriously expect me to come again?

Hilda (conceals a half-teasing smile). Yes, indeed; I did expect that of you.

Solness. That I should come back to your home and take you away with me?

Hilda. Just like a troll—yes.

Solness. And make a princess of you?

Hilda. That's what you promised.

Solness. And give you a kingdom as well?

Hilda (looks up at the ceiling). Why not? Of course it need not have been an actual, every-day sort of kingdom.

Solness. But something else just as good?

Hilda. Yes, at least as good. *(Looks at him a moment.)* I thought, if you could build the highest church-towers in the world, you could surely manage to raise a kingdom of one sort or another as well.

Solness (shakes his head). I can't quite make you out, Miss Wangel.

Hilda. Can you not? To me it seems all so simple.

Solness. No, I can't make up my mind whether you mean all you say, or are simply having a joke with me.

Hilda (smiles). Making fun of you, perhaps? I, too?

Solness. Yes, exactly. Making fun—of both of us. *(Looks at her.)* Is it long since you found out that I was married?

Hilda. I have known it all along. Why do you ask me that?

Solness (lightly). Oh, well, it just occurred to me. *(Looks earnestly at her and says in a low voice.)* What have you come for?

Hilda. I want my kingdom. The time is up.

Solness (laughs involuntarily). What a girl you are!

Hilda (gaily). Out with my kingdom, Mr. Solness! *(Raps with her fingers.)* The kingdom on the table!

Solness (pushing the rocking-chair nearer and sitting down). Now, seriously speaking—what have you come for? What do you really want to do here?

Hilda. Oh, first of all, I want to go around and look at all the things that you have built.

Solness. That will give you plenty of exercise.

Hilda. Yes, I know you have built a tremendous lot.

Solness. I have indeed—especially of late years.

Hilda. Many church-towers among the rest? Immensely high ones?

Solness. No. I build no more church-towers now. Nor churches either.

Hilda. What do you build, then?

Solness. Homes for human beings.

Hilda (reflectively). Couldn't you build a little—a little bit of a church-tower over these homes as well?

Solness (starting). What do you mean by that?

Hilda. I mean—something that points—points up into the free air. With the vane at a dizzy height.

Solness (pondering a little). Strange that you should say that—for that is just what I am most anxious to do.

Hilda (impatiently). Why don't you do it, then?

Solness (shakes his head). No, the people will not have it.

Hilda. Fancy their not wanting it!

Solness (more lightly). But now I am building a new home for myself—just opposite here.

Hilda. For yourself?

Solness. Yes. It is almost finished. And on that there is a tower.

Hilda. A high tower?

Solness. Yes.

Hilda. Very high?

Solness. No doubt people will say it is too high—too high for a dwelling-house.

Hilda. I'll go out and look at that tower the first thing to-morrow morning.

Solness (sits resting his cheek on his hand and gazes at her). Tell me, Miss Wangel—what is your name? Your Christian name, I mean?

Hilda. Why, Hilda, of course.

Solness (as before). Hilda? Indeed?

Hilda. Don't you remember that? You called me Hilda yourself—that day when you misbehaved.

Solness. Did I really?

Hilda. But then you said "little Hilda"; and I didn't like that.

Solness. Oh, you didn't like that, Miss Hilda?

Hilda. No, not at such a time as that. But—"Princess Hilda"—that will sound very well, I think.

Solness. Very well indeed. Princess Hilda of—of—what was to be the name of the kingdom?

Hilda. Pooh! I won't have anything to do with that stupid kingdom. I have set my heart upon quite a different one!

Solness (has leaned back in the chair, still gazing at her). Isn't it strange——? The more I think of it now, the more it seems to me as though I had gone about all these years torturing myself with—h'm——

Hilda. With what?

Solness. With the effort to recover something—some experience, which I seemed to have forgotten. But I never had the least inkling of what it could be.

Hilda. You should have tied a knot in your pockethandkerchief, Mr. Solness.

Solness. In that case, I should simply have had to go racking my brains to discover what the knot could mean.

Hilda. Oh, yes, I suppose there are trolls of that kind in the world, too.

Solness (rises slowly). What a good thing it is that you have come to me now.

Hilda (looks deeply into his eyes). Is it a good thing?

Solness. For I have been so lonely here. I have been gazing so helplessly at it all. *(In a lower voice.)* I must tell you—I have begun to be so afraid—so terribly afraid of the younger generation.

Hilda (with a little snort of contempt). Pooh—is the younger generation a thing to be afraid of?

Solness. It is indeed. And that is why I have locked and barred myself in. *(Mysteriously.)* I tell you the younger generation will one day come and thunder at my door! They will break in upon me!

Hilda. Then I should say you ought to go out and open the door to the younger generation.

Solness. Open the door?

Hilda. Yes. Let them come in to you on friendly terms, as it were.

Solness. No, no, no! The younger generation—it means retribution, you see. It comes, as if under a new banner, heralding the turn of fortune.

Hilda (rises, looks at him and says with a quivering twitch of her lips). Can I be of any use to you, Mr. Solness?

Solness. Yes, you can indeed! For you, too, come—under a new banner, it seems to me. Youth marshalled against youth——!

[DR. HERDAL *comes in by the hall-door.*

Dr. Herdal. What—you and Miss Wangel here still?

Solness. Yes. We have had no end of things to talk about.

Hilda. Both old and new.

Dr. Herdal. Have you really?

Hilda. Oh, it has been the greatest fun. For Mr. Solness—he has such a miraculous memory. All the least little details he remembers instantly.

[MRS. SOLNESS *enters by the door on the right.*

Mrs. Solness. Well, Miss Wangel, your room is quite ready for you now.

Hilda. Oh, how kind you are to me!

Solness (to MRS. SOLNESS). The nursery?

Mrs. Solness. Yes, the middle one. But first let us go in to supper.

Solness (nods to HILDA). Hilda shall sleep in the nursery, she shall.

Mrs. Solness (looks at him). Hilda?

Solness. Yes, Miss Wangel's name is Hilda. I knew her when she was a child.

Mrs. Solness. Did you really, Halvard? Well, shall we go? Supper is on the table.

[*She takes* DR. HERDAL'S *arm and goes out with*

him to the right. HILDA *has meanwhile been collecting her travelling things.*

Hilda (softly and rapidly to SOLNESS*).* Is it true, what you said? Can I be of use to you?

Solness (takes the things from her). You are the very being I have needed most.

Hilda (looks at him with happy, wondering eyes and clasps her hands). But then, great heavens——!

Solness (eagerly). What——?

Hilda. Then I have my kingdom!

Solness (involuntarily). Hilda——!

Hilda (again with the quivering twitch of her lips). Almost—I was going to say.

　　　　　[*She goes out to the right,* SOLNESS *follows her.*

ACT II

A prettily furnished small drawing-room in SOLNESS'S *house.
In the back, a glass door leading out to the verandah
and garden. The right-hand corner is cut off trans-
versely by a large bay-window, in which are flower-
stands. The left-hand corner is similarly cut off by a
transverse wall, in which is a small door papered like
the wall. On each side, an ordinary door. In front,
on the right, a console table with a large mirror over it.
Well-filled stands of plants and flowers. In front, on
the left, a sofa with a table and chairs. Further back,
a bookcase. Well forward in the room, before the bay
window, a small table and some chairs. It is early in
the day.*

SOLNESS *sits by the little table with* RAGNAR BROVIK'S *portfolio open in front of him. He is turning the drawings
over and closely examining some of them.* MRS. SOL-
NESS *moves about noiselessly with a small watering-pot,
attending to her flowers. She is dressed in black as
before. Her hat, cloak and parasol lie on a chair near
the mirror. Unobserved by her,* SOLNESS *now and
again follows her with his eyes. Neither of them
speaks.*

KAIA FOSLI *enters quietly by the door on the left.*

Solness *(turns his head, and says in an off-hand tone of
indifference).* Well, is that you?

Kaia. I merely wished to let you know that I have come.

Solness. Yes, yes, that's all right. Hasn't Ragnar come,
too?

Kaia. No, not yet. He had to wait a little while to see the doctor. But he is coming presently to hear——

Solness. How is the old man to-day?

Kaia. Not well. He begs you to excuse him; he is obliged to keep his bed to-day.

Solness. Why, of course; by all means let him rest. But now, get to work.

Kaia. Yes. *(Pauses at the door.)* Do you wish to speak to Ragnar when he comes?

Solness. No—I don't know that I have anything particular to say to him.

> [KAIA *goes out again to the left.* SOLNESS *remains seated, turning over the drawings.*

Mrs. Solness (over beside the plants). I wonder if he isn't going to die now, as well?

Solness (looks up to her). As well as who?

Mrs. Solness (without answering). Yes, yes—depend upon it, Halvard, old Brovik is going to die, too. You'll see that he will.

Solness. My dear Aline, ought you not to go out for a little walk?

Mrs. Solness. Yes, I suppose I ought to.

> [*She continues to attend to the flowers.*

Solness (bending over the drawings). Is she still asleep?

Mrs. Solness (looking at him). Is it Miss Wangel you are sitting there thinking about?

Solness (indifferently). I just happened to recollect her.

Mrs. Solness. Miss Wangel was up long ago.

Solness. Oh, was she?

Mrs. Solness. When I went in to see her, she was busy putting her things in order.

> [*She goes in front of the mirror and slowly begins to put on her hat.*

Solness (after a short pause). So we have found a use for one of our nurseries after all, Aline.

Mrs. Solness. Yes, we have.

Solness. That seems to me better than to have them all standing empty.

Mrs. Solness. That emptiness is dreadful; you are right there.

Solness (closes the portfolio, rises and approaches her). You will find that we shall get on far better after this, Aline Things will be more comfortable. Life will be easier—especially for you.

Mrs. Solness (looks at him). After this?

Solness. Yes, believe me, Aline——

Mrs. Solness. Do you mean—because she has come here?

Solness (checking himself). I mean, of course— when once we have moved into the new house.

Mrs. Solness (takes her cloak). Ah, do you think so, Halvard? Will it be better then?

Solness. I can't think otherwise. And surely you think so, too?

Mrs. Solness. I think nothing at all about the new house.

Solness (cast down). It's hard for me to hear you say that; for you know it is mainly for your sake that I have built it.

[*He offers to help her on with her cloak.*

Mrs. Solness (evades him). The fact is, you do far too much for my sake.

Solness (with a certain vehemence). No, no, you really mustn't say that, Aline! I cannot bear to hear you say such things!

Mrs. Solness. Very well, then I won't say it, Halvard.

Solness. But I stick to what *I* said. You'll see that things will be easier for you in the new place.

Mrs. Solness. O heavens—easier for me——!

Solness (eagerly). Yes, indeed they will! You may be quite sure of that! For you see—there will be so very, very much there that will remind you of your own home——

Mrs. Solness. The home that used to be father's **and** mother's—and that was burnt to the ground——

Solness (in a low voice). Yes, yes, my poor Aline. That was a terrible blow for you.

Mrs. Solness (breaking out in lamentation). You may build as much as ever you like, Halvard—you can never build up again a real home for me!

Solness (crosses the room). Well, in heaven's name, let us talk no more about it, then.

Mrs. Solness. Oh, yes, Halvard, I understand you very well. You are so anxious to spare me—and to find excuses for me, too—as much as ever you can.

Solness (with astonishment in his eyes). You! Is it you—yourself, that you are talking about, Aline?

Mrs. Solness. Yes, who else should it be but myself?

Solness (involuntarily to himself). That, too!

Mrs. Solness. As for the old house, I wouldn't mind so much about that. When once misfortune was in the air—why——

Solness. Ah, you are right there. Misfortune will have its way—as the saying goes.

Mrs. Solness. But it's what came of the fire—the dreadful thing that followed——! That is the thing! That, that, that!

Solness (vehemently). Don't think about that, Aline!

Mrs. Solness. Ah, that is exactly what I cannot help thinking about. And now, at last, I must speak about it, too; for I don't seem able to bear it any longer. And then never to be able to forgive myself——

Solness (exclaiming). Yourself——!

Mrs. Solness. Yes, for I had duties on both sides—both towards you and towards the little ones. I ought to have hardened myself—not to have let the horror take such hold upon me—nor the grief for the burning of my old home. *(Wrings her hands.)* Oh, Halvard, if I had only had the strength!

Solness (softly, much moved, comes closer). Aline—you

must promise me never to think these thoughts any more.—
Promise me that, dear!

Mrs. Solness. Oh, promise, promise! One can promise anything.

Solness (clenches his hands and crosses the room). Oh, but this is hopeless, hopeless! Never a ray of sunlight! Not so much as a gleam of brightness to light up our home!

Mrs. Solness. This is no home, Halvard.

Solness. Oh no, you may well say that. *(Gloomily).* And God knows whether you are not right in saying that it will be no better for us in the new house, either.

Mrs. Solness. It will never be any better. Just as empty —just as desolate—there as here.

Solness (vehemently). Why in all the world have we built it then? Can you tell me that?

Mrs. Solness. No; you must answer that question for yourself.

Solness (glances suspiciously at her). What do you mean by that, Aline?

Mrs. Solness. What do I mean?

Solness. Yes, in the devil's name! You said it so strangely—as if you had hidden some meaning in it.

Mrs. Solness. No, indeed, I assure you——

Solness (comes closer). Oh, come now—I know what I know. I have both my eyes and my ears about me, Aline— you may depend upon that!

Mrs. Solness. Why, what are you talking about? What is it?

Solness (places himself in front of her). Do you mean to say you don't find a kind of lurking, hidden meaning in the most innocent word I happen to say?

Mrs. Solness. *I,* do you say? *I* do that?

Solness (laughs). Ho-ho-ho! It's natural enough, Aline! When you have a sick man on your hands——

Mrs. Solness (anxiously). Sick? Are you ill, Halvard?

Solness (violently). A half-mad man then! A crazy man! Call me what you will.

Mrs. Solness (feels blindly for a chair and sits down). Halvard—for God's sake——

Solness. But you are wrong, both you and the doctor. I am not in the state you imagine.

> [*He walks up and down the room.* MRS. SOLNESS
> *follows him anxiously with her eyes. Finally
> he goes up to her.*

Solness (calmly). In reality there is nothing whatever the matter with me.

Mrs. Solness. No, there isn't, is there? But then what is it that troubles you so?

Solness. Why this, that I often feel ready to sink under this terrible burden of debt——

Mrs. Solness. Debt, do you say? But you owe no one anything, Halvard!

Solness (softly, with emotion). I owe a boundless debt to you—to you—to you, Aline.

Mrs. Solness (rises slowly). What is behind all this? You may just as well tell me at once.

Solness. But there is nothing behind it; I have never done you any wrong—not wittingly and wilfully, at any rate. And yet—and yet it seems as though a crushing debt rested upon me and weighed me down.

Mrs. Solness. A debt to me?

Solness. Chiefly to you.

Mrs. Solness. Then you are—ill after all, Halvard.

Solness (gloomily). I suppose I must be—or not far from it. *(Looks towards the door to the right, which is opened at this moment.)* Ah! now it grows lighter.

> [HILDA WANGEL *comes in. She has made some
> alteration in her dress and let down her skirt.*

Hilda. Good morning, Mr. Solness!

Solness (nods). Slept well?

Hilda. Quite deliciously! Like a child in a cradle. Oh —I lay and stretched myself like—like a princess!

Solness (smiles a little). You were thoroughly comfortable then?

Hilda. I should think so.

Solness. And no doubt you dreamed, too.

Hilda. Yes, I did. But that was horrid.

Solness. Was it?

Hilda. Yes, for I dreamed I was falling over a frightfully high, sheer precipice. Do you never have that kind of dream?

Solness. Oh yes—now and then——

Hilda. It's tremendously thrilling—when you fall and fall——

Solness. It seems to make one's blood run cold.

Hilda. Do you draw your legs up under you while you are falling?

Solness. Yes, as high as ever I can.

Hilda. So do I.

Mrs. Solness (takes her parasol). I must go into town now, Halvard. *(To* HILDA.*)* And I'll try to get one or two things that you may require.

Hilda (making a motion to throw her arms round her neck). Oh, you dear, sweet Mrs. Solness! You are really much too kind to me! Frightfully kind——

Mrs. Solness (deprecatingly, freeing herself). Oh, not at all. It's only my duty, so I am very glad to do it.

Hilda (offended, pouts). But really, I think I am quite fit to be seen in the streets—now that I've put my dress to rights. Or do you think I am not?

Mrs. Solness. To tell you the truth, I think people would stare at you a little.

Hilda (contemptuously). Pooh! Is that all? That only amuses me.

Solness (with suppressed ill-humour). Yes, but people

might take it into their heads that you were mad, too, you see.

Hilda. Mad? Are there so many mad people here in town, then?

Solness (points to his own forehead). Here you see one, at all events.

Hilda. You—Mr. Solness!

Mrs. Solness. Oh, don't talk like that, my dear Halvard!

Solness. Have you not noticed that yet?

Hilda. No, I certainly have not. *(Reflects and laughs a little.)* And yet—perhaps in one single thing.

Solness. Ah, do you hear that, Aline?

Mrs. Solness. What is that one single thing, Miss Wangel?

Hilda. No, I won't say.

Solness. Oh, yes, do!

Hilda. No, thank you—I am not so mad as that.

Mrs. Solness. When you and Miss Wangel are alone, I daresay she will tell you, Halvard.

Solness. Ah—you think she will?

Mrs. Solness. Oh, yes, certainly. For you have known her so well in the past. Ever since she was a child—you tell me.

[*She goes out by the door on the left.*

Hilda (after a little while). Does your wife dislike me very much?

Solness. Did you think you noticed anything of the kind?

Hilda. Did you not notice it yourself?

Solness (evasively). Aline has become exceedingly shy with strangers of late years.

Hilda. Has she really?

Solness. But if only you could get to know her thoroughly——! Ah! she is so good—so kind—so excellent a creature——

Hilda (impatiently). But if she is all that—what made her say that about her duty?

Solness. Her duty?

Hilda. She said that she would go out and buy something for me, because it was her duty. Oh, I can't bear that ugly, horrid word!

Solness. Why not?

Hilda. It sounds so cold and sharp and stinging. Duty—duty—duty. Don't you think so, too? Doesn't it seem to sting you?

Solness. H'm—haven't thought much about it.

Hilda. Yes, it does. And if she is so good—as you say she is—why should she talk in that way?

Solness. But, good Lord, what would you have had her say, then?

Hilda. She might have said she would do it because she had taken a tremendous fancy to me. She might have said something like that—something really warm and cordial, you understand.

Solness (looks at her). Is that how you would like to have it?

Hilda. Yes, precisely. *(She wanders about the room, stops at the bookcase and looks at the books.)* What a lot of books you have.

Solness. Yes, I have got together a good many.

Hilda. Do you read them all, too?

Solness. I used to try to. Do you read much?

Hilda. No, never! I have given it up. For it all seems so irrelevant.

Solness. That is just my feeling.

> [HILDA *wanders about a little, stops at the small table, opens the portfolio and turns over the contents.*

Hilda. Are all these drawings yours?

Solness. No, they are drawn by a young man whom I employ to help me.

Hilda. Some one you have taught?

Solness. Oh, yes, no doubt he has learnt something from one, too.

Hilda (sits down). Then I suppose he is very clever. *(Looks at a drawing.)* Isn't he?

Solness. Oh, he might be worse. For my purpose——

Hilda. Oh, yes—I'm sure he is·frightfully clever.

Solness. Do you think you can see that in the drawings?

Hilda. Pooh—these scrawlings! But if he has been learning from you——

Solness. Oh, so far as that goes—there are plenty of people that have learnt from me and have come to little enough for all that.

Hilda (looks at him and shakes her head). No, I can't for the life of me understand how you can be so stupid.

Solness. Stupid? Do you think I am so very stupid?

Hilda. Yes, I do indeed. If you are content to go about here teaching all these people——

Solness (with a slight start). Well, and why not?

Hilda (rises, half serious, half laughing). No indeed, Mr. Solness! What can be the good of that? No one but you should be allowed to build. You should stand quite alone—do it all yourself. Now you know it.

Solness (involuntarily). Hilda——!

Hilda. Well!

Solness. How in the world did that come into your head?

Hilda. Do you think I am so very far wrong, then?

Solness. No, that's not what I mean. But now I'll tell you something.

Hilda. Well?

Solness. I keep on—incessantly—in silence and alone—brooding on that very thought.

Hilda. Yes, that seems to me perfectly natural.

Solness (looks somewhat searchingly at her). Perhaps you have noticed it already?

Hilda. No, indeed I haven't.

Solness. But just now—when you said you thought I was—off my balance? In one thing, you said——

Hilda. Oh, I was thinking of something quite different.

Solness. What was it?

Hilda. I am not going to tell you.

Solness (crosses the room). Well, well—as you please. *(Stops at the bow-window.)* Come here, and I will show you something.

Hilda (approaching). What is it?

Solness. Do you see—over there in the garden——?

Hilda. Yes?

Solness (points). Right above the great quarry——?

Hilda. That new house, you mean?

Solness. The one that is being built, yes. Almost finished.

Hilda. It seems to have a very high tower.

Solness. The scaffolding is still up.

Hilda. Is that your new house?

Solness. Yes.

Hilda. The house you are soon going to move into?

Solness. Yes.

Hilda (looks at him). Are there nurseries in that house, too?

Solness. Three, as there are here.

Hilda. And no child,

Solness. And there never will be one.

Hilda (with a half-smile). Well, isn't it just as I said——?

Solness. That——?

Hilda. That you are a little—a little mad after all.

Solness. Was that what you were thinking of?

Hilda. Yes, of all the empty nurseries I slept in.

Solness (lowers his voice). We have had children—Aline and I.

Hilda (looks eagerly at him). Have you——?

Solness. Two little boys. They were of the same age.

Hilda. Twins, then.

Solness. Yes, twins. It's eleven or twelve years ago now.

Hilda (cautiously). And so both of them——? You have lost both the twins, then?

Solness (with quiet emotion). We kept them only about three weeks. Or scarcely so much. *(Bursts forth.)* Oh, Hilda, I can't tell you what a good thing it is for me that you have come! For now at last I have some one I can talk to!

Hilda. Can you not talk to—her, too?

Solness. Not about this. Not as I want to talk and must talk. *(Gloomily.)* And not about so many other things, either.

Hilda (in a subdued voice). Was that all you meant when you said you needed me?

Solness. That was mainly what I meant—at all events, yesterday. For to-day I am not so sure——*(Breaking off.)* Come here and let us sit down, Hilda. Sit there on the sofa —so that you can look into the garden. *(*HILDA *seats herself in the corner of the sofa.* SOLNESS *brings a chair closer.)* Should you like to hear about it?

Hilda. Yes, I shall love to sit and listen to you.

Solness (sits down). Then I will tell you all about it.

Hilda. Now I can see both the garden and you, Mr. Solness. So now, tell away! Begin!

Solness (points towards the bow-window). Out there on the rising ground—where you see the new house——

Hilda. Yes?

Solness. Aline and I lived there in the first years of our married life. There was an old house up there that had be-longed to her mother; and we inherited it, and the whole of the great garden with it.

Hilda. Was there a tower on that house, too?

Solness. No, nothing of the kind. From the outside it

looked like a great, dark, ugly wooden box; but all the same, it was snug and comfortable enough inside.

Hilda.   Then did you pull down the ramshackle old place?

Solness.   No, it burnt down.

Hilda.   The whole of it?

Solness.   Yes.

Hilda.   Was that a great misfortulne for you?

Solness.   That depends on how you look at it.   As **a** builder, the fire was the making of me——

Hilda.   Well, but——?

Solness.   It was just after the birth of the two little boys——

Hilda.   The poor little twins, yes.

Solness.   They came healthy and bonny into the world. And they were growing too—you could see the difference from day to day.

Hilda.   Little children do grow quickly at first.

Solness.   It was the prettiest sight in the world to see Aline lying with the two of them in her arms.—But then came the night of the fire——

Hilda (excitedly).   What happened?   Do tell me!   Was any one burnt?

Solness.   No, not that.   Every one got safe and sound out of the house——

Hilda.   Well, and what then——?

Solness.   The fright had shaken Aline terribly.   The alarm—the escape—the break-neck hurry—and then the ice-cold night air—for they had to be carried out just as they lay—both she and the little ones.

Hilda.   Was it too much for them?

Solness.   Oh no, they stood it well enough.   But Aline fell into a fever, and it affected her milk.   She would insist on nursing them herself; because it was her duty, she said. And both our little boys, they—*(clenching his hands.)*—they—oh!

Hilda.   They did not get over that?

Solness.   No, that they did not get over.   That was how we lost them.

Hilda.   It must have been terribly hard for you.

Solness.   Hard enough for me; but ten times harder for Aline.   *(Clenching his hands in suppressed fury.)*   Oh, that such things should be allowed to happen here in the world!   *(Shortly and firmly.)*   From the day I lost them, I had no heart for building churches.

Hilda.   Did you not like the church-tower in our town?

Solness.   I didn't like it.   I know how free and happy I felt when the tower was finished.

Hilda.   *I* know that, too.

Solness.   And now I shall never—never build anything of that sort again!   Neither churches nor church-towers.

Hilda (nods slowly).   Nothing but houses for people to live in.

Solness.   Homes for human beings, Hilda.

Hilda.   But homes with high towers and pinnacles upon them.

Solness.   If possible.   *(Adopts a lighter tone.)*   But, as I said before, that fire was the making of me—as a builder, I mean.

Hilda.   Why don't you call yourself an architect, like the others?

Solness.   I have not been systematically enough taught for that.   Most of what I know, I have found out for myself.

Hilda.   But you succeeded all the same.

Solness.   Yes, thanks to the fire.   I laid out almost the whole of the garden in villa lots; and there I was able to build after my own heart.   So I came to the front with a rush.

Hilda (looks keenly at him).   You must surely be a very happy man, as matters stand with you.

Solness (gloomily).   Happy?   Do you say that, too— like all the rest of them?

Hilda. Yes, I should say you must be. If you could only cease thinking about the two little children——

Solness (slowly). The two little children—they are not so easy to forget, Hilda.

Hilda (somewhat uncertainly). Do you still feel their loss so much—after all these years?

Solness (looks fixedly at her, without replying). A happy man you said——

Hilda. Well, now, are you not happy—in other respects?

Solness (continues to look at her). When I told you all this about the fire—h'm——

Hilda. Well?

Solness. Was there not one special thought that you— that you seized upon?

Hilda (reflects in vain). No. What thought should that be?

Solness (with subdued emphasis). It was simply and solely by that fire that I was enabled to build homes for human beings. Cosy, comfortable, bright homes, where father and mother and the whole troop of children can live in safety and gladness, feeling what a happy thing it is to be alive in the world—and most of all to belong to each other—in great things and in small.

Hilda (ardently). Well, and is it not a great happiness for you to be able to build such beautiful homes?

Solness. The price, Hilda! The terrible price I had to pay for the opportunity!

Hilda. But can you never get over that?

Solness. No. That I might build homes for others, I had to forego—to forego for all time—the home that might have been my own. I mean a home for a troop of children —and for father and mother, too.

Hilda (cautiously). But need you have done that? For all time, you say?

Solness (nods slowly). That was the price of this happiness that people talk about. *(Breathes heavily.)* This happiness—h'm—this happiness was not to be bought any cheaper, Hilda.

Hilda (as before). But may it not come right even yet?

Solness. Never in this world—never. That is another consequence of the fire—and of Aline's illness afterwards.

Hilda (looks at him with an indefinable expression). And yet you build all these nurseries?

Solness (seriously). Have you never noticed, Hilda, how the impossible—how it seems to beckon and cry aloud to one?

Hilda (reflecting). The impossible? *(With animation.)* Yes, indeed! Is that how you feel too?

Solness. Yes, I do.

Hilda. There must be—a little of the troll in you, too.

Solness. Why of the troll?

Hilda. What would you call it, then?

Solness (rises). Well, well, perhaps you are right. *(Vehemently).* But how can I help turning into a troll, when this is how it always goes with me in everything—in everything!

Hilda. How do you mean?

Solness (speaking low, with inward emotion). Mark what I say to you, Hilda. All that I have succeeded in doing, building, creating—all the beauty, security, cheerful comfort—ay, and magnificence, too—*(Clenches his hands.)* Oh, is it not terrible even to think of——!

Hilda. What is so terrible?

Solness. That all this I have to make up for, to pay for —not in money, but in human happiness. And not with my own happiness only, but with other people's, too. Yes, yes, do you see that, Hilda? That is the price which my position as an artist has cost me—and others. And every single day I have to look on while the price is paid for me anew. Over again, and over again—and over again for ever!

Hilda (rises and looks steadily at him). Now I can see that you are thinking of—of her.

Solness. Yes, mainly of Aline. For Aline—she, too, had her vocation in life, just as much as I had mine. *(His voice quivers.)* But her vocation has had to be stunted, and crushed and shattered—in order that mine might force its way to—to a sort of great victory. For you must know that Aline—she, too, had a talent for building.

Hilda. She! For building?

Solness (shakes his head). Not houses and towers, and spires—not such things as I work away at——

Hilda. Well, but what then?

Solness (softly, with emotion). For building up the souls of little children, Hilda. For building up children's souls in perfect balance, and in noble and beautiful forms. For enabling them to soar up into erect and full-grown human souls. That was Aline's talent. And there it all lies now—— unused and unusable for ever—of no earthly service to any one—just like the ruins left by a fire.

Hilda. Yes, but even if this were so——?

Solness. It is so! It is so! I know it!

Hilda. Well, but in any case it is not your fault.

Solness (fixes his eyes on her and nods slowly). Ah, that is the great, terrible question. That is the doubt that is gnawing me—night and day.

Hilda. That?

Solness. Yes. Suppose the fault was mine—in a certain sense.

Hilda. Your fault! The fire!

Solness. All of it; the whole thing. And yet, perhaps— I may not have had anything to do with it.

Hilda (looks at him with a troubled expression). Oh, Mr. Solness—if you can talk like that, I am afraid you must be—ill, after all.

Solness. H'm—I don't think I shall ever be of quite sound mind on that point.

[RAGNAR BROVIK *cautiously opens the little door in the left-hand corner.* HILDA *comes forward.*

Ragnar (when he sees HILDA*).* Oh. I beg pardon, Mr.
Solness——　　　　　　　[*He makes a movement to withdraw.*
Solness. No, no, don't go. Let us get it over.
Ragnar. Oh, yes—if only we could.
Solness. I hear your father is no better?
Ragnar. Father is fast growing weaker—and therefore
I beg and implore you to write a few kind words for me on
one of the plans! Something for father to read before
he——

Solness (vehemently). I won't hear anything more about
those drawings of yours!
Ragnar. Have you looked at them?
Solness. Yes—I have.
Ragnar. And they are good for nothing? And *I* am
good for nothing, too?
Solness (evasively). Stay here with me, Ragnar. You
shall have everything your own way. And then you can
marry Kaia and live at your ease—and happily, too, who
knows? Only don't think of building on your own account.
Ragnar. Well, well, then I must go home and tell father
what you say—I promised I would.—Is this what I am to
tell father—before he dies?
Solness (with a groan). Oh tell him—tell him what you
will, for me. Best to say nothing at all to him! *(With a
sudden outburst).* I cannot do anything else, Ragnar!
Ragnar. May I have the drawings to take with me?
Solness. Yes, take them—take them by all means!
They are lying there on the table.
Ragnar (goes to the table). Thanks.
Hilda (puts her hand on the portfolio). No, no; leave
them here.
Solness. Why?
Hilda. Because I want to look at them, too.
Solness. But you have been—— *(To* RAGNAR*).*
Well, leave them here, then.
Ragnar. Very well.

Solness. And go home at once to your father.

Ragnar. Yes. I suppose I must.

Solness (as if in desperation). Ragnar—you must not ask me to do what is beyond my power! Do you hear, Ragnar? You must not!

Ragnar. No, no. I beg your pardon——

> [*He bows and goes out by the corner door.* HILDA *goes over and sits down on a chair near the mirror.*

Hilda (looks angrily at SOLNESS). That was a very ugly thing to do.

Solness. Do you think so, too?

Hilda. Yes, it was horrible ugly—and hard and bad and cruel as well.

Solness. Oh, you don't understand my position.

Hilda. No matter——. I say you ought not to be like that.

Solness. You said yourself, only just now, that no one but *I* ought to be allowed to build.

Hilda. *I* may say such things—but you must not.

Solness. I most of all, surely, who have paid so dear for my position.

Hilda. Oh yes—with what you call domestic comfort—and that sort of thing.

Solness. And with my peace of soul into the bargain.

Hilda (rising). Peace of soul! *(With feeling.)* Yes, yes, you are right in that! Poor Mr. Solness—you fancy that——

Solness (with a quiet, chuckling laugh). Just sit down again, Hilda, and I'll tell you something funny.

Hilda (sits down; with intent interest). Well?

Solness. It sounds such a ludicrous little thing; for, you see, the whole story turns upon nothing but a crack in í chimney.

Hilda. No more than that?

Solness. No, not to begin with.

[*He moves a chair nearer to* HILDA *and sits down.*

Hilda (impatiently, taps on her knee). Well, now for the crack in the chimney!

Solness. I had noticed the split in the flue long, long before the fire. Every time I went up into the attic, I looked to see if it was still there.

Hilda. And it was?

Solness. Yes; for no one else knew about it.

Hilda. And you said nothing?

Solness. Nothing.

Hilda. And did not think of repairing the flue either?

Solness. Oh, yes, I thought about it—but never got any further. Every time I intended to set to work, it seemed just as if a hand held me back. Not to-day, I thought— to-morrow; and nothing ever came of it.

Hilda. But why did you keep putting it off like that?

Solness. Because I was revolving something in my mind. *(Slowly, and in a low voice.)* Through that little black crack in the chimney, I might, perhaps, force my way upwards—as a builder.

Hilda (looking straight in front of her). That must have been thrilling.

Solness. Almost irresistible—quite irresistible. For at that time it appeared to me a perfectly simple and straightforward matter. I would have had it happen in the wintertime—a little before midday. I was to be out driving Aline in the sleigh. The servants at home would have made huge fires in the stoves.

Hilda. For, of course, it was to be bitterly cold that day?

Solness. Rather biting, yes—and they would want Aline to find it thoroughly snug and warm when she came home.

Hilda. I suppose she is very chilly by nature?

Solness. She is. And as we drove home, we were to see the smoke.

Hilda. Only the smoke?

Solness. The smoke first. But when we came up to the

garden gate, the whole of the old timber-box was to be a rolling mass of flames.—That is how I wanted it to be, you see.

Hilda. Oh why, why could it not have happened so!

Solness. You may well say that, Hilda.

Hilda. Well, but now listen, Mr. Solness. Are you perfectly certain that the fire was caused by that little crack in the chimney?

Solness. No, on the contrary—I am perfectly certain that the crack in the chimney had nothing whatever to do with the fire.

Hilda. What?

Solness. It has been clearly ascertained that the fire broke out in a clothes-cupboard—in a totally different part of the house.

Hilda. Then what is all this nonsense you are talking about the crack in the chimney?

Solness. May I go on talking to you a little, Hilda?

Hilda. Yes, if you'll only talk sensibly——

Solness. I will try.   [*He moves his chair nearer.*

Hilda. Out with it, then, Mr. Solness.

Solness (confidentially). Don't you agree with me, Hilda, that there exist special, chosen people who have been endowed with the power and faculty of desiring a thing, craving for a thing, willing a thing—so persistently and so—so inexorably—that at last it has to happen? Don't you believe that?

Hilda (with an indefinable expression in her eyes). If that is so, we shall see, one of these days, whether *I* am one of the chosen.

Solness. It is not one's self alone that can do such great things. Oh, no—the helpers and the servers—they must do their part, too, if it is to be of any good. But they never come of themselves. One has to call upon them very persistently—inwardly, you understand.

Hilda. What are these helpers and servers?

Solness. Oh, we can talk about that some other time. For the present, let us keep to this business of the fire.

Hilda. Don't you think that fire would have happened all the same—even without your wishing for it?

Solness. If the house had been old Knut Brovik's, it would never have burnt down so conveniently for him. I am sure of that; for he does not know how to call for the helpers—no, nor for the servers, either. *(Rises in unrest.)* So you see, Hilda—it is my fault, after all, that the lives of the two little boys had to be sacrificed. And do you think it is not my fault, too, that Aline has never been the woman she should and might have been—and that she most longed to be?

Hilda. Yes, but if it is all the work of those helpers and servers——?

Solness. Who called for the helpers and servers? It was I! And they came and obeyed my will. *(In increasing excitement.)* That is what people call having the luck on your side; but I must tell you what this sort of luck feels like! It feels like a great raw place here on my breast. And the helpers and servers keep on flaying pieces of skin off other people in order to close my sore!— But still the sore is not healed—never, never! Oh, if you knew how it can sometimes gnaw and burn.

Hilda (looks attentively at him). You are ill, Mr. Solness. Very ill, I almost think.

Solness. Say mad; for that is what you mean.

Hilda. No, I don't think there is much amiss with your intellect.

Solness. With what then? Out with it!

Hilda. I wonder whether you were not sent into the world with a sickly conscience.

Solness. A sickly conscience? What devilry is that?

Hilda. I mean that your conscience is feeble—too delicately built, as it were—hasn't strength to take a grip of things—to lift and bear what is heavy.

Solness (growls). H'm! May I ask, then, what sort of conscience one ought to have?

Hilda. I should like your conscience to be—to be thoroughly robust.

Solness. Indeed? Robust, eh? Is your own conscience robust, may I ask?

Hilda. Yes, I think it is. I have never noticed that it wasn't.

Solness. It has not been put very severely to the test, I should think.

Hilda (with a quivering of the lips). Oh, it was no such simple matter to leave father—I am so awfully fond of him.

Solness. Dear me! for a month or two——

Hilda. I think I shall never go home again.

Solness. Never? Then why did you leave him?

Hilda (half-seriously, half-banteringly). Have you forgotten that the ten years are up?

Solness. Oh nonsense. Was anything wrong at home? Eh?

Hilda (quite seriously). It was this impulse within me that urged and goaded me to come—and lured and drew me on, as well.

Solness (eagerly). There we have it! There we have it, Hilda! There is a troll in you, too, as in me. For it's the troll in one, you see—it is that that calls to the powers outside us. And then you must give in—whether you will or no.

Hilda. I almost think you are right, Mr. Solness.

Solness (walks about the room). Oh, there are devils innumerable abroad in the world, Hilda, that one never sees.

Hilda. Devils, too?

Solness (stops). Good devils and bad devils; light-haired devils and black-haired devils. If only you could always tell whether it is the light or dark ones that have got hold of you! *(Paces about.)* Ho-ho! Then it would be simple enough.

Hilda (follows him with her eyes). Or if one had a really vigorous, radiantly healthy conscience—so that one dared to do what one would.

Solness (stops beside the console table). I believe, now, that most people are just as puny creatures as I am in that respect.

Hilda. I shouldn't wonder.

Solness (leaning against the table). In the sagas—— Have you read any of the old sagas?

Hilda. Oh, yes! When I used to read books, I——

Solness. In the sagas you read about vikings, who sailed to foreign lands, and plundered and burned and killed men——

Hilda. And carried off women——

Solness. ——and kept them in captivity——

Hilda. ——took them home in their ships——

Solness. ——and behaved to them like—like the very worst of trolls.

Hilda (looks straight before her, with a half-veiled look). I think that must have been thrilling.

Solness (with a short, deep laugh). To carry off women,

Hilda. To be carried off.

Solness (looks at her a moment). Oh, indeed.

Hilda (as if breaking the thread of the conversation). But what made you speak of these vikings, Mr. Solness?

Solness. Why, those fellows must have had robust consciences, if you like! When they got home again, they could eat, and drink and be as happy as children. And the women, too! They often would not leave them on any account. Can you understand that, Hilda?

Hilda. Those women I can understand exceedingly well.

Solness. Oho! Perhaps you could do the same yourself?

Hilda. Why not?

Solness. Live—of your own free will—with a ruffian like that?

Hilda. If it was a ruffian I had come to love——

Solness. Could you come to love a man like that?

Hilda. Good heavens, you know very well one can't choose whom one is going to love.

Solness (looks meditatively at her). Oh, no, I suppose it is the troll within one that's responsible for that.

Hilda (half-laughing). And all those blessed devils, that you know so well—both the light-haired and the dark-haired ones.

Solness (quietly and warmly). Then I hope with all my heart that the devils will choose carefully for you, Hilda.

Hilda. For me they have chosen already—once and for all.

Solness (looks earnestly at her). Hilda—you are like a wild bird of the woods.

Hilda. Far from it. I don't hide myself away under the bushes.

Solness. No, no. There is rather something of the bird of prey in you.

Hilda. That is nearer it—perhaps. *(Very earnestly.)* And why not a bird of prey? Why should not *I* go a-hunting—I, as well as the rest. Carry off the prey I want—if only I can get my claws into it and do with it as I will.

Solness. Hilda—do you know what you are?

Hilda. Yes, I suppose I am a strange sort of bird.

Solness. No. You are like a dawning day. When I look at you—I seem to be looking towards the sunrise.

Hilda. Tell me, Mr. Solness—are you certain that you have never called me to you? Inwardly, you know?

Solness (softly and slowly). I almost think I must have.

Hilda. What did you want with me?

Solness. You are the younger generation, Hilda.

Hilda (smiles). That younger generation that you are so afraid of?

Solness (nods slowly). And which, in my heart, I yearn towards so deeply.

[HILDA *rises, goes to the little table and fetches*
RAGNAR BROVIK'S *portfolio.*

Hilda (holds out the portfolio to him). We were talking
of these drawings——

Solness (shortly, waving them away). Put those things
away! I have seen enough of them.

Hilda. Yes, but you have to write your approval on
them.

Solness. Write my approval on them? Never!

Hilda. But the poor old man is lying at death's door!
Can't you give him and his son this pleasure before they are
parted? And perhaps he might get the commission to carry
them out, too.

Solness. Yes, that is just what he would get. He has
made sure of that—has my fine gentleman!

Hilda. Then, good heavens—if that is so—can't you tell
the least little bit of a lie for once in a way?

Solness. A lie? *(Raging.)* Hilda—take those devil's
drawings out of my sight!

Hilda (draws the portfolio a little nearer to herself).
Well, well, well—don't bite me.—You talk of trolls—but I
think you go on like a troll yourself. *(Looks around.)*
Where do you keep your pen and ink?

Solness. There is nothing of the sort in here.

Hilda (goes towards the door). But in the office where
that young lady is——

Solness. Stay where you are, Hilda!—I ought to tell a
lie, you say. Oh, yes, for the sake of his old father I might
well do that—for in my time I have crushed him, trodden
him under foot——

Hilda. Him, too?

Solness. I needed room for myself. But this Ragnar—
he must on no account be allowed to come to the front.

Hilda. Poor fellow, there is surely no fear of that. If
he has nothing in him——

Solness (comes closer, looks at her and whispers). If

Ragnar Brovik gets his chance, he will strike me to the earth. Crush me—as I crushed his father.

Hilda. Crush you? Has he the ability for that?

Solness. Yes, you may depend upon it he has the ability! He is the younger generation that stands ready to knock at my door—to make an end of Halvard Solness.

Hilda (looks at him with quiet reproach). And yet you would bar him out. Fie, Mr. Solness!

Solness. The fight I have been fighting has cost heart's blood enough.—And I am afraid, too, that the helpers and servers will not obey me any longer.

Hilda. Then you must go ahead without them. There is nothing else for it.

Solness. It is hopeless, Hilda. The luck is bound to turn. A little sooner or a little later. Retribution is in-exorable.

Hilda (in distress, putting her hands over her ears). Don't talk like that! Do you want to kill me? To take from me what is more than my life?

Solness. And what is that?

Hilda. The longing to see you great. To see you, with a wreath in your hand, high, high up upon a church-tower. *(Calm again.)* Come, out with your pencil now. You must have a pencil about you?

Solness (takes out his pocket-book). I have one here.

Hilda (lays the portfolio on the sofa-table). Very well. Now let us two sit down here, Mr. Solness. (SOLNESS *seats himself at the table.* HILDA *stands behind him, lean-ing over the back of the chair.)* And now we will write on the drawings. We must write very, very nicely and cor-dially—for this horrid Ruar—or whatever his name is.

Solness (writes a few words, turns his head and looks at her). Tell me one thing, Hilda.

Hilda. Yes!

Solness. If you have been waiting for me all these ten years——

Hilda. What then?

Solness. Why have you never written to me? Then I could have answered you.

Hilda (hastily). No, no, no! That was just what I did not want.

Solness. Why not?

Hilda. I was afraid the whole thing might fall to pieces. —But we were going to write on the drawings, Mr. Solness.

Solness. So we were.

Hilda (bends forward and looks over his shoulder while he writes). Mind now, kindly and cordially! Oh how I hate —how I hate this Ruald——

Solness (writing). Have you never really cared for any one, Hilda?

Hilda (harshly). What do you say?

Solness. Have you never cared for any one?

Hilda. For any one else, I suppose you mean?

Solness (looks up at her). For any one else, yes. Have you never? In all these ten years? Never?

Hilda. Oh, yes, now and then. When I was perfectly furious with you for not coming.

Solness. Then you did take an interest in other people, too?

Hilda. A little bit—for a week or so. Good heavens, Mr. Solness, you surely know how such things come about.

Solness. Hilda—what is it you have come for?

Hilda. Don't waste time talking. The poor old man might go and die in the meantime.

Solness. Answer me, Hilda. What do you want of me?

Hilda. I want my kingdom.

Solness. H'm——

> [*He gives a rapid glance towards the door on the left and then goes on writing on the drawings. At the same moment* MRS. SOLNESS *enters; she has some packages in her hand.*

Mrs. Solness. Here are a few things I have got for you, Miss Wangel. The large parcels will be sent later on.

Hilda. Oh, how very, very kind of you!

Mrs. Solness. Only my simple duty. Nothing more than that.

Solness (reading over what he has written). Aline!

Mrs. Solness. Yes?

Solness. Did you notice whether the—the book-keeper was out there?

Mrs. Solness. Yes, of course, she was out there.

Solness (puts the drawings in the portfolio). H'm——

Mrs. Solness. She was standing at the desk, as she always is—when *I* go through the room.

Solness (rises). Then I'll give this to her and tell her that——

Hilda (takes the portfolio from him). Oh, no, let me have the pleasure of doing that! *(Goes to the door, but turns.)* What is her name?

Solness. Her name is Miss Fosli.

Hilda. Pooh, that sounds too cold! Her Christian name, I mean?

Solness. Kaia—I believe.

Hilda (opens the door and calls out). Kaia, come in here! Make haste! Mr. Solness wants to speak to you.

[KAIA FOSLI *appears at the door.*

Kaia (looking at him in alarm). Here I am——?

Hilda (handing her the portfolio). See here, Kaia! You can take this home; Mr. Solness has written on them now.

Kaia. Oh, at last!

Solness. Give them to the old man as soon as you can.

Kaia. I will go straight home with them.

Solness. Yes, do. Now Ragnar will have a chance of building for himself.

Kaia. Oh, may he come and thank you for all——?

Solness (harshly). I won't have any thanks! Tell him that from me.

Kaia. Yes, I will——

Solness. And tell him at the same time that henceforward I do not require his services—nor yours either.

Kaia (softly and quiveringly). Not mine either?

Solness. You will have other things to think of now and to attend to; and that is a very good thing for you. Well, go home with the drawings now, Miss Fosli. At once! Do you hear?

Kaia (as before). Yes, Mr. Solness.

[*She goes out.*

Mrs. Solness. Heavens! what deceitful eyes she has.

Solness. She? That poor little creature?

Mrs. Solness. Oh—I can see what I can see, Halvard. —— Are you really dismissing them?

Solness. Yes.

Mrs. Solness. Her as well?

Solness. Was not that what you wished?

Mrs. Solness. But how can you get on without her——? Oh, well, no doubt you have some one else in reserve, Halvard.

Hilda (playfully). Well, I for one am not the person to stand at that desk.

Solness. Never mind, never mind—it will be all right, Aline. Now all you have to do is to think about moving into our new home—as quickly as you can. This evening we will hang up the wreath—*(Turns to Hilda.)*—right on the very pinnacle of the tower. What do you say to that, Miss Hilda?

Hilda (looks at him with sparkling eyes). It will be splendid to see you so high up once more.

Solness. Me!

Mrs. Solness. For heaven's sake, Miss Wangel, don't imagine such a thing! My husband!—when he always gets so dizzy!

Hilda. He get dizzy! No, I know quite well he does not!

Mrs. Solness. Oh, yes, indeed he does.

Hilda. But I have seen him with my own eyes right up at the top of a high church-tower!

Mrs. Solness. Yes, I hear people talk of that; but it is utterly impossible——

Solness (vehemently). Impossible—impossible, yes! But there I stood all the same!

Mrs. Solness. Oh, how can you say so, Halvard? Why, you can't even bear to go out on the second-story balcony here. You have always been like that.

Solness. You may perhaps see something different this evening.

Mrs. Solness (in alarm). No, no, no! Please God I shall never see that. I will write at once to the doctor—and I am sure he won't let you do it.

Solness. Why, Aline——!

Mrs. Solness. Oh, you know you're ill, Halvard. This proves it! Oh God—Oh God!

[*She goes hastily out to the right.*

Hilda (looks intently at him). Is it so, or is it not?

Solness. That I turn dizzy?

Hilda. That my master builder dares not—cannot—climb as high as he builds?

Solness. Is that the way you look at it?

Hilda. Yes.

Solness. I believe there is scarcely a corner in me that is safe from you.

Hilda (looks towards the bow-window). Up there, then. Right up there——

Solness (approaches her). You might have the topmost room in the tower, Hilda—there you might live like a princess.

Hilda (indefinably, between earnest and jest). Yes, that is what you promised me.

Solness. Did I really?

Hilda. Fie, Mr. Solness! You said I should be a prin-cess, and that you would give me a kingdom. And then you went and——Well!

Solness (cautiously). Are you quite certain that this is not a dream—a fancy, that has fixed itself in your mind?

Hilda (sharply). Do you mean that you did not do it?

Solness. I scarcely know myself. *(More softly.)* But now I know so much for certain, that I——

Hilda. That you——? Say it at once!

Solness. —that I ought to have done it.

Hilda (exclaims with animation). Don't tell me you can ever be dizzy!

Solness. This evening, then, we will hang up the wreath —Princess Hilda.

Hilda (with a bitter curve of the lips). Over your new home, yes.

Solness. Over the new house, which will never be a home for me.

[*He goes out through the garden door.*
Hilda (looks straight in front of her with a far-away ex-pression and whispers to herself. The only words audible are) —frightfully thrilling——

ACT III

The large, broad verandah of Solness's *dwelling-house. Part of the house, with outer door leading to the verandah, is seen to the left. A railing along the verandah to the right. At the back, from the end of the verandah, a flight of steps leads down to the garden below. Tall old trees in the garden spread their branches over the verandah and towards the house. Far to the right, in among the trees, a glimpse is caught of the lower part of the new villa, with scaffolding round so much as is seen of the tower. In the background the garden is bounded by an old wooden fence. Outside the fence, a street with low, tumble-down cottages.*

Evening sky with sun-lit clouds.

On the verandah, a garden bench stands along the wall of the house, and in front of the bench a long table. On the other side of the table, an arm-chair and some stools. All the furniture is of wicker-work.

Mrs. Solness, *wrapped in a large white crape shawl, sits resting in the arm-chair and gazes over to the right. Shortly after,* Hilda Wangel *comes up the flight of steps from the garden. She is dressed as in the last act and wears her hat. She has in her bodice a little nosegay of small common flowers.*

Mrs. Solness (turning her head a little). Have you been round the garden, Miss Wangel?

Hilda. Yes, I have been taking a look at it.

Mrs. Solness. And found some flowers, too, I see.

359

Hilda.   Yes, indeed!   There are such heaps of them in among the bushes.

Mrs. Solness.   Are there really?   Still?   You see I scarcely ever go there.

Hilda (closer).   What!   Don't you take a run down into the garden every day, then?

Mrs. Solness (with a faint smile).   I don't "run" anywhere, nowadays.

Hilda.   Well, but do you not go down now and then to look at all the lovely things there?

Mrs. Solness.   It has all become so strange to me.   I am almost afraid to see it again.

Hilda.   Your own garden!

Mrs. Solness.   I don't feel that it is mine any longer.

Hilda.   What do you mean——?

Mrs. Solness.   No, no, it is not—not—not as it was in my mother's and father's time.   They have taken away so much—so much of the garden, Miss Wangel.   Fancy—they have parcelled it out—and built houses for strangers— people that I don't know.   And they can sit and look in upon me from their windows.

Hilda (with a bright expression).   Mrs. Solness!

Mrs. Solness.   Yes!

Hilda.   May I stay here with you a little?

Mrs. Solness.   Yes, by all means, if you care to.

> [HILDA *moves a stool close to the arm-chair and sits down.*

Hilda.   Ah—here one can sit and sun oneself like a cat.

Mrs. Solness (lays her hand softly on HILDA's *neck).*   It is nice of you to be willing to sit with me.   I thought you wanted to go in to my husband.

Hilda.   What should I want with him?

Mrs. Solness.   To help him, I thought.

Hilda.   No, thank you.   And besides, he is not in.   He is over there with the workmen.   But he looked so fierce that I did not care to talk to him.

Mrs. Solness. He is so kind and gentle in reality.

Hilda. He!

Mrs. Solness. You do not really know him yet, Miss Wangel.

Hilda (looks affectionately at her). Are you pleased at the thought of moving over to the new house?

Mrs. Solness. I ought to be pleased; for it is what Halvard wants——

Hilda. Oh, not just on that account, surely.

Mrs. Solness. Yes, yes, Miss Wangel; for it is only my duty to submit myself to him. But very often it is dreadfully difficult to force one's mind to obedience.

Hilda. Yes, that must be difficult indeed.

Mrs. Solness. I can tell you it is—when one has so many faults as I have——

Hilda. When one has gone through so much trouble as you have——

Mrs. Solness. How do you know about that?

Hilda. Your husband told me.

Mrs. Solness. To me he very seldom mentions these things.——Yes, I can tell you I have gone through more than enough trouble in my life, Miss Wangel.

Hilda (looks sympathetically at her and nods slowly). Poor Mrs. Solness. First of all there was the fire——

Mrs. Solness (with a sigh). Yes, everything that was mine was burnt.

Hilda. And then came what was worse.

Mrs. Solness (looking inquiringly at her). Worse?

Hilda. The worst of all.

Mrs. Solness. What do you mean?

Hilda (softly). You lost the two little boys.

Mrs. Solness. Oh, yes, the boys. But, you see, that was a thing apart. That was a dispensation of Providence; and in such things one can only bow in submission—yes, and be thankful, too.

Hilda. Then you are so?

Mrs. Solness. Not always, I am sorry to say. I know well enough that it is my duty—but all the same I cannot.

Hilda. No, no, I think that is only natural.

Mrs. Solness. And often and often I have to remind myself that it was a righteous punishment for me——

Hilda. Why?

Mrs. Solness. Because I had not fortitude enough in misfortune.

Hilda. But I don't see that——

Mrs. Solness. Oh, no, no, Miss Wangel—do not talk to me any more about the two little boys. We ought to feel nothing but joy in thinking of them; for they are so happy —so happy now. No, it is the small losses in life that cut one to the heart—the loss of all that other people look upon as almost nothing.

Hilda (lays her arms on MRS. SOLNESS's *knees and looks up at her affectionately).* Dear Mrs. Solness—tell me what things you mean!

Mrs. Solness. As I say, only little things. All the old portraits were burnt on the walls. And all the old silk dresses were burnt, that had belonged to the family for generations and generations. And all mother's and grandmother's lace—that was burnt, too. And only think—the jewels, too! *(Sadly.)* And then all the dolls.

Hilda. The dolls?

Mrs. Solness (choking with tears). I had nine lovely dolls.

Hilda. And they were burnt, too?

Mrs. Solness. All of them. Oh, it was hard—so hard for me.

Hilda. Had you put by all these dolls, then? Ever since you were little?

Mrs. Solness. I had not put them by. The dolls and I had gone on living together.

Hilda. After you were grown up?

Mrs. Solness. Yes, long after that.

Hilda. After you were married, too?

Mrs. Solness. Oh, yes, indeed. So long as he did not see it——. But they were all burnt up, poor things. No one thought of saving them. Oh, it is so miserable to think of. You mustn't laugh at me, Miss Wangel.

Hilda. I am not laughing in the least.

Mrs. Solness. For you see, in a certain sense, there was life in them, too. I carried them under my heart—like little unborn children.

> [DR. HERDAL, *with his hat in his hand, comes out through the door and observes* MRS. SOLNESS *and* HILDA.

Dr. Herdal. Well, Mrs. Solness, so you are sitting out here catching cold?

Mrs. Solness. I find it so pleasant and warm here to-day.

Dr. Herdal. Yes, yes. But is there anything going on here? I got a note from you.

Mrs. Solness (rises). Yes, there is something I must talk to you about.

Dr. Herdal. Very well; then perhaps we had better go in. *(To* HILDA.) Still in your mountaineering dress, Miss Wangel?

Hilda (gaily, rising). Yes—in full uniform! But to-day I am not going climbing and breaking my neck. We two will stop quietly below and look on, doctor.

Dr. Herdal. What are we to look on at?

Mrs. Solness (softly, in alarm, to HILDA). Hush, hush— for God's sake! He is coming. Try to get that idea out of his head. And let us be friends, Miss Wangel. Don't you think we can?

Hilda (throws her arms impetuously round MRS. SOLNESS'S *neck).* Oh, if we only could!

Mrs. Solness (gently disengages herself). There, there there! There he comes, doctor. Let me have a word with you.

Dr. Herdal. Is it about him?

Mrs. Solness. Yes, to be sure it's about him. Do come in.

> [*She and the doctor enter the house. Next moment* SOLNESS *comes up from the garden by the flight of steps. A serious look comes over* HILDA's *face.*

Solness (glances at the house-door, which is closed cautiously from within). Have you noticed, Hilda, that as soon as I come, she goes?

Hilda. I have noticed that as soon as you come, you make her go.

Solness. Perhaps so. But I cannot help it. *(Looks observantly at her.)* Are you cold, Hilda? I think you look cold.

Hilda. I have just come up out of a tomb.

Solness. What do you mean by that?

Hilda. That I have got chilled through and through, Mr. Solness.

Solness (slowly). I believe I understand——

Hilda. What brings you up here just now?

Solness. I caught sight of you from over there.

Hilda. But then you must have seen her too?

Solness. I knew she would go at once if I came.

Hilda. Is it very painful for you that she should avoid you in this way?

Solness. In one sense, it's a relief as well.

Hilda. Not to have her before your eyes?

Solness. Yes.

Hilda. Not to be always seeing how heavily the loss of the little boys weighs upon her?

Solness. Yes. Chiefly that.

> [HILDA *drifts across the verandah with her hands behind her back, stops at the railing and looks out over the garden.*

Solness (after a short pause). Did you have a long talk with her?

[HILDA *stands motionless and does not answer.*

Solness.   Had you a long talk, I asked?

[HILDA *is silent as before.*

Solness.   What was she talking about, Hilda?

[HILDA *continues silent.*

Solness.   Poor Aline!   I suppose it was about the little boys.

Hilda (a nervous shudder runs through her; then she nods hurriedly once or twice).

Solness.   She will never get over it—never in this world. *(Approaches her.)*   Now you are standing there again like a statue; just as you stood last night.

Hilda (turns and looks at him, with great serious eyes), I am going away.

Solness (sharply).   Going away!

Hilda.   Yes.

Solness.   But I won't allow you to!

Hilda.   What am I to do here now?

Solness.   Simply to be here, Hilda!

Hilda (measures him with a look).   Oh, thank you.   You know it wouldn't end there.

Solness (heedlessly).   So much the better!

Hilda (vehemently).   I cannot do any harm to one whom I know!   I can't take away anything that belongs to her.

Solness.   Who wants you to do that?

Hilda (continuing).   A stranger, yes! for that is quite a different thing!   A person I have never set eyes on.   But one that I have come into close contact with——!   Oh, no! Oh, no!   Ugh!

Solness.   Yes, but I never proposed you should.

Hilda.   Oh, Mr. Solness, you know quite well what the end of it would be.   And that is why I am going away.

Solness.   And what is to become of me when you are gone?   What shall I have to live for then?—After that?

Hilda (with the indefinable look in her eyes).   It is surely not so hard for you. You have your duties to her. Live for those duties.

Solness. Too late. These powers—these—these——

Hilda. —devils——

Solness. Yes, these devils! And the troll within me as well—they have drawn all the life-blood out of her. *(Laughs in desperation.)* They did it for my happiness! Yes, yes! *(Sadly.)* And now she is dead—for my sake. And I am chained alive to a dead woman. *(In wild anguish.)* I—I who cannot live without joy in life!

> [HILDA *moves round the table and seats herself on the bench, with her elbows on the table, and her head supported by her hands.*

Hilda (sits and looks at him awhile). What will you build next?

Solness (shakes his head). I don't believe I shall build much more.

Hilda. Not those cosy, happy homes for mother and father, and for the troop of children?

Solness. I wonder whether there will be any use for such homes in the coming time.

Hilda. Poor Mr. Solness! And you have gone all these ten years—and staked your whole life—on that alone.

Solness. Yes, you may well say so, Hilda.

Hilda (with an outburst). Oh, it all seems to me so foolish—so foolish!

Solness. All what?

Hilda. Not to be able to grasp at your own happiness—at your own life! Merely because some one you know happens to stand in the way!

Solness. One whom you have no right to set aside.

Hilda. I wonder whether one really has not the right! And yet, and yet——. Oh, if one could only sleep the whole thing away!

> [*She lays her arms flat on the table, rests the left*

> *side of her head on her hands and shuts her
> eyes.*

Solness (turns the arm-chair and sits down at the table).
Had you a cosy, happy home—up there with your father,
Hilda?

Hilda (without stirring, answers as if half asleep). I
had only a cage.

Solness. And you are determined not to go back to it?

Hilda (as before). The wild bird never wants to go into
the cage.

Solness. Rather range through the free air——

Hilda (still as before). The bird of prey loves to
range——

Solness (lets his eyes rest on her). If only one had the
viking-spirit in life——

*Hilda (in her usual voice; opens her eyes but does not
move).* And the other thing? Say what that was!

Solness. A robust conscience.

> [HILDA *sits erect on the bench, with animation.
> Her eyes have once more the sparkling expres-
> sion of gladness.*

Hilda (nods to him). I know what you are going to
build next!

Solness. Then you know more than I do, Hilda.

Hilda. Yes, builders are such stupid people.

Solness. What is it to be then?

Hilda (nods again). The castle.

Solness. What castle?

Hilda. My castle, of course.

Solness. Do you want a castle now?

Hilda. Don't you owe me a kingdom, I should like to
know?

Solness. You say I do.

Hilda. Well—you admit you owe me this kingdom.
And you can't have a kingdom without a royal castle, I
should think!

Solness (more and more animated). Yes, they usually go together.

Hilda. Good! Then build it for me! This moment!

Solness (laughing). Must you have that on the instant, too?

Hilda. Yes, to be sure! For the ten years are up now, and I am not going to wait any longer. So—out with the castle, Mr. Solness!

Solness. It's no light matter to owe you anything, Hilda.

Hilda. You should have thought of that before. It is too late now. So—*(tapping the table)*—the castle on the table! It is my castle! I will have it at once!

Solness (more seriously, leans over towards her, with his arms on the table). What sort of castle have you imagined, Hilda?

[*Her expression becomes more and more veiled. She seems gazing inwards at herself.*

Hilda (slowly). My castle shall stand on a height—on a very great height—with a clear outlook on all sides, so that I can see far—far around.

Solness. And no doubt it is to have a high tower!

Hilda. A tremendously high tower. And at the very top of the tower there shall be a balcony. And I will stand out upon it——

Solness (involuntarily clutches at his forehead). How can you like to stand at such a dizzy height——?

Hilda. Yes, I will, right up there will I stand and look down on the other people—on those that are building churches, and homes for mother and father and the troop of children. And you may come up and look on at it, too.

Solness (in a low tone). Is the builder to be allowed to come up beside the princess?

Hilda. If the builder will.

Solness (more softly). Then I think the builder will come.

Hilda (nods). The builder—he will come.

Solness. But he will never be able to build any more. Poor builder!

Hilda (animated). Oh yes, he will! We two will set to work together. And then we will build the loveliest—the very loveliest—thing in all the world.

Solness (intently). Hilda—tell me what that is!

Hilda (looks smilingly at him, shakes her head a little, pouts and speaks as if to a child). Builders—they are such very—very stupid people.

Solness. Yes, no doubt they are stupid. But now tell me what it is—the loveliest thing in the world—that we two are to build together?

Hilda (is silent a little while, then says with an indefinable expression in her eyes). Castles in the air.

Solness. Castles in the air?

Hilda (nods). Castles in the air, yes! Do you know what sort of thing a castle in the air is?

Solness. It is the loveliest thing in the world, you say.

Hilda (rises with vehemence and makes a gesture of repulsion with her hand). Yes, to be sure it is! Castles in the air—they are so easy to take refuge in. And so easy to build, too—(looks scornfully at him)—especially for the builders who have a—a dizzy conscience.

Solness (rises). After this day we two will build together, Hilda.

Hilda (with a half-dubious smile). A real castle in the air?

Solness. Yes. One with a firm foundation under it.

> [RAGNAR BROVIK *comes out from the house. He is carrying a large, green wreath with flowers and silk ribbons.*

Hilda (with an outburst of pleasure). The wreath! Oh, that will be glorious!

Solness (in surprise). Have you brought the wreath, Ragnar?

Ragnar. I promised the foreman I would.

Solness (relieved). Ah, then I suppose your father is better?

Ragnar. No.

Solness. Was he not cheered by what I wrote?

Ragnar. It came too late.

Solness. Too late!

Ragnar. When she came with it he was unconscious. He had had a stroke.

Solness. Why, then, you must go home to him! You must attend to your father!

Ragnar. He does not need me any more.

Solness. But surely you ought to be with him.

Ragnar. She is sitting by his bed.

Solness (rather uncertainly). Kaia?

Ragnar (looking darkly at him). Yes—Kaia.

Solness. Go home, Ragnar—both to him and to her. Give me the wreath.

Ragnar (suppresses a mocking smile). You don't mean that you yourself——?

Solness. I will take it down to them myself. *(Takes the wreath from him.)* And now you go home; we don't require you to-day.

Ragnar. I know you do not require me any more; but to-day I shall remain.

Solness. Well, remain then, since you are bent upon it.

Hilda (at the railing). Mr. Solness, I will stand here and look on at you.

Solness. At me!

Hilda. It will be fearfully thrilling.

Solness (in a low tone). We will talk about that presently, Hilda.

> [*He goes down the flight of steps with the wreath and away through the garden.*

Hilda (looks after him, then turns to RAGNAR). I think you might at least have thanked him.

Ragnar. Thanked him? Ought I to have thanked him?

Hilda. Yes, of course you ought!

Ragnar. I think it is rather you I ought to thank.

Hilda. How can you say such a thing?

Ragnar (without answering her). But I advise you to take care, Miss Wangel! For you don't know him rightly yet.

Hilda (ardently). Oh, no one knows him as I do!

Ragnar (laughs in exasperation). Thank him, when he has held me down year after year! When he made father disbelieve in me—made me disbelieve in myself! And all merely that he might——!

Hilda (as if divining something). That he might——? Tell me at once!

Ragnar. That he might keep her with him.

Hilda (with a start towards him). The girl at the desk.

Ragnar. Yes.

Hilda (threateningly, clenching her hands). That is not true! You are telling falsehoods about him!

Ragnar. I would not believe it either until to-day—when she said so herself.

Hilda (as if beside herself). What did she say? I will know! At once! at once!

Ragnar. She said that he had taken possession of her mind—her whole mind—centred all her thoughts upon himself alone. She says that she can never leave him—that she will remain here, where he is——

Hilda (with flashing eyes). She will not be allowed to!

Ragnar (as if feeling his way). Who will not allow her?

Hilda (rapidly). He will not either!

Ragnar. Oh no—I understand the whole thing now. After this, she would merely be—in the way.

Hilda. You understand nothing—since you can talk like that! No, *I* will tell you why he kept hold of her.

Ragnar. Well then, why?

Hilda. In order to keep hold of you.

Ragnar. Has he told you so?

Hilda. No, but it is so. It must be so! *(Wildly.)*
I will—I will have it so!

Ragnar. And at the very moment when you came—he
let her go.

Hilda. It was you—you that he let go. What do you
suppose he cares about strange women like her?

Ragnar (reflects). Is it possible that all this time he has
been afraid of me?

Hilda. He afraid! I would not be so conceited if I
were you.

Ragnar. Oh, he must have seen long ago that I had
something in me, too. Besides—cowardly—that is just
what he is, you see.

Hilda. He! Oh, yes, I am likely to believe that!

Ragnar. In a certain sense he is cowardly—he, the great
master builder. He is not afraid of robbing others of their
life's happiness—as he has done both for my father and for
me. But when it comes to climbing up a paltry bit of scaffolding—he will do anything rather than that.

Hilda. Oh, you should just have seen him high, high up
—at the dizzy height where I once saw him.

Ragnar. Did you see that?

Hilda. Yes, indeed I did. How free and great he looked
as he stood and fastened the wreath to the church-vane!

Ragnar. I know that he ventured that, once in his life—
one solitary time. It is a legend among us younger men.
But no power on earth would induce him to do it again.

Hilda. To-day he will do it again!

Ragnar (scornfully). Yes, I daresay!

Hilda. We shall see it!

Ragnar. That neither you nor I will see.

Hilda (with uncontrollable vehemence). I will see it! I
will and must see it!

Ragnar. But he will not do it. He simply dare not do it.
For you see he cannot get over this infirmity—master
builder though he be.

[MRS. SOLNESS *comes from the house on to the verandah.*

Mrs. Solness (looks around). Is he not here? Where has he gone to?

Ragnar. Mr. Solness is down with the men.

Hilda. He took the wreath with him.

Mrs. Solness (terrified). Took the wreath with him! Oh, God! oh, God! Brovik—you must go down to him! Get him to come back here!

Ragnar. Shall I say you want to speak to him, Mrs. Solness?

Mrs. Solness. Oh, yes, do!—No, no—don't say that *I* want anything! You can say that somebody is here, and that he must come at once.

Ragnar. Good. I will do so, Mrs. Solness.

[*He goes down the flight of steps and away through the garden.*

Mrs. Solness. Oh, Miss Wangel, you can't think how anxious I feel about him.

Hilda. Is there anything in this to be so terribly frightened about?

Mrs. Solness. Oh, yes; surely you can understand. Just think, if he were really to do it! If he should take it into his head to climb up the scaffolding!

Hilda (eagerly). Do you think he will?

Mrs. Solness. Oh, one can never tell what he might take into his head. I am afraid there is nothing he mightn't think of doing.

Hilda. Aha! Perhaps you too think that he is— well——?

Mrs. Solness. Oh, I don't know what to think about him now. The doctor has been telling me all sorts of things; and putting it all together with several things I have heard him say——

[DR. HERDAL *looks out, at the door*

Dr. Herdal. Is he not coming soon?

Mrs. Solness. Yes, I think so. I have sent for him at any rate.

Dr. Herdal (advancing). I am afraid you will have to go in, my dear lady——

Mrs. Solness. Oh, no! Oh, no! I shall stay out here and wait for Halvard.

Dr. Herdal. But some ladies have just come to call on you——

Mrs. Solness. Good heavens, that too! And just at this moment!

Dr. Herdal. They say they positively must see the ceremony.

Mrs. Solness. Well, well, I suppose I must go to them after all. It is my duty.

Hilda. Can't you ask the ladies to go away?

Mrs. Solness. No, that would never do. Now that they are here, it is my duty to see them. But do you stay out here in the meantime—and receive him when he comes.

Dr. Herdal. And try to occupy his attention as long as possible——

Mrs. Solness. Yes, do, dear Miss Wangel. Keep a firm hold of him as ever you can.

Hilda. Would it not be best for you to do that?

Mrs. Solness. Yes; God knows that is my duty. But when one has duties in so many directions——

Dr. Herdal (looks towards the garden). There he is coming.

Mrs. Solness. And I have to go in!

Dr. Herdal (to Hilda). Don't say anything about my being here.

Hilda. Oh, no! I daresay I shall find something else to talk to Mr. Solness about.

Mrs. Solness. And be sure you keep firm hold of him. I believe you can do it best.

[Mrs. Solness *and* Dr. Herdal *go into the house.*

HILDA *remains standing on the verandah.* SOL-
NESS *comes from the garden, up the flight of
steps.*

Solness. Somebody wants me, I hear.

Hilda. Yes; it is I, Mr. Solness.

Solness. Oh, is it you, Hilda? I was afraid it might be
Aline or the Doctor.

Hilda. You are very easily frightened, it seems!

Solness. Do you think so?

Hilda. Yes; people say that you are afraid to climb
about—on the scaffoldings, you know.

Solness. Well, that is quite a special thing.

Hilda. Then it is true that you are afraid to do it?

Solness. Yes, I am.

Hilda. Afraid of falling down and killing yourself?

Solness. No, not of that.

Hilda. Of what, then?

Solness. I am afraid of retribution, Hilda.

Hilda. Of retribution? *(Shakes her head.)* I don't
understand that.

Solness. Sit down and I will tell you something.

Hilda. Yes, do! At once!

　　[*She sits on a stool by the railing and looks ex-
　　　pectantly at him.*

Solness (throws his hat on the table). You know that I
began by building churches.

Hilda (nods). I know that well.

Solness. For, you see, I came as a boy from a pious
home in the country; and so it seemed to me that this
church-building was the noblest task I could set myself.

Hilda. Yes, yes.

Solness. And I venture to say that I built those poor
little churches with such honest and warm and heartfelt
devotion that—that——

Hilda. That——? Well?

Solness. Well, that I think that he ought to have been pleased with me.

Hilda. He? What he?

Solness. He who was to have the churches, of course! He to whose honour and glory they were dedicated.

Hilda. Oh, indeed! But are you certain, then, that—that he was not—pleased with you?

Solness (scornfully). He pleased with me! How can you talk so, Hilda? He who gave the troll in me leave to lord it just as it pleased. He who bade them be at hand to serve me, both day and night—all these—all these——

Hilda. Devils——

Solness. Yes, of both kinds. Oh, no, he made me feel clearly enough that he was not pleased with me. *(Mysteriously.)* You see, that was really the reason why he made the old house burn down.

Hilda. Was that why?

Solness. Yes, don't you understand? He wanted to give me the chance of becoming an accomplished master in my own sphere—so that I might build all the more glorious churches for him. At first I did not understand what he was driving at; but all of a sudden it flashed upon me.

Hilda. When was that?

Solness. It was when I was building the church-tower up at Lysanger.

Hilda. I thought so.

Solness. For you see, Hilda—up there, amidst those new surroundings, I used to go about musing and pondering within myself. Then I saw plainly why he had taken my little children from me. It was that I should have nothing else to attach myself to. No such thing as love and happiness, you understand. I was to be only a master builder—nothing else. And all my life long I was to go on building for him. *(Laughs.)* But I can tell you nothing came of that!

Hilda. What did you do, then?

Solness. First of all, I searched and tried my own heart——

Hilda. And then?

Solness. Then I did the impossible—I no less than he.

Hilda. The impossible?

Solness. I had never before been able to climb up to a great, free height. But that day I did it.

Hilda (leaping up). Yes, yes, you did!

Solness. And when I stood there, high over everything, and was hanging the wreath over the vane, I said to him: Hear me now, thou Mighty One! From this day forward I will be a free builder—I, too, in my sphere—just as thou in thine. I will never more build churches for thee—only homes for human beings.

Hilda (with great sparkling eyes). That was the song that I heard through the air!

Solness. But afterwards his turn came.

Hilda. What do you mean by that?

Solness (looks despondently at her). Building homes for human beings—is not worth a rap, Hilda.

Hilda. Do you say that now?

Solness. Yes, for now I see it. Men have no use for these homes of theirs—to be happy in. And I should not have had any use for such a home, if I had had one. *(With a quiet, bitter laugh.)* See, that is the upshot of the whole affair, however far back I look. Nothing really built; not anything sacrificed for the chance of building. Nothing, nothing! the whole is nothing.

Hilda. Then you will never build anything more?

Solness (with animation). On the contrary, I am just going to begin!

Hilda. What, then? What will you build? Tell me at once!

Solness. I believe there is only one possible dwelling-place for human happiness—and that is what I am going to build now.

Hilda (looks fixedly at him). Mr. Solness—you mean our castle?

Solness. The castles in the air—yes.

Hilda. I am afraid you would turn dizzy before we got half-way up.

Solness. Not if I can mount hand in hand with you, Hilda.

Hilda (with an expression of suppressed resentment). Only with me? Will there be no others of the party?

Solness. Who else should there be?

Hilda. Oh—that girl—that Kaia at the desk. Poor thing—don't you want to take her with you, too?

Solness. Oho! Was it about her that Aline was talking to you?

Hilda. Is it so—or is it not?

Solness (vehemently). I will not answer such a question. You must believe in me, wholly and entirely!

Hilda. All these ten years I have believed in you so utterly—so utterly.

Solness. You must go on believing in me!

Hilda. Then let me see you stand free and high up!

Solness (sadly). Oh Hilda—it is not every day that I can do that.

Hilda (passionately). I will have you do it! I will have it! *(Imploringly.)* Just once more, Mr. Solness! Do the impossible once again!

Solness (stands and looks deep into her eyes). If I try it, Hilda, I will stand up there and talk to him as I did that time before.

Hilda (in rising excitement). What will you say to him?

Solness. I will say to him: Hear me, Mighty Lord—thou may'st judge me as seems best to thee. But hereafter I will build nothing but the loveliest thing in the world——

Hilda (carried away). Yes—yes—yes!

Solness. —build it together with a princess, whom I love——

Hilda. Yes, tell him that! Tell him that!

Solness. Yes. And then I will say to him: Now I shall go down and throw my arms round her and kiss her——

Hilda. —many times! Say that!

Solness. —many, many times, I will say.

Hilda. And then——?

Solness. Then I will wave my hat—and come down to the earth—and do as I said to him.

Hilda (with outstretched arms). Now I see you again as I did when there was song in the air.

Solness (looks at her with his head bowed). How have you become what you are, Hilda?

Hilda. How have you made me what I am?

Solness (shortly and firmly). The princess shall have her castle.

Hilda (jubilant, clapping her hands). Oh, Mr. Solness——! My lovely, lovely castle. Our castle in the air!

Solness. On a firm foundation.

> [*In the street a crowd of people has assembled, vaguely seen through the trees. Music of wind instruments is heard far away behind the new house.*

> [MRS. SOLNESS, *with a fur collar round her neck,* DOCTOR HERDAL *with her white shawl on his arm, and some ladies, come out on the verandah.* RAGNAR BROVIK *comes at the same time up from the garden.*

Mrs. Solness (to RAGNAR). Are we to have music, too?

Ragnar. Yes. It's the band of the Mason's Union. *(To* SOLNESS.) The foreman asked me to tell you that he is ready now to go up with the wreath.

Solness (takes his hat). Good. I will go down to him myself.

Mrs. Solness (anxiously). What have you to do down there, Halvard?

Solness (curtly). I must be down below with the men.

Mrs. Solness. Yes, down below—only down below.

Solness. That is where I always stand—on everyday occasions.

> [*He goes down the flight of steps and away through the garden.*

Mrs. Solness (calls after him over the railing). But do beg the man to be careful when he goes up? Promise me that, Halvard!

Dr. Herdal (to Mrs. Solness*).* Don't you see that I was right? He has given up all thought of that folly.

Mrs. Solness. Oh, what a relief! Twice workmen have fallen, and each time they were killed on the spot. *(Turns to* Hilda.*)* Thank you, Miss Wangel, for having kept such a firm hold upon him. I should never have been able to manage him.

Dr. Herdal (playfully). Yes, yes, Miss Wangel, you know how to keep firm hold on a man, when you give your mind to it.

> [Mrs. Solness *and* Dr. Herdal *go up to the ladies, who are standing nearer to the steps and looking over the garden.* Hilda *remains standing beside the railing in the foreground.* Ragnar *goes up to her.*

Ragnar (with suppressed laughter, half whispering). Miss Wangel—do you see all those young fellows down in the street?

Hilda. Yes.

Ragnar. They are my fellow-students, come to look at the master.

Hilda. What do they want to look at him for?

Ragnar. They want to see how he daren't climb to the top of his own house.

Hilda. Oh, that is what those boys want, is it?

Ragnar (spitefully and scornfully). He has kept us down so long—now we are going to see him keep quietly down below himself.

Hilda. You will not see that—not this time.

Ragnar (smiles). Indeed! Then where shall we see him?

Hilda. High—high up by the vane! That is where you will see him!

Ragnar (laughs). Him! Oh, yes, I daresay!

Hilda. His will is to reach the top—so at the top you shall see him.

Ragnar. His will, yes; that I can easily believe. But he simply cannot do it. His head would swim round, long, long before he got half-way. He would have to crawl down again on his hands and knees.

Dr. Herdal (points across). Look! There goes the foreman up the ladders.

Mrs. Solness. And of course he has the wreath to carry, too. Oh, I do hope he will be careful!

Ragnar (stares incredulously and shouts). Why, but it's——

Hilda (breaking out in jubilation). It is the master builder himself!

Mrs. Solness (screams with terror). Yes, it is Halvard! Oh, my great God——! Halvard! Halvard!

Dr. Herdal. Hush! Don't shout to him!

Mrs. Solness (half beside herself). I must go to him! I must get him to come down again!

Dr. Herdal (holds her). Don't move, any of you! Not a sound!

Hilda (immovable, follows SOLNESS *with her eyes).* He climbs and climbs. Higher and higher! Higher and higher! Look! Just look!

Ragnar (breathless). He must turn now. He can't possibly help it.

Hilda. He climbs and climbs. He will soon be at the top now.

Mrs. Solness. Oh, I shall die of terror. I cannot bear to see it.

Dr. Herdal. Then don't look up at him.

Hilda. There he is standing on the topmost planks. Right at the top!

Dr. Herdal. Nobody must move! Do you hear?

Hilda (exulting, with quiet intensity). At last! At last! Now I see him great and free again!

Ragnar (almost voiceless). But this is im——

Hilda. So I have seen him all through these ten years. How secure he stands! Frightfully thrilling all the same. Look at him! Now he is hanging the wreath round the vane.

Ragnar. I feel as if I were looking at something utterly impossible.

Hilda. Yes, it is the impossible that he is doing now! *(With the indefinable expression in her eyes.)* Can you see any one else up there with him?

Ragnar. There is no one else.

Hilda. Yes, there is one he is striving with.

Ragnar. You are mistaken.

Hilda. Then do you hear no song in the air, either?

Ragnar. It must be the wind in the tree-tops.

Hilda. *I* hear a song—a mighty song! *(Shouts in wild jubilation and glee.)* Look, look! Now he is waving his hat! He is waving it to us down here! Oh, wave, wave back to him. For now it is finished! *(Snatches the white shawl from the Doctor, waves it and shouts up to* SOLNESS.*)* Hurrah for Master Builder Solness!

Dr. Herdal. Stop! Stop! For God's sake——!

[*The ladies on the verandah wave their pocket-handkerchiefs, and the shouts of "Hurrah" are taken up in the street below. Then they are suddenly silenced, and the crowd bursts out into a shriek of horror. A human body, with planks and fragments of wood, is vaguely perceived crashing down behind the trees.*

Mrs. Solness and the Ladies (at the same time).   He is falling!   He is falling!

> [MRS. SOLNESS *totters, falls backwards, swooning, and is caught, amid cries and confusion, by the ladies.   The crowd in the street breaks down the fence and storms into the garden.   At the same time* DR. HERDAL, *too, rushes down thither.   A short pause.*

Hilda (stares fixedly upwards and says, as if petrified).   My Master Builder.

Ragnar (supports himself, trembling, against the railing).   He must be dashed to pieces—killed on the spot.

One of the Ladies (whilst MRS. SOLNESS *is carried into the house)*.   Run down for the doctor——

Ragnar.   I can't stir a foot——

Another Lady.   Then call to some one!

Ragnar (tries to call out).   How is it?   Is he alive?

A Voice (below in the garden).   Mr. Solness is dead!

Other Voices (nearer).   The head is all crushed.——He fell right into the quarry.

Hilda (turns to RAGNAR *and says quietly)*.   I can't see him up there now.

Ragnar.   This is terrible.   So, after all, he could not do it.

Hilda (as if in quiet spell-bound triumph).   But he mounted right to the top.   And I heard harps in the air. *(Waves her shawl in the air, and shrieks with wild intensity.)*   My—my Master Builder!